Individuals in Society

Individuals in Society

A Modern Introduction to Sociology

James A. Kitchens

North Texas State University

Leobardo F. Estrada

North Texas State University

Charles E. Merrill Publishing Company
A Bell & Howell Company
Columbus, Ohio 43216

Published by
Charles E. Merrill Publishing Company
A Bell & Howell Company
Columbus, Ohio 43216

Library of Congress Catalog Card Number: 73-88244

ISBN: 0-675-08858-5

3 4 5 6 7 8 9—80 79 78 77 76 75

Cover illustration by Will Chenoweth

Printed in the United States of America

To Benjamin,
whose potential presence
gave the incentive

Preface

Your study of sociology can and ought to be fun, especially in an introductory course. This statement is true despite the fact that sociology is a serious academic discipline which prepares people for lifelong careers of able and useful service. Most students, reading about sociology and taking an introductory course in the subject, are not, however, going to pursue a career in sociology. After all, not all who take a biology course will be biologists, nor will all who take astronomy be astronomers.

Perhaps, like most students in an introductory class, you are interested in sociology as an avocation. That is, you are curious about how people act and the reasons for their actions. You are yourself a part of the phenomenon under study and so have a vital stake in the answers to your questions. You will become, rather than a professional sociologist, an informed observer of the social scene as a dentist, lawyer, businessperson, homemaker, or any one of a host of other occupational pigeonholes which make up American life. Your principle interest is in learning about the social phenomena which will continue to surround you throughout your life.

Learning about those phenomena is a captivating experience. A competent, interesting teacher interacting with a group of creative students can bring the intriguing facts of social life to light. Like the fish that swims the ocean, you are surrounded by interesting life forms. Unlike the fish, you can use your imagination and intellect to study these forms and to understand them. Should you choose, you may life out your life (as many people do) unaware of these forms of social existence. But if you wish, you may become aware of them, understand how they work, and comprehend their meaning and influence upon you.

This book is designed to assist you in the happy task of learning about your social existence. It makes no effort to be comprehensive. Selectivity is a necessity in a field like sociology, which covers a wide range of phenomena. The book is based upon the authors' sincere wish to make sociology understandable. We want you to be struck by the fact that sociology is interesting. Because you will learn about factors which influence your life (in the past, present, and future), we want your curiosity to be aroused. And when you close the book after reading the last page, we want you to be better informed about your own social experience and about your society.

The authors wish to thank those writers of books which have performed the task of whetting their appetite for sociology. And we want, also, to thank the dedicated teachers who have offered guidance and stimulation in pursuing the increasingly intriguing experience of learning about social life. Special thanks is due to Dr. Alvin Bertrand and Dr. Vernon J. Parenton of Louisiana State University and Dr. Charles Tolbert and Dr. Harold Osborne of Baylor University. Thanks are in order, also, to North Texas State University and the Department of Sociology for providing the interaction context in which the authors could enjoy the refreshing interchange with young men and women who were curious about the sociological task.

And now, read on. We are confident that a meaningful experience will be yours in the weeks ahead and, quite possibly, this experience will also be fun.

Contents

Individuals in Society

PART ONE

The Sociological Perspective

Chapter 1

Cognitive Objectives

This chapter is designed to present the sociological perspective. It will help you to understand the special way a sociologist looks at human behavior. You should gain the following important information from this chapter:

1. *A definition of sociology*
2. *What "patterns of behavior" are*
3. *Why Auguste Comte is important in the development of sociology*
4. *What science is and how it differs from other ways of "knowing"*
5. *The difference between the "experimental design" and the* ex post facto *design in scientific studies*
6. *The limitations in using the scientific method in sociological research*
7. *The methods sociologists use to collect information*
8. *What a social theory is*
9. *How scientific method acts as a bridge between theory and observable data*

Doing the Sociological Thing

Our society supports the axiom, "The only thing that never changes is that everything changes." The mass media remind us daily of the rocket-like pace of events among which individuals live out their lives. The constant swirl of events which surrounds our daily experience caused Alvin Toffler to speak of "future shock." By this term, Toffler intended to convey the notion that changes come so rapidly that the individual's ability to adapt is taxed, perhaps beyond its limit. The effect upon the social experience is not unlike a shock which, like electricity, may be too much for the person's system.[1]

These increasingly rapid changes in the social experience of people is at least one reason for the urgent need for sociological understanding of our times. The problems of society impinge on the individual at every level of his living and coping with the social scene is made easier by understanding the forces which affect our lives. Beyond that, adequate solutions to social problems are to be found only when the problems themselves are correctly understood. Just as the final cure for cancer is probably dependent upon man's discovery of the causes of the disease, so the forces of social organization which debilitate the system and cause its "dis-ease" must be revealed if useful and humane solutions are to be discovered and implemented.

So here you are in an introductory course in an academic discipline which claims to study the relationships between individuals and the structure of society. It is, of course, too much to expect that one course in sociology will be able to clarify all the problems of our

3

society, much less their cause and solution. The science of sociology has not developed to such an extent, and a few short months is obviously not time enough for so ambitious a task. There are, however, several important ideas which this text and this course will introduce to you.

You will learn some interesting facts, including how many people live in urban areas, the relationships between urban slum residence and juvenile delinquency, and the changes in patterns of family life. Perhaps you will learn other facts by viewing movies or reading books and articles about child rearing, Harlem, Appalachia, drug addiction, prostitution, the youth culture, religion, homosexuality, or animal behavior. Sociology can supply you with interesting facts and images of how life in society is lived.

You will learn the meanings of many new words which you may or may not have heard before. Alienation, socialization, relative deprivation, deviancy, norms, social organization, society, group interaction, and polygyny are some of these words. Some are words which you now use but which have a different meaning to the sociologist. These words and their sociological meaning will give you a way of analyzing and understanding how life in society is lived.

Your mental horizons will be broadened as you read of people in other countries or different regions of this nation. You will understand how some American traditions are formed, how they are maintained, how they are challenged, and how they have changed. Sociology can show you how life is lived by different kinds of people in our society.

Perhaps the most important result which you will receive from this text will be a perspective which will help you to describe and to explain the human phenomena you see everyday. The sociological imagination, as C. Wright Mills calls it, is concerned with the impact of social relationships upon individual behavior.[2] Many of the facts you will learn as well as the new words you will learn to use are designed to illuminate those social relationships. The perspective of sociology or its point of view is concerned with how those relationships affect your behavior.

Now, we want you to meet Sammy. Sammy is a faceless American until we give him the characteristics of a group we would like him to represent. We can change Sammy's appearance (including his sex), his dress, his income, his education, and his lifestyle to make him a member of any American group we desire. If we shade his skin, give him little education, and visualize him as poor, Sammy could be a member of a minority racial group who lives in an urban ghetto. If we give him a good education, adequate income, a home in the suburbs (and probably a light skin), Sammy could be a representative of the middle class. If he has a chauffer, goes on safaris, owns lots of stocks and bonds (or companies, or land, etc.), and belongs to a country club, Sammy could be a member of the upper crust. Or Sammy could be young, have long hair, and go to college. Sammy could be an Indian on a reservation, a Mexican-American in the Southwest, a farmer in Alabama, a sergeant in the Army, an alcoholic on skid row, a child in Seattle, an aged adult in a nursing home, or a patient in a hospital.

Sammy is a single human being who lives with other human beings. He takes part in groups of all sizes and descriptions. No matter his sex, age, color, religion, or place of residence, Sammy comes in contact with groups. He and others like him form families, churches, schools, friendships, neighborhoods, labor unions, gangs, car pools, PTAs, fraternities, sororities, civic clubs, and so forth. He interacts with others—he has an effect on others and they have an effect on him.

Sammy's behavior, along with the behavior of the other Sammys he bumps into, is the object of our study. He is an interesting person and we want to know what makes Sammy act like he does. When we know what makes Sammy tick we will understand ourselves better. The way Sammy's groups function will illuminate the manner in which our groups function.

Sociology, then, deals with life. The living, ongoing process of people in action is the core of sociology. Sociology's subject matter includes all stages of the human life cycle—work, play, marriage, child rearing, and death. Each person receives the impact of social relationships, and life is the process of adjusting to that impact and living out its dictates. This is the perspective of sociology and it is this imaginative way of looking at life which, hopefully, you will get from this course.

THE SOCIOLOGICAL VIEWPOINT

A starting point for us is this statement: sociologists are interested in studying Sammy and his groups. The word "group" is understood by sociologists as collections of people (including a total society) like clubs, churches, family, friends, congregations, and audiences within which Sammy interacts. Sociologists want to know what effect the group has on Sammy's behavior. They want to know how the group functions, what it does, and how Sammy reacts to the group. The sociologist seeks the answers to two important questions. The first is: How do Sammy and his group behave? That is, what exactly is Sammy's behavior, and what are the characteristics of the group—its size, objectives, and activities? Sociologists look at human behavior and attempt to describe it. The second question is: Why do Sammy and his group act as they do? Hence, sociologists seek to understand the reasons Sammy acts like he does, and what his activity means. They ask related questions: What influence does the group exert on Sammy? What makes the group click? How is it held together? What makes the group change or what keeps the group from changing?

Sociology, defined formally, is the scientific study of human behavior in group life. Later in this chapter, we will explore what the term scientific means. Now it is sufficient to say that a scientific study is built on the collection of data from real life, systematically and objectively analyzed. As a study of human behavior in groups, sociology is concerned with social facts. Emile Durkheim (1858–1917), French sociologist, defined a social fact to be "external to the individual (that is, neither psychological nor biological in origin) and constraining upon the individual (that is, determinative of behavior)."[3] Sociology seeks to isolate and understand the *social* factors which help to determine how people live and why they behave as they do.

Since sociologists seek to know how and why individuals act like they do in various groups in which they participate, they look for patterns of behavior, that is, large numbers of people acting in similar or somewhat similar ways. Alan Bates, in *The Sociological Enterprise,* says:

> The sociologist is interested in organized social behavior. Put very generally, this means that behavior which links together individuals or groups of individuals is not random or haphazard. It has the properties of orderliness, pattern, repetitiveness, hence predictability. Here is a college classroom. During a particular semester at nine o'clock each morning, Monday through Friday, the room is filled with college students. Each goes without hesitation to a certain chair. A minute or two later a professor enters, stands at the front of the classroom, facing the students, and begins to talk. Most of the students write in notebooks. A few whisper covertly to one another. At the end of fifty minutes a bell rings, the professor ends his comments, the students close their notebooks, and all leave the room. We have here an identification and short description of an instance of social organization even though it does not use the technical language of sociology. It is clear that the behavior of these persons with respect to each other is patterned.[4]

He notes further: "What is crucial for (the sociologist) is that all these persons, despite their differences, behave with respect to each other in an orderly, predictable fashion."[5]

Sociologists, then, are interested in the forms and consequences of the activity of human beings in relation to each other. And their aim is to establish a body of knowledge about human societies and interaction which will be useful in explaining and predicting behavior in group life.

THE ORIGINS OF SOCIOLOGY

The word sociology was coined in 1839 by a Frenchman named August Comte (1798–1857). Comte was an intellectual who wrote and lectured on social conditions in France during the confusion and disorganization which followed the French Revolution.

Comte's major contribution lay in his insistence that a science of society (sociology) was possible. He divided history, including the history of a scholarly discipline, into three phases.

The *theological phase* is characterized by those who explain phenomena by making reference to the gods. Ordinarily, these divine beings who control events are predominately human in their attributes. That is, they are characterized as jealous, angry, loving, stupid, vengeful, or benevolent depending on their mood. All events or experiences (i.e., the birth of a baby, a storm, a successful hunt, etc.) are explained as resulting from willful superhuman beings.

The *metaphysical phase* represents a reawakening of faith in human reason. The explanation of any phenomena relies on nature and natural laws, interpreted rationally. Hence, events and experiences are analyzed logically and rational explanations are used to explain them.

During the *positivistic phase* phenomena are analyzed by the scientific method. (For Comte, positivism was science.) Observation (including actual recording of data), experiment, and objectivity are used to explain phenomena. The positivists use logic as did the metaphysicians of the previous period, but they add the need for observation and objectivity in determining the cause and effect of events and experiences.

Comte's point in analyzing these three stages of history was to note that the positivistic method had been applied to astronomy, chemistry, physics, and biology. These were scientific disciplines already well developed in Comte's day. Now, according to Comte, we may apply the scientific method to the study of human societies. In other words, a science of sociology is possible.

Sociology as Comte envisioned it would have two major divisions. The first he termed *statics,* which refers to how societies or groups are held together and achieve stability. Statics refers to the sociologist's interest in *order.* The other division of sociology is *dynamics,* which is concerned with how and why societies change. Thus, the core of sociology, according to Comte, is the application of the methods of science to the order and the changes in human groups and societies.

WHAT IS SCIENCE?

Perhaps this is the point at which we should discuss the meaning of the word science. What is the scientific method, and how does scientific knowledge differ from other knowledge? In order to determine this, we first need to determine what types of knowledge exist. Usually four categories of knowledge are named.

Pragmatic Knowledge

This branch of knowledge is the "how to" kind. It is displayed in statements like, "I know how to make an 'A' in physics," or "I know how to build a bird house," or "I know how to make money." Much of our knowledge is of the "how to" variety. The test of this kind of knowledge is: Does it work? If not, it is incorrect or untrue.

Moral or Religious Knowledge

This is knowledge of right and wrong, good or bad, superior or inferior. It makes judgments on art forms, beauty, and the actions of people. The source of this knowledge is either divine revelation or persons considered to be authoritative. One "knows" that the Mona Lisa is a beautiful work of art because art critics agree that it is. Or one "knows" that working on Sunday, committing adultery, wearing cosmetics, eating pork, or engaging in some other activity is wrong (evil or sinful) because one's church says it is. The test of the truth of this type of knowledge is whether it conforms with the pronouncements of those one considers to be in authority.

Philosophic Knowledge

Philosophy may generally be regarded as systematic theories concerning the essence or ultimate nature of reality. It is based on the laws of reason, or logic supplemented by direct intuition. Its truth is judged by the principles of logical reasoning. For example, various philosophers have raised questions concerning the nature of man. That is, who or what is man? What is his purpose? Is he capable of controlling himself and his destiny? Hobbes, a seventeenth century thinker, felt man was basically evil and strong social controls were necessary to keep man from destroying himself. Rousseau, his contemporary, viewed man as inherently good, and strong social controls as a corrupting influence on the otherwise peaceful, loving nature of man. Each of these thinkers attempted to base his concepts of man on reason and to build a system of thought which was logical and conformed to the principles of rational thinking.

Scientific Knowledge

This kind of knowing is based on a combination of logical reasoning and factual or empirical evidence. The scientist, like the philosopher, uses logic, experience, and intuition to set up a theory of how what he wishes to study works. For example, the scientist may assume, logically, that a group of rats who are forced to live in a very crowded cage will show more deviant or unusual behavior (like aggressiveness, homosexuality, cannibalism, etc.) than rats who are not overly crowded. This we may say is a theory. The scientist then checks the theory against the actual facts by performing an experiment in which a number of rats are crowded into a small space and an equal number of rats are placed in a much larger and uncrowded space. Then, by observation, the scientist rates the differences in behavior of the two groups of rats. The theory may be correct or incorrect. Scientific knowledge is tested, therefore, by the question, does what I predict correspond to observable data?

Scientific knowledge is tested by observation.

Scientific knowledge is also distinguished from the other types of knowledge in the following ways:

1. The scientist asks only those questions which can be answered by sensory observation. The question "Is God dead?" is a religious

or philosophical question, not a scientific question. When we ask whether the idea that God is dead affects church attendance, we are asking a question which science can help us answer.

2. The scientist stresses objectivity. This means that the scientist attempts to reduce the possible distortions in observation and analysis which may occur due to his or her personal attitudes, emotions, values, and likes and dislikes.

3. Tests from which scientific knowledge is drawn must be repeatable. That is, the conclusions of a study can be duplicated by other investigators.

4. The scientist looks for natural causes and does not consider supernatural ones. Explanations made in terms of some cause which does not itself have a cause have no place in science. This does not mean that all scientists are atheists. It simply means that the scientist is looking for natural, not supernatural, causes and can never conclude a study, regardless of personal religious beliefs, with words like "God did this."

Sociology as Science

The sociologist attempts to apply these standards of scientific knowledge to his study of human behavior in group life. But the aspiring social scientist must keep in mind certain limitations imposed upon all social investigators that are not necessarily applicable to the chemist, physicist, or biologist. Since social subjects are human beings and not rats or monkeys, or chemicals in a test tube, the sociologist can artificially manipulate his subject matter only to a certain point. One can take infant monkeys away from their mothers and study the effect of surrogate mothers upon them. But one cannot do the same with human infants. Deliberate manipulation of subject matter in such a manner is referred to as *experimental design.* Using such a method, the scientist divides his subjects (monkeys, peanuts, chemicals) into two similar groups. One group, called the experimental group, is exposed to a test event while the other group, called the control group, is not. Differences due to the introduction of the event may then be measured by comparing the two groups.

The sociologist is limited, then, in the use of the experimental method. If, for example, his interest is in the effect of education on income, he cannot deliberately withhold education from a specified group of children in order to discover the disadvantages they incur as a result of this limitation. The social scientist must find people who, due to the natural processes of life, have been denied an education. The real disadvantage of this *ex post facto* approach is that the physical scientist in the laboratory can more completely control all the other variables affecting the phenomenon under study. The social scientist cannot as successfully keep these variables under control.

An additional limitation which the sociologist experiences is due to the fact that the social observer is a part of the phenomenon under study. The sociologist is investigating society and is at the same time an active member of that society. Being enmeshed in one's subject matter makes it more difficult for him to avoid having personal values and attitudes disturb one's objectivity.

Finally, sociologists study human beings, and humans are capable of investing their acts with meaning and purpose. One must not only observe the acts of humans, but must somehow untangle the meaning or symbolism they attach to their activity. For example, merely counting the number of people voting for a specific candidate is one thing, but trying to determine why they did so (i.e., to get at the meaning behind their activity) is an entirely different matter. Counting the number of arrests of juvenile delinquents who live in slum areas in major cities is a matter of checking the police records or some other record of criminal offenses, but determining the relationship between the slum's social environment and criminally deviant acts is not that simple. What are the values and attitudes of delinquent adolescents? What home conditions do the delinquents come from? What are the educational opportunities and disadvantages of delinquents? Is an adolescent who breaks a law more likely to get arrested if he is from a slum area? All these, and a host of other questions, must be answered to understand the meaning of delinquent behavior.

A wink, a handshake, a raised fist, are all symbolic acts!

SOCIOLOGICAL METHODS

Earlier it was stated that scientific knowledge is based upon a combination of logic and factual evidence. The scientist constructs a logical theory about the phenomenon in question. The theory consists of the scientist's perception of how this specific aspect of life works. He may devise the theory by reading the ideas and studies of other people; he may combine several ideas to conceive another idea; or his theory might be based upon an intelligent hunch. At any rate, the scientist presents a set of logically related sets of propositions which appear to explain why a specific phenomenon or aspect of social life works like it does.

After clearly establishing the theory, the scientist proceeds to collect information from the real world to determine whether and the degree to which the theory correctly describes reality. In other words, the researcher establishes some kind of experiment with which to observe the phenomena around which the study is built.

Matilda White Riley describes the process with the scheme shown below.[6] The bridge between one's theory and the small slice of reality one is studying is called methods. One goes from the logically derived theory to real life by means of specifically designed methods of data collection. After collecting the data, one submits them to proper

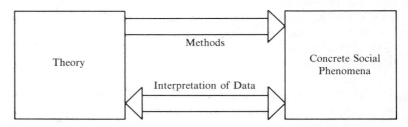

analysis using statistical techniques and then modifies the theory to conform to what has been discovered, throws it out as incorrect, or becomes satisfied that the theory correctly describes that with which it is concerned.

Some of the methods commonly used by sociologists to collect data include questionnaires, interviews, case studies, observation, participant observation, and interpretations of available data.

Mailed Questionnaires

In using this method, the investigator makes a list of questions which the respondent is to answer and mails the questionnaire to each person selected for questioning. The advantages of this method are that it is relatively inexpensive and that many people may be studied at once. Of course, there is the risk that some (perhaps many) people will fail to return the questionnaire. The researcher must be very careful that each question is phrased in such a manner that is easily grasped by the reader and that it actually asks for the kind of information needed. If a question is unclear or may be interpreted in a number of different ways, the information received in response may be unreliable.

Personal Interview

This method, like the questionnaire, is based upon a list of written questions (called an interview schedule). However, unlike the mailed questionnaire, the questions are asked in a face-to-face situation in which the interviewer records the answers of the respondent. The most serious limitation with personal interview is the time and expense involved in conducting the interviews. In some cases, the researcher also may have trouble finding the chosen respondent and securing his permission to ask the questions.

Case Method

Sometimes researchers will choose only a few respondents (a common number is ten) for in-depth interviews or possibly a series of interviews over a specified period of time. (The latter is called a panel study.) Tapes, cameras, or other methods of recording the opinions, ideas, and behavior of the selected individuals may be utilized. Sometimes historical documents like biographies, diaries, and personal letters may also be used to collect in-depth information from the respondent.

Observation

There are times when asking questions is either impossible or unnecessary. For example, the investigator may be interested in the patterns of play in a school, or the way individuals act in a PTA meeting. In these situations, asking questions would disrupt the natural processes the investigator wishes to observe. By unobtrusively observing the individuals in action and recording observations, the sociologist can plot the activity on a diagram (called a sociogram) or write out a narrative describing the activity observed.

Participant Observation

This method adds the ingredient of participation to the observation method. The investigator may actually go and live for a period of time in the environment in which he is interested and record what he experiences and observes. He may, for example, ask permission to sit in as an outsider during a series of seances to study the phenomenon of spiritualism. In other words, this method is employed when the sociologist feels it is necessary to put himself into the situation to discover its nature. He must be especially careful to guard against subjectivity in all phases of the activity. As a participant, one cannot allow personal biases to color observations and recording of data.

Interpretations of Available Data

The researcher may use data collected by the Census Bureau or other federal, state, or local agencies. Frequently, these agencies will collect information useful to the sociologist. Available data are usually reorganized, and statistically tested to look for significant trends or changes in behavioral events, such as marriage rates, birth rates, unemployment, inflation, court dispositions, and crime rates. When the social scientist has access to these data, they can be fruitfully used to test some sociological theories.

SOCIOLOGICAL METHODS AT WORK

Let us say that for some reason you were interested in studying the effect parental pressures have on students' achievement in school. You, as a sociologist, would be attempting to investigate the impact of a significant reference group upon an individual's behavior. How would you proceed in order to develop a theory which might be tested by empirical research?

First, you might begin by attempting to isolate specific areas of this broad topic in order to limit your theory to manageable proportions. Your major topic is the impact of family pressures upon a student's behavior. Two important words appear in this statement: *behavior* and *pressures.*

Behavior includes activities as well as attitudes and involves life both in and out of school. It includes relationships to teachers, other students, close friends, and the opposite sex, attitudes toward grades and school, feelings about parents, as well as a host of other types of phenomena. Pressures might encompass parental attitudes, parental achievements (i.e., the parents' business and educational accomplishments), overt statements of the parents, and the accomplishment of brothers or sisters in school. Your task is to select specific aspects of behavior and pressures to investigate. Attempting to look at all elements involved would make your research, unless you had sufficient time and resources for an exhaustive study, too broad and general.

Suppose then that you decided to limit your concern to the relationship of parental achievement to the student's academic accomplishments as reflected in grade point average and participation in extra-curricular activities. Thus the basic question which you are going to consider is: What relationship, if any, exists between parental accomplishment and student achievement?

Theoretically, you might think that students whose father and mother, and perhaps siblings, were high achievers in school and in business or other ventures would be likely to experience pressures to do well in school. These pressures would come in the form of encouragement through overt statements like "How are you doing in history?" or through providing extra books, materials, or money for tutors. Pressure might stem from statements such as "Remember, your brother was president of his class" or "Your father always did well in physics." You would also need to keep in mind that such a student would have been exposed to years of these subtle influences.

Therefore, pressures to do well in any given year of school might issue from these past, rather than present, experiences. Lower-achieving families, you might suppose, would be less likely to place these pressures on the student.

Thus far you have made several assumptions. The first is an assumption which all sociologists make, namely that an individual's behavior is in part directed by the groups in which that person participates. (So important is the influence of the family on shaping the individual that some would argue that this statement is not an assumption.) Second, you have assumed that high-achieving families are at the same time families which put high pressure for achievement on their members (in this case the sons and daughters; in other cases, the pressure for accomplishment may be on the parents). Third, you have assumed that families of relative low achievement tend to place less pressure for academic performance on their members. Finally, you have assumed that higher pressure for achievement will result in higher achievement.

These assumptions fit into a set of logically ordered propositions.

1. Parents who are high achievers socially and academically provide opportunities, encouragement, and examples of social and academic performance for their sons and daughters.
2. Opportunities, encouragement, and examples of achievement form the basis of pressure for students from high-achieving families to do well in school.
3. Higher pressure for achievement leads to higher achievement.
4. Therefore, students whose families are high achievers will perform better in school than those whose families are low achievers.

This set of statements is your theory. It serves to explain, at least in part, the phenomenon you are studying. The last statement is a testable hypothesis. In this example, the method of data collection to test the theory will be a questionnaire.

A sample of students would be asked to respond to questions about their parents' academic and social achievement. For example, questions about the parents' occupations, income, and number of years completed in school could be asked. You would also want to know the types and number of social clubs and organizations in which parents hold membership. Answers to these questions would allow you to know the level of achievement of the parents of students selected in your sample. The parents could be ranked into high achievers and low achievers.

Similar questions would be asked of the students themselves. Their grade point average, their interest in making good grades, the number of clubs to which they belong, the degree of participation in these clubs and other extra-curricular activities are among the kinds of information necessary to measure their level of achievement. You would also want to determine whether the student feels pressured.

Support for your hypothesis would consist of finding that students from high-achieving families are themselves high achievers. Finding this support would tend to confirm the general framework of the hypothesis and thus substantiate your theory.

One word of caution must be stated before leaving this example of theory and research. This example has been oversimplified and therefore leaves out a number of important steps in theory building. No mention was made of the necessity of wide reading in the area you intend to investigate. Other research and writing which deals with the phenomenon you are studying bears fruitful results in clarifying your own thinking. Wild hunches and illogical reasoning can be controlled by reading what others have concluded. Reviewing the literature is also beneficial in helping the researcher to tie the study to the larger body of knowledge from past scientific social research.

Further, you must be careful not to assume that one factor (the high-achieving family in our example) is the single *cause* of another (the high-achieving student). This error of reductionism causes the researcher to overlook other variables which may work in a causal manner. To say that high-achieving students are more likely to come from high-achieving families is not to say that the family level of accomplishment is the only source of pressure for performance placed on the student.

SUMMARY

Sociology is a discipline dealing with the behavior of human beings in interaction with other human beings. It seeks to build a body of knowledge useful in describing and explaining human activities in societies, groups, and other types of collections of people.

The origins of sociology may be attributed to the writings of August Comte. He insisted that the scientific method could be applied to the activities of human societies and he gave a basic framework for the development of this new discipline.

The goal of sociology is knowledge that is accurate and therefore a description of the way real life actually works. This is, of course, the goal of any science. However, the social scientist must recognize the limitations of the scientific method in dealing with the subject matter under consideration. Because it is people which the social scientist studies, (1) he cannot always deliberately manipulate them so as to control the link of behavior he wishes to research, (2) he is a part of the general topic under study and must beware of biasing the investigations through personal prejudices, and (3) his subject's behavior is always meaningful and symbolic (at least to the subject) and the social scientist is as interested in the meaning of the behavior as the description of the behavior itself.

Notes

1. Alvin Toffler, *Future Shock* (New York: Random House, 1970).

2. C. W. Mills, *The Sociological Imagination* (New York: Oxford University Press, 1959).

3. See Harry Elmer Barnes, *An Introduction to the History of Sociology,* abridged ed. (Chicago: University of Chicago Press, 1966), pp. 210–11.

4. Alan P. Bates, *The Sociological Enterprise* (Boston: Houghton Mifflin Company, 1967), pp. 6–7.

5. Ibid., p. 7.

6. Matilda White Riley, *Sociological Research* (New York: Harcourt, Brace and World, 1963).

Thinking
Sociologically

1.   Pretend that you are one of three astronauts on the moon and have met with great misfortune. Your moon rover has broken down two hundred miles from the main capsule. A decision must be made as to which items to take on the journey back to the mother ship. Rank the following ten items according to their importance for assuring the survival of the space crew. Do not consult with anyone else as you rank the most important item with a "1" and the least important item as "10."

_____magnetic compass

_____ten gallons of water

_____box of matches

_____collapsible raft

_____stellar map of the moon's constellations

_____eighty feet of rope

_____case of food concentrate

_____three 100 lb. tanks of oxygen

_____transistorized heating unit

_____bandages and medicine

Now break up into groups and decide as a group on a ranking of the ten items. How different are the group scores from your own scores? Did someone in your group have more influence than anyone else? How did your group reach a consensus on the rankings? Do you think that working in groups has an effect on your behavior?

2.   Begin to notice how predictable human behavior is—at a football game, at a movie, in the classroom, in a family, at work, on the highways. Look for patterns of behavior as people behave in a similar fashion. Behavior is predictable because people follow patterns. Think about weddings. As an example, list five or six things that are similar about almost all weddings. Notice the songs, the clothing (of both participants and guests), the statements and vows, and people's behavior both during and after the wedding.

3. Given the assumption that the higher the social class the greater the probability of college attendance of youngsters, what hypothesis could you make to explain why some persons of high social class do not go to college?

PART TWO

Society, Culture, and Personality

Chapter 2

Cognitive Objectives

Chapter two is designed to present the sociological meaning of the word "group," to outline the characteristics of all groups, and to describe various types of groups. As you read the chapter look for the following:

1. *A definition of social interaction*
2. *The importance of the concept of interaction in understanding the social group*
3. *A definition of social group*
4. *The characteristics of a social group*
5. *The processes which give a group solidarity and help to keep it going*
6. *The meaning of the words norm, role, and position*
7. *The meaning of the different type norms: folkways, mores, law*
8. *The characteristics of primary and secondary type relationships*
9. *The importance of Charles Horton Cooley in differentiating types of groups*
10. *The meaning of the words* gemeinschaft *and* geselleschaft

The Shape of the Social Group

When you look at a house you see bricks, mortar, windows, doors, and a roof. What you do not see are pipes running along certain patterns to parts of the house, electrical wires going in all directions, rafters, studs, and thousands of nails. All those things which you can see and all the things that are hidden from your eyes form the structure of the house, giving it stability and its unique shape.

Societies also have structure, and when you see a society (or a segment of one) in action—like a congregation worshipping, or the United States Senate voting on a bill, or twenty-two men knocking heads on a football field—you see a part of the structure of a society. But, as with the house, a part of the structure is hidden from the eyes. Take a football game, for example. Each man on the field has a specific assignment for each play, and all the players know and (usually) abide by both written and unwritten rules for the game. But when spectators view the game, they do not actually see the appointed tasks of each man nor the actual rules of the game. What they see is twenty-two young men dressed in flashy uniforms, running around on green turf with white lines, and trying to do something with an egg-shaped, brown ball. But the rules and the individual responsibilities of each player give the game a shape, a structure. Because football has a social structure, it makes sense both to those playing and those watching. Without its structure, the game would be chaos. Imagine what would happen if one team suddenly decided to play football using tennis rules or if the quarterback decided he wanted to take the air out of

the ball. Without the rules, and without the players abiding by the rules, the game would not make sense. It would have no structure.

This chapter has as its aim a description of those things which give society a shape and keep it orderly and non-chaotic. We may call those things the basic elements in social structure. The best way to approach that subject is to begin with the definition of a social group.

WHERE TWO OR THREE ARE GATHERED TOGETHER

George Lundburg has defined a human group as "any set of two or more persons who take each other into account in their actions and are thus held together and set apart from others by virtue of their interaction."[1] Actually this statement is much more nearly a description of social interaction than a definition of a group. But its utility for us is in that very fact, since interaction is an integral part of a group. A group, however, is more than interaction, as we shall see later.

When two people "take each other into account in their actions," they are interacting. For example, when two persons converge at a

Two people may make a group.

single door at a given moment and one steps slightly to the side to allow the other to enter the door first, they are interacting since they are taking each other into account in their actions. Their behavior is predictable and organized in that they follow certain unwritten rules. If one is older than the other, ordinarily the older person is allowed to go first. Usually, a quiet "thank you" is expected for this polite behavior. But does this brief interaction constitute a human group? May the two persons so fleetingly taking each other into account in their actions be said to be a group?

Interaction is at the heart of the human group. This fact leads to at least three other considerations. First, a group consists of at least two persons who take part in the interaction. Second, there is some common goal or objective which they are seeking to achieve. The objective may be no more than the pleasant experience of being together as on a date, or it may be a formal, explicit goal such as a pact or contract between two parties. Examples of the latter might be a small unit of combat volunteers whose purpose is to destroy a cache of enemy ammunition or a homebuilder who contracts to build homes for a property owner. In the third place, interaction takes place on the basis of mutually shared rules of behavior. This means that the participants are guided by rules laid down by the group and shared by all those interacting. Like the goals, the rules may be informal, unwritten understandings of how behavior is to be carried out (like the expectation that people in a theatre will remain relatively quiet while watching a performance). Or they may be formal, codified rules such as parliamentary procedure or rules for behavior in a Boy Scout pack meeting. These rules serve to make the interaction smooth and act as barriers to a confused, disorganized situation.

Now we are ready to put all this information together and look at what it means. A group, sociologically defined, is two or more persons interacting to achieve some goal and guided by socially determined rules. Two people playing tennis, four people riding in a car pool, two people on a date, three people working for the telephone company, a family—all these are social groups.

The examples just mentioned may be called elemental groups. That is, they are groups made up of relatively small numbers of people in which interaction is on a direct or face-to-face basis. They are to be distinguished from large scale organizations or multi-group structures. These larger groupings are made up of a number of smaller elemental groups. For example, a university is a multi-group structure. A host of elemental groups such as maintenance people, dormmates, biology faculty, tennis team, and so forth are tied together into a larger structure recognized as having a special shape or organization. An entire society, like American society, may be viewed as a distinctive group composed of a numerous multi-group structures.

American society is composed of individuals who share a basic culture and who define themselves as part of a group called "Americans" and who interact by taking part in the social structure in an orderly manner.

TWO OR THREE DO NOT ALWAYS MAKE A GROUP

It takes more than simply physical proximity to constitute a human group. In fact, nearness may not even be necessary. A son who is away from home in college or in the Army remains a part of his family group. Yet six people sitting side by side watching a movie may have a minimum of interaction and no common goal and therefore, though only inches apart, they do not form a group. To be more explicit, a collection of people must have certain characteristics to be defined as a group. These qualities appear to be a part of all human groups.

Boundary Maintenance

Every group seeks self-preservation by establishing precise boundaries which are designed to protect the integrity of the group from the social environment. Sociologists refer to this characteristic as *boundary maintenance.* There are rules for membership—qualifications which each member must have. For example, not just anyone may be a *bona fide* member of a group such as a college class. First, a student has to be enrolled in the college, and here too certain standards must be met. One must go through the rigors and expense of registering for the class. Thus by having rules of membership, the group keeps outsiders out.

Uniforms, badges, or membership certificates are also used in maintaining boundaries. These external signs of membership give a kind of psychological identification to the group member. It should be noted here that these symbols may not always be formal. For example, sandals, blue jeans, tee shirts, and long hair may be viewed as the uniform of certain persons who are a part of the youth culture. These are as effective as an army uniform for identification of group members.

Self-preservation helps to protect the integrity of the group by giving the group a social identification. When members can identify the group and perceive themselves as a part of the group, an "in" feeling occurs. Outsiders are kept out by virtue of the social boundaries which further intensifies the members' feelings of belonging since he can separate himself and his group from non-members.

The mechanisms used by the group to establish boundaries can also help facilitate the easy movement of an individual from one group to which he belongs to another. For example, the businessman wears a suit and tie to work. These are badges of membership in certain groups. In the evening he changes to the uniform of his bowling team and thereby identifies with the bowling group. Various branches of the armed services provide social boundaries in the form of differing uniforms for each branch. Within each branch explicit badges are worn (stripes, medals) which further differentiate between groups. Thus, self-preservation through boundary maintenance has to do with the means by which a group keeps outsiders out and gives insiders an "in" feeling.

Movement toward Equilibrium

A second characteristic of all groups appears to be the tendency toward balance or *equilibrium*. Groups normally seek balance and attempt to protect themselves from change induced from external factors. The effort to maintain equilibrium does not always mean that groups (elemental or multi-group structures) are completely resistant to any change. Equilibrium may mean, as George Homans says, that a change in one element is followed by changes in all other elements so as to reduce the impact of the original change.[2] The birth of their first child is definitely a change for a young couple. It disturbs the status quo and changes old habits and patterns of behavior. To offset the disruption of normal activities, each member must be willing to change his mode of life in order to achieve a new equilibrium. In a similar manner, student demands for a greater voice in university affairs have resulted in a series of internal changes in administration policies in order to achieve a new equilibrium.

Cohesiveness

A third characteristic is *cohesiveness*. This characteristic has to do with the attachment and relationship of group members to each other or, in other words, with harmonious internal relations. Through both formal and informal communications and through control of members' behavior, individuals are regulated in their relationship to one another. Members who disrupt the integration and whose behavior does not change when subjected to controls are excluded from the group. The recalcitrant individual's exclusion from the group may come as a transfer or promotion in a large scale organization, or the person may be snubbed by a small informal group. An individual may be blackballed, his contract may not be renewed, or he may be fired.

The exclusion of nonconformist individuals is based on the integrative need of the group.

Tension

All groups appear at one time or another to be characterized by *tension*. Group members do not always interact in a harmonious manner and because this is true, conflict appears to be a natural component of group life. This malintegration is termed tension and, although never sought as a characteristic by the group, it seems to be a part of group life. Maladjustment of group members may arise because the rules are not clear (breakdown in communication), because the rules are not known, or because the rules simply are not obeyed. Individuals may develop vested interests counter to the objectives of the group, power grabs may arise, or new personalities may be introduced. All these elements may create a conflict situation.

Groups sometimes provide mechanisms to reduce tension. For example, explicitly written documents (like constitutions, bylaws, job specifications, contracts, or other legal documents) are used to spell out the rules exactly. Contracting parties sometimes go before the courts or other negotiating bodies for settlement of disputes. Tension-reducing mechanisms even include such things as the authoritative statement of the father concerning which of two quarrelling children actually owns a toy.

Conflict is not without its positive qualities. The tension that arises in a group may result in a compromise situation which in effect makes for more effective group work, greater harmony, and an improved situation. Beneficial policy changes in large organizations may occur because a large number of people create a crisis by complaint. The same is true on a smaller scale when, for example, a wife gets upset because she perceives her husband's behavior to be inadequate for one reason or another. The point which is vital to understand is, however, that despite the potential creativity of a conflict situation, the group seeks to reduce tension and correct the conflict by reestablishing harmony.

Goals

Finally, groups are characterized by *goals*. No group exists which does not function toward the achievement of some goal. The *specific* objective may be nothing more than the interaction itself as, for example, when two persons of the opposite sex enjoy each other's company for an evening. Usually this activity is called a date and serves a number of functions besides the enjoyment of the interaction.

On the other hand, some groups have exactly worded, rigid objectives for which the group is designed to accomplish. For example, a committee may be established by a fraternity to investigate possible places to have a weekend picnic. The purpose of the interaction of this committee is oriented around the securing of useful information on picnic sites for the consideration of the fraternity.

Robert Merton has distinguished between manifest and latent functions.[3] Manifest functions may be said to be those objectives which are clearly designed to be accomplished by the group. These functions are purposely sought as objectives by the group. Latent functions, on the other hand, are goals which are accomplished as by-products of group interaction. For example, schools are expressly designed to teach the three Rs (and other curriculum matter) and to transmit cultural values (like patriotism, honesty, cooperation) from one generation to another. These are the manifest functions of the school. Its latent functions are its work as a dating agency and its baby sitting services (i.e., keeping boys and girls off the streets).

CONTINUING THE GROUP

In sum, a group is two or more persons interacting to achieve some goal and guided by socially determined rules. It is characterized by boundary maintenance, equilibrium, integration, tension, and goal orientation. All groups have these characteristics, yet some groups exist for only a short time while others seem to go on forever. What keeps some groups going?

Charles Loomis helps us answer that question. He has described six master processes which are methods of insuring continuity of the group.[4] These master processes are the mechanisms which develop group solidarity and help to maintain the group over a long period of time.

Communication

This concept refers to the processes by which information, attitudes, and beliefs are transmitted through the group. Communication, as used here, may also refer to methods by which information, attitudes, and beliefs are created by group interaction. It is not so much that one member says "Here is an attitude for all to share," and then through communication channels the attitude is transmitted to other members of the group. Individual sentiments are not so easily swayed. Rather, the interaction of the group hammers out individual attitudes through debates, rap sessions, and arguments. This, too, is communication.

Group Morale

Here, the focal point is the actual methods used to keep outsiders out and give insiders an "in" feeling. Groups maintain their solidarity and keep themselves going by actually practicing boundary maintenance.

Clothing may be worn as a badge to help a person belong to a group or to keep him out.

Recently one writer attended a panel discussion on narcotics. The meeting was well attended by long-haired college students. One panel member, an older man dressed in a business suit and sporting neatly trimmed hair, attempted to identify with the "long hairs" by adopting their jargon. He was hardly two minutes into his presentation when it became apparent that the "long hairs" had drawn the boundaries of their group with him on the outside. He had attempted to wear one of their badges by speaking their lingo, but they rejected him from their group. (It might be said, in his defense, that he rejected another of their badges—he said smoking pot is wrong.)

Socialization

The process by which a new recruit is taught the skills, rules, and values necessary to successful participation in the group is called socialization. When parents tell little Johnny that he must not take things which belong to other people, they are engaging in the process of socialization. When the professor says on the first day of class, "No one may come into this class late," he is in the process of transmitting the rules to the group and is socializing class members.

Social Control

Groups devise means to insure obedience to the rules and to control deviancy. Formal punishment like prison sentences or fines are designed to insure conformity to the rules. More informal, but just as effective, is ostracism which is practiced in small, friendship groups. A person whose behavior is counter to the rules of the group is snubbed and made to feel like an outsider, etc. The ostracism is designed to make the deviating individual conform or become so uncomfortable that he will leave the group.

The term *sanction* is used to describe these controls. Explicitly, sanctions refer to rewards and may be both positive and negative. To act as expected is to receive praise, applause, or other forms of social approval. To deviate frequently results in expression of disapproval.

Systemic Linkage

This term refers to the connections which exist between the group and other social systems (groups) around it. The college class, which is a group, is linked to the total university, another social system. In fact, the university may be viewed as a total system which is a mass of interconnected systems or subsystems.

Institutionalization

Institutionalization refers to the establishing of a specific type of behavior as appropriate. That is, institutionalization is the creating of new rules. Most frequently this process takes place by a new, or even deviant, pattern of behavior merely being defined or redefined as appropriate. Take the miniskirt as an example. Fifteen years ago it would have been considered immoral by many in our society. Today, most of the society finds it perfectly appropriate, even desirable.

HOW TO KEEP EVERYBODY DRIVING
ON THE RIGHT

It is time now to look a little more carefully at those rules which guide the behavior of individuals in social living. The interaction of people

is based on these rules and without them no group is possible. Imagine how it would be on a major highway if no rule existed about which side of the road one is to drive on.

It was said earlier that social structure gives society a shape or an arrangement. Another way of putting it is to say that social organization arises from the structure of society. Organization gives order to society and keeps it from becoming chaos, and this order is based upon certain basic elements which are the rules of the game mentioned previously. Just as the carpenter nails together the boards and lays the bricks to give arrangement to building materials to shape a house, so people operating according to the basic elements (or rules) give society a shape or organization. The following are the basic elements of social structure.

Norms

Put at its simplest, a norm is the behavior which is expected in a given context. This expectation is shared by the people involved. Norms extend from such a simple thing as saying "excuse me" when you sneeze to international law covering prisoners of war. They make behavior predictable. That is, since norms are *expected* types of behavior, we know in advance what another person is likely to do in a given situation. In addition to giving order to social life, they save a lot of time. People do not have to determine what they are supposed to do in a given context. By knowing the rules, one knows in advance what is expected.

Take a normal (there's our word norm again) classroom situation. Students know before the class even meets the first time what to expect from the teacher. Depending on the type of subject matter, the instructor will enter the classroom close to the beginning of the hour, call the roll, lecture or read or lead a discussion, and leave when the class meeting is concluded. The orderliness of it as well as its predictability is based on the fact that both teacher and students are acting according to shared behavioral expectations (norms).

When the noon hour approaches, students make their way to the cafeteria (a behavioral expectation of our society is that people eat a mid-day meal). Once there, they form lines as each awaits the time to be served. They sit at tables and booths (rather than on the floor), eat with forks (rather than fingers), wipe their mouths on napkins (rather than on their sleeves), and wait until their afternoon class meeting, confident that the professor will appear in the right place at the correct time. All this noontime behavior is based upon norms.

Usually norms are divided into three types depending upon their importance to the group and the punishment which they bear if broken. There are *folkways* which are traditional rules of the simplest level having little or no functional necessity and bearing little punishment. For example, norms that a lady be permitted to go through a door before a gentleman, that a man takes off his hat in an elevator, or that we stand when the national anthem is played are folkways. Their source is in religion, expediency, or custom.

The second type of norm has more importance to group life and therefore is more severly punished when broken. These norms are called *mores* (singular is *mos*). Examples of mores might be the general expectation that a person will keep the vows which he makes when he marries. Mores stem primarily from expediency. That is, certain types of behavior are necessary for a society to survive.

It is necessary to note, however, that social survival usually means maintaining the status quo. That is, mores keep change from occurring so rapidly that the social organization would be completely destroyed. Some mores do change and societies continue to survive. Witness, for example, the changes which have taken place in dating patterns in the last two decades. But the point here is that mores are

replaced by new mores which effectively allow a society to continue or to survive.

The last type of norm is a *law*. When a mos is officially codified (i.e., written down), it becomes a law. A very necessary element in social survival is limiting the taking of human life. A mos of our society is that people will not kill other citizens without a just cause. (We will not stop here to discuss all the meanings of the word "kill" or what a "just cause" is.) So we officially codify this mos and make murder unlawful.

Some laws are treated more like mores than laws. Many laws associated with morality, e.g., laws against adultery or fornication, are simply not enforced by agencies such as the police and the courts. Public opinion and individual sanctions are used to enforce these laws. Others, like the so-called "blue laws" which forbid the sale of certain type of merchandise on Sunday, are enforced by the legal structure. One may easily see, however, that other businessmen would have a vested interest in seeing that a competitor obeyed the blue laws, which may help explain why these laws are narrowly enforced.

Role

Norms are behavioral expectations and are the smallest element in social structure. If we take all the norms which guide a person's behavior while carrying out a single function in a specific context, we have a role. A role then is simply a cluster of norms which pertain to the performance of a single function. It is not at all unlike a "role" which an actor plays. He says the lines, shows the emotion, and carries out the activity which his "part" or role calls for in the play.

Take a father, for example. He has several roles which he plays in his family. He is a provider, disciplinarian, teacher, companion, sex partner, etc. If we isolate one of these for a moment, we can see how it is but a bundle of behavioral expectations. His teacher role includes the following norms. He will help give his children the information and skills they need to become independent adults. He will set an example of responsible adulthood for his children. He will answer his children's questions as accurately and honestly as possible. These norms, and others, combine to form the teacher role for the father in today's American family. It is assumed in our society that when a man marries and decides to have a family, he will fill the role of teacher, among others. Thus we are dealing with a pattern of behavior which for a large segment of our society is predictable because it is based on shared behavioral expectations (norms) that cluster about the performance of a single function (role).

Position

If we consider for a moment all the roles which a person performs in a single group, we may term this cluster of roles a *position*. Each person plays roles in a number of groups. The father we mentioned previously might also be a church member, a lodge officer, catcher for a softball team, and a committee chairman for the PTA. He will also be part of many informal groups like friendship cliques, and so on. In each of these groups this man has a single position which is the constellation of all the roles he performs in each. The content of the roles are, in turn, the composite of norms or behavior which is expected of his performance in the group.

Human interaction, in summary, takes place on the basis of rules of behavior which are shared by those interacting. These rules, called norms, give orderliness and predictability to human activity. Without these rules no social life would be possible.

TYPES OF RELATIONSHIPS

A high school student worked in a large supermarket. He was expected to be at work at a precise time, punch a time clock, work until an exact time for lunch, report back in exactly thirty minutes, and work until a specific time in the evening. The conversation he had with the manager the day he was hired was his last except for an occasional "Good morning, Mr. Caraway" in passing. He was told precisely what his job was to be, and he was to do that job and no other.

Later, still in high school, he went to work for a small corner grocery store. The time schedule was not nearly so rigid and there were many friendly conversations with the owner of the store. The job he was to do was not precisely defined and he was expected to pitch in wherever he was needed and to take a personal interest in the work of the total store.

The experience of the student was different in the two grocery stores because each one represents a different group, each characterized by a certain type of relationship. The small corner grocery was characterized by *primary* type relationships while the supermarket was, for the most part, more *secondary* in nature.

Primary and Secondary

Charles Horton Cooley, around the turn of the century, first identified primary relationships.[5] He said that this type of relationship is intimate and usually face-to-face, includes sentimentality, and emphasizes cooperation. Usually we experience primary relationships in the family, friendship groups, peer groups, and the smaller, more closely tied groups in which we participate. These groups are called *primary groups.*

Cooley referred to these relationships as primary for a number of reasons. First, they seem to be basic and universal to all human societies. Second, they are primary in the sense that this is the first type of relationship that the infant experiences. They therefore play a fundamental role in the social development of the child. In the third place, and most important, through these relationships the individual internalizes and becomes identified with the beliefs, values, and purposes of the society.

A primary relationship is one, then, in which the persons involved are related to one another in sentimental, personal, and informal ways. *Secondary* relationships, on the other hand, are less personal, less intimate, and more formalized.

How many secondary groups do you participate in?

A word of caution should be interjected at this point. Primary and secondary relationships and groups are ideal types. That is, they are *logical* extremes and do not exist in reality. There is no primary group that does not possess some secondary relationships and vice versa. Our most important primary group, the family, may at times possess some secondary characteristics. After all, it is begun by the formal signing of a legal document (the marriage certificate), and wills, insurance policies, birth certificates, and other formal statements are a part of the modern family. On the other hand, even in groups with many secondary characteristics one may develop friendly, informal, and even intimate relationships. Therefore, one generally speaks of groups as more or less primary or more or less secondary depending upon the type of relationships which seem to describe the group most accurately.

A somewhat fuller treatment of the same general topic was introduced by Ferdinand Tönnies (1855–1936), a German sociologist.[6] Tönnies (pronounced "turn yees"), who witnessed the unification of Germany and its beginnings of industrialization, was interested in developing types of societies to help explain the changes he observed in Germany. He spoke of *gemeinschaft* (community) and *gesellschaft* (society). The basis of the former is sentiment or natural will (*wesenwille*). Gesellschaft-like societies are based on rational will (i.e., logical, formal contracts).

Tönnies further differentiated between the two types of society in the following manner. In a gemeinschaft-like setting, fellowship, kinship ties and neighborliness are emphasized. Customs, traditions, and family rules become important in determining behavior and a man's word is his bond. Folkways and mores are almost sacred and there is a genuine resistance to change. There is an emphasis on harmony and concord. Religion and superstition are integral parts of such a society and intimate aspects of the individual's life.

Gesellschaft-like societies are based upon rational calculation. Exchanges of goods and services are controlled by many social agencies, and written laws and contracts take the place of verbal agreements. Traditions are not nearly so hallowed and change is not as seriously challenged.

It may be observed that the gemeinschaft-like society is one in which primary groups and primary relationships predominate. Conversely, gesellschaft-like society is characteristically made up of secondary groups and secondary type relationships. The gemeinschaft-like society is more primitive and agrarian whereas industrial, urban, mass societies are more gesellschaft-like in character.

SUMMARY

Sociology, it was said in chapter one, is the scientific study of human behavior in group life. This chapter has had as its purpose clarifying the word "group." We noted that a group is comprised of at least two people interacting to achieve some objective and guided by socially determined rules of behavior. Five characteristics of the group were listed: boundary maintenance, equilibrium, integration, tension, and goal orientation. Norms were discussed along with roles (clusters of norms) and positions (clusters of roles). Next, it was noted that groups can be classified into two ideal types according to whether the nature of their characteristic type of relationship is more primary or secondary. Finally, it was pointed out that total societies could be described by their predominant type of group.

Notes

1. George A. Lundburg, et. al., *Sociology,* 4th ed. (New York: Harper and Row, 1963), p. 73

2. George C. Homans, *The Human Group* (New York: Harcourt and Brace, 1950), pp. 303–4.

3. Robert K. Merton, *Social Theory and Social Structure* (New York: The Free Press, 1957), pp. 17–84.

4. Charles Loomis, *Social Systems: Essays on their Persistence and Change* (Princeton, N.J.: D. Van Nostrand, 1960), pp. 30–36.

5. Charles H. Cooley, *Social Organization* (New York: Scribner, 1909), pp. 23–24.

6. Ferdinand Tönnies, *Community and Society,* trans. Charles P. Loomis (E. Lansing, Mich.: Michigan State University Press, 1957).

Thinking
Sociologically

1.   Begin to look for "shared behavioral expectations" in the interaction of individuals around you. As a class, for example, divide up into small groups of four to six people. One person in each group will engage in certain type activities on the campus or in some other public place, while each other member of the group observes from some spot. One person, for example, can first stand on the sidewalk. Notice what people do as they pass the individual standing there. Next, have the person sit on the sidewalk. Now notice how the reactions differ toward this individual. Then have the individual lie down on the sidewalk. Can you see a different set of reactions? Consider how people would react if the individual lying there were only partially clothed. Would you expect different reactions toward him if this behavior had taken place in a different place? For example, what if the individual were standing and then sitting and then lying beside a swimming pool. Could you expect a different set of reactions on the basis of "shared behavioral expections"?

2.   Look in your closet and see how many "badges" and "uniforms" are there which you wear to identify yourself as a member of a specific group. Look for things associated with your age group and sex. Don't leave out things like "Sunday" clothes, "masculine" or "feminine" clothes, cowboy boots, lapel pins, or clothes associated exclusively with particular activities. List the differences between your vocabulary and that of your parents. Are these examples of "boundary maintenance" which set your age group apart from that of your parents?

3.   Select a primary group and a secondary group in which you participate. Can you see elements of the five characteristics of a social group in both of these? Do you feel more comfortable and at ease in some of these groups than you do in others? Is your sense of comfort related in any way to the concepts of gemeinschaft and geselleschaft?

4.   The old saying is that rules (or norms) are made to be broken. Try deliberately breaking a few of our time honored folkways and see

how quickly you are sanctioned. For example, turn your chair around in class and face away from the instructor. Or when sitting at a table with a small group of students begin moving objects like cups, glasses, ash trays, and books immediately in front of one person. Put these things in about the spot which the person's plate would be if he were eating. Move the objects slowly, one at a time, with a few minutes pause between each move. What facial expression, gestures, and words does the person use to try to keep you from doing this?

Chapter 3

Cognitive
Objectives

Chapter three is concerned with the subject of culture and is designed to investigate the meaning of culture, the human need for culture, and how culture affects human behavior. The following are points of emphasis which you should look for as you read this chapter:

1. *The difference between human behavior and the behavior of other primates (monkeys and chimpanzees, for example)*
   a. *What is meant when one says the difference is a matter of degree?*
   b. *How does this argument differ with those who say that human behavior is a difference of kind?*
2. *What is a symbol? What does the ability to symbolize have to do with tool making?*
3. *The definition of culture*
4. *What values are and what some of the dominant values of American society are*
5. *How culture affects human behavior—its role in relationship with the situation, personality, perception of the norms, definition of the situation, and social control*
6. *The meaning of cultural relativism*
7. *The importance of ethnocentrism*

The Rules of the Game

Sociologists, we have said, are interested in human behavior in group life. We have surveyed rather closely the meaning of the word "group" as used by the sociologist. Now let us turn to the words "human behavior" and see what light the sociological perspective can cast upon them. Let's begin with a question: What makes human behavior unique?

MAN AND APE

Man is a primate. That is, man shares many physical characteristics with monkeys, chimpanzees, and gorillas. Of course, man is a separate species. (Species refers to a group of organisms capable of interbreeding and bearing living young.) Man, as a separate species, shares physiological qualities with other primates but is physically distinct. Apparently, about five million years ago, a common ancestor gave rise to both the great apes and man. (The theory of evolution does not teach that man descended from the apes; rather, we are told both man and the apes came from a common source.)

Despite the existence of a common ancestor for man and apes, even a non-expert can see that there are significant differences between human and nonhuman primates, both physiologically and behaviorally. Our question is, what are the differences in behavior and what causes them?

Up until two decades ago, it was fashionable to say simply that the differences in human and nonhuman primate behavior are a matter of degree. That is, man and the apes are capable of approximately the same kind of behavior, only man, due to certain physical equipment which he possesses, is capable of more of it. Proponents of this position noted several reasons for man's superior position. (1) He has a bigger brain than the ape. The cranial capacity (brain size) of the average human is approximately 1350 centimeters while the chimpanzee has a cranial capacity of approximately 55 centimeters. Because man has a bigger brain, he can think faster and more efficiently than can the chimp. The larger capacity also led to the development of speech which allows for increased communication among humans. (2) Man stands upright whereas apes walk on all fours. Man's upright posture freed his hands to carry things, which led to his ability to manipulate objects and also developed in man the capacity (and therefore the desire) to collect things. (3) Man has an opposable thumb, which means that his thumb can be placed in a position opposite the fingers. Man's hands, therefore allowed him to handle tools in an efficient manner. he would become a skilled craftsman making fine pottery, sophisticated weapons, sharp tools, etc.

Thus the difference between man and chimps, said the proponents of this older theory, is a matter of degree. His bigger brain gives him an advantage which his second cousin does not have. He is capable of faster thought, and has free hands and an opposable thumb.

Then, in 1949, Leslie White, an anthropologist writing in *The Science of Culture,* noted that we are dealing with a difference in *kind.* [1] In the larger brain of man resides an ability which does not exist, even in a smaller degree, in a chimp: man has the ability to *symbolize.* Man can conceptualize; he can think abstractly. This means that man can visualize an image in his mind and then imprint that image on a set of materials to create in reality what had been a mental image. Man can make tools and then produce tools to make tools. True, chimps do sometimes use twigs in a tool-like fashion. However, no chimp is known to have made a pocket knife to whittle out a stick to be used as some kind of instrument, and chimps do not save tools to be used again and again.

White is saying that man operates on a symbolizing level and nonhuman primates operate on the level of *signs.* A sign is any object or event the function of which is to signify some other object or event. The word "halt" to a man is a symbol since it has meaning and the user has assigned the meaning to the word. To a dog, the same combination of sounds ("halt") is a sign. He has been conditioned to cease movement when he hears the word. The conditioning has come only after many experiences of trial and error. No amount of explanation will suffice to convey the meaning of the word to the dog. For

Referees make frequent use of symbols.

him, any word ("go," "run," "blip") could be associated by training with the cessation of movement.

Man's brain allows him to symbolize. White says that a symbol can be anything the meaning of which is determined by the user. For example, take a few straight lines on a page. In themselves, the lines mean nothing. However, humans assign different meanings to various arrangements of these lines. In the margin are two symbols. These marks are nothing but combinations of straight lines on a page. But to many Americans one set of marks symbolizes reverence, things Godly, and is a call for dedicated service and sacrifice. The other conjures up feelings of aversion, fear, and even hate.

MAN AND INSTINCTS

Man's behavior, we have seen, is unique because it is meaningful or symbolic behavior. Most of what we do has some meaning to us and to others with whom we are interacting. When the young man says to the young lady, "I love you," he intends to convey some meaning to her. Both he and she understand the meaning conveyed in those words. (Sometimes, however, the meaning intended by words or gestures of the user and the meaning perceived by the other are not the same.) Some of our actions as humans are still on the purely biological or physical level and have no meaning. For example, when a person sneezes, he intends no meaning. The sneeze is simply a physical reaction to certain elements in a person's immediate environment. When, however, the sneezer says "Excuse me" and another person says "Bless you" after the sneeze, once again the persons involved are on the meaningful level.

A man builds a house and a bird builds a nest. Are they doing the same thing? And even more important, is their behavior caused by the same forces? The bird, we are told, builds its nest by *instinct.* It is biologically programmed to build the nest at a specific time and in a specific way. All members of a species use the same type of materials and fashion their nests in precisely the same manner. In man, the process of building a house is *learned,* not instinctual. In fact, if instinct is defined as a particular pattern or way of doing things which is fixed by the genetic make-up of the individual, man has no instincts. It seems that as man has come to depend more and more on his symbolic brain, he has become increasingly more dependent upon learning rather than instincts. In his 3.5 million years of history on earth, he has lost one instinct after another until now all his patterns of behavior are learned.

Humans are *taught* how to behave. Even the most basic of human reactions, like sexuality, is learned. Children must be taught what it means to be men and women in a certain society. For example, in our society, the male is usually expected to be the sexual aggressor and pursue the female. However, this pattern is learned, not instinctual. In some societies, the male is passive and is sought out by the female.

Some animal behavior is also learned. The infant monkey must interact with others of his species to learn much of proper monkey behavior. A monkey reared in isolation and then returned to his natural habitat cannot survive. He has been denied the privilege of learning what monkeys must know to live in the wild. But monkeys, unlike humans, do not add to the body of knowledge which the former generation has taught them.

So far, what we have seen in this chapter is that man thinks and behaves symbolically and his patterns of behavior are learned. We are ready now to look at one word which combines both of these ideas and describes the process by which man's meaningful behavior is learned. That word is *culture.*

A human built this because of learning. A bird will nest here because of instinct.

MAN AND CULTURE

The word culture, as used by the sociologist, is quite different from its usage in popular language. We frquently hear people say things like, "She is a very cultured person." Such a statement implies that the person being described is trained in the arts or knows the rules of etiquette or speaks proper English. Sophistication, grace, and charm is the popular meaning of culture. Such is *not* the meaning of the word when used by the sociologist.

E. B. Tylor, an anthropologist of the nineteenth century, defined culture as "that complex whole which includes knowledge, belief, art, law, morals, customs, and any other capabilities and habits acquired by man as a member of society."[2] Leslie White put it a little bit differently. He said that culture includes: acts, or patterns of behavior; objects, or tools and things made by tools; ideas, or beliefs and knowledge; and sentiments, or attitudes and values.[3]

Culture is man's social inheritance and the physical objects involved in that inheritance. All the social things which are taught and transmitted by one generation to the next is culture. Use your imagination for a moment and picture a human being reared in complete isolation from other human beings. Such a person probably could not walk. His words would be grunts. He would know nothing about controlling his bowels, eating habits, simple arithmetic, reading, watching television, bicycles, automobiles, money, clothing, shaking hands, waving good-bye, loving, or being loved. Such a person would be less than human. The qualities which the person would have lost in being isolated are his social inheritance. Such a person would be ignorant of all the learned and expected ways of life which are shared by members of a society. When we visualize all that this person loses by his isolation, we begin to understand culture and its importance.

It is quite easy to separate what is biological and what is cultural in source. Take as an example a rather commonplace experience. You are walking across the campus and pass a flower garden in which an elderly man wearing faded overalls is hoeing. He is whistling a tune, like "Rock of Ages," and he smiles at you and says, "Hello." Much of this event is based on biology. The man is Caucasian (or what we commonly call white). His hair is curly, turning grey, and rather sparse on top. He has two feet, is standing upright, and appears to have all the other physical traits of a normal human being. These are factors associated with his genetics. The word he used to greet you ("hello") and that he greeted you rather than ignoring you, is culturally based. That he wears overalls and not a "G-string" or a flowing robe is also determined by his culture. The instrument he uses for digging, the hoe, is also a part of his culture. In another society he might have been using another implement like a sharpened stick or piece of wood with a stone affixed to its end. His smile, which was a way of showing friendliness and acceptance, is also part of his culture.

Culture then refers to the mass of learned patterns of behavior which is passed from one generation to the next. It is meaningful behavior. That I am capable of clenching my fist is inherited biologically. But that my clenched fist symbolizes anger, readiness to fight, or frustration is learned. It is part of my culture because it has meaning which I have learned from interaction with others. It is a part of my social inheritance.

CULTURE AND VALUES

In the previous chapter we noted that social life would be impossible without rules of conduct. Without norms, human interaction would have no order; it would be chaotic. The rules of conduct (norms) are a part of the culture which man inherits through interaction with others.

People follow patterns of behavior which they have learned. Their acts have meaning and are a part of their culture.

Culture also provides members of a society with values. Values are standards used in a society to determine what is important or of worth. They measure the capacity of an idea, object, or experience to satifsy a human desire. Values, then, are feelings associated with what is desirable or undesirable. The point here is that these standards of what is valuable stem from our culture.

Norms are associated with values in the sense that values are a kind of umbrella under which norms are worked out. A society may have eight or ten or a dozen values. From these values come expected behavioral patterns (norms). Which comes first, values or norms, is a question much like the chicken and egg dilemma. We have chickens, therefore, we have eggs and we have eggs, therefore, we have chickens; no one can say which came first. In the same sense, the way we behave determines what our values are, and what our values are determines the way we behave.

Some of the values which sociologists have isolated as characteristic of the American society are listed below. Obviously, this list of values does not include all the values present in this society. Some important

What values important in this person's culture are illustrated here?

subcultural differences in value structures are completely overlooked. For example, certain groups would challenge some of the values and add others. This list of values includes some of the most general principals which appear to be characteristic of middle-class society.

Achievement of Success—Americans place a premium upon success, usually measured by dollars and cents. From the youngest age, American children are taught to compete (grades in school, little league city championships, etc.) and the object is to win or at least to achieve well in comparison to other competitors. This attitude is summed up in the motto of the U. S. Army: "The difficult we do immediately, the impossible takes a little longer."

Freedom—The concept of freedom in our society implies that large areas of choice should be left open to the individual. Freedom does not mean the absence of restraint. This value implies that each individual should be allowed the privilege of deciding among the alternatives available. The removal of restraints would create a chaotic situation leading to anarchy and confusion. For example, consider the pilot of an airplane. So long as he operates within the boundaries of his instruments and the laws of aerodynamics, he is free to navigate the skies. The moment he rejects the limitations of his instruments and these laws, he is no longer free but lost and possibly in danger.

Equality—By equality, Americans usually mean that every individual should have equal access to the opportunity to make decisions implied in the ideals of freedom. Americans do not believe that everybody possesses (or should possess) equal amounts of intelligence, education, or material possessions. This value places a premium upon the ideal that all should be allowed to develop the fullest of their potentials and go as far as their incentive will take them.

Individuality—Americans measure good or bad in terms of the individual. How good or bad is defined is not the issue at this point. What is implied in this value is the belief in the worth of the individual.

Education—Because an informed electorate is so important to democracy, and because of the stress on freedom and individuality characteristic of democratic societies, Americans place great value on education. We believe that economic and social problems can be lessened and cured with education.

Progress—Americans define progress not only as change, but change for the better. Usually, progress has to do with technological advances. But, however defined, this society deems it not desirable but imperative that progress be achieved.

Happiness—Generally, people in our society believe that life should be enjoyable and that pleasure is better than pain. This value is closely related to both individualism and progress.

Conformity—The American demand for conformity serves to balance the values of freedom and individuality. Conformity implies that individuals exercising their own decisions will be given freedom but not too much freedom.

Gunnar Myrdal, in a book entitled *An American Dilemma,* pointed out that a society's values may emphasize one thing and the norms may call for something entirely contradictory.[4] Myrdal was writing about the racial crisis in this nation and he noted that American values stress equality while its norms are discriminatory. A restaurant owner, for example, may subscribe to the value of equality as would most of the customers of the restaurant. But the "white only" sign remains over the entrance of the business because if one allowed

non-whites to patronize the business, white customers would find another place to eat. The societal value stresses equality but the expected behavior is discriminatory. The American creed of equality, liberty, and freedom and the actual practices of Americans are out of kilter and thus Americans confront a dilemma which, to be resolved, demands a change in the norms.

Values change, but slowly. Technological advances along with urbanization have caused our society to shift from an agrarian, rural nation to a mass, urban society. Most of the values listed above were hammered out in the rural history of this nation, especially the emphasis on individualism. In recent decades we have seen the acceptance of governmental activity as a positive value in an increasing number of fields. From compulsory social security to taxing the individuals personal income to controls on prices and wages and the protection against both economic depression and inflation, we have turned increasingly to governmental controls. It may be that America's emphasis on "rugged individualism" and the historical changes which are taking place in our society are incompatible. The philosophy that "government is best which governs least" may be a thing of the past. We are becoming increasingly a geselleschaft-like society and such an urban and completely industrialized society may demand a strong centralized government if individuals are to survive.

CULTURE AND BEHAVIOR

Culture exists, and man is dependent upon it. The process of learning from childhood what others expect and what one may expect from others is the process of internalizing one's culture. The individual learns the values, roles, norms, traditions, language, and so on in such a way that the individual becomes almost unaware of them. One's reaction to one's culture becomes almost automatic. So natural to the person are certain ways of behaving, thinking, and believing that one does these things like breathing. Like the squirrel that lives in (but is unaware of) the forest, so a human lives within (and may be unaware of) a culture.

Human behavior is affected by at least six elements and culture is only one. These six elements all act in unison to guide the individual's actual behavior. They are culture, personality, situation, perception of the norms, definition of the situation, and social control.

1. *Culture* represents the ideal, the norms and values of the society. It serves as a kind of blueprint guiding human behavior.
2. *Personality* refers to the psychological and biological limitations of the individual.

3. *Situation* involves the physical limitations of time and space.
4. *Perception of norms* means the individual's awareness of how he is supposed to act in the specific circumstances.
5. *Definition of the situation* is the individual's evaluation of both the social and physical environment that surrounds the situation.
6. *Social control* refers to the extent of punishment involved if the person deviates from the expected.

Let's see now if we can understand how all this works. Suppose a couple is about to get married. The wedding is an aspect of their behavior or activity which is designed to accomplish their goal of marriage. Each of these six behavioral elements will come to bear on this wedding.

Culture

The expectations in our society is that two people will have a formal wedding ceremony. The ideal usually involves a wedding gown, church, flowers, minister, rice, and an automobile on which "Just Married" has been scrawled with white shoe polish. This is the popular idea (the blueprint, or ideal) for a formal wedding ceremony in our society. But not every wedding takes place according to the ideal. Many marriages, perhaps most, follow some alternative pattern depending on other elements.

Personality

Perhaps the young man to be married is not religious. He may therefore prefer to have the wedding in a courthouse. Or maybe, on the basis of personality factors, the couple wants a small private wedding in the home of a friend. The psychological factors of personality may alter the ideal.

Situation

Big weddings cost money, and the couple may be short of cash. Though they may wish for all the trimmings of a big church wedding, their financial limitations may prohibit this. The actual financial situation must be taken into account in their plans. Lack of time because of some element in the situation may also prohibit a big wedding.

Perception of the Norms

In this case, it is hard to imagine an American couple that is unaware of the norms. Nonetheless, it must be said that one must know the norms before one may obey them. Where the various members of the wedding party are to stand during the ceremony, who is to say and do what and at what time in the proceedings are examples of norms which must be perceived if they are to be obeyed. Embarrassing mistakes could occur because someone fails to perceive a norm during the wedding.

Definition of the Situation

Actual plans for the wedding must take into account all of the above. A non-religious young man may "give in" to the wishes of his religious fiancee for a church wedding. Or, knowing that a big church wedding has always been the wish of his daughter, a father may borrow money to see that she gets what she wants. Or, since the daughter of the Jones' (who must be kept up with) had a very expensive wedding, the Smiths must see that their daughter has just as good a wedding, if not better. People's behavior is determined, in part, by their definition of the situation.

Social Control

Norms have a kind of toleration limit built around them. Within these limits one may deviate without punishment, beyond them some kind of punishment is experienced. In the case of the wedding, so long as the couple has a ceremony which is legal, no serious punishment will result. Let them simply begin living together, however, and some rather extreme types of social control might result.

Redefinitions

Though we may not be aware of it, these behavioral elements are at work every time at least two people are interacting. Culture, which tells us how we *ought* to act, is but one part of those factors which determine behavior. The demands of culture are filtered through all six aspects before behavioral decisions are made. For the most part, however, people tend to act within the bounds of the norms. And when large numbers of people deviate from the norms over a period of time, cultural redefinition may take place, and the deviating behavior is redefined as appropriate. If, for example, enough couples got married in blue jeans, this specific behavior could be accepted as appropriate.

If our culture defined ghosts as real, most of us would believe in ghosts. If the dominant values of our society were non-materialistic, few of us would seek materialistic status symbols. The frequent changes in music, clothing styles, hair length, and slang expressions among the younger generation is a cultural phenomenon. The type of music one should listen to (and enjoy), the style of clothing one should wear, etc., is an aspect of culture. These rules for behavior that tell us how we ought to behave change by redefinition. Thus for one period of time and during another the Beatles are "in." Bob Dylan is popular, perhaps acid rock is next, and then comes bittersweet folk rock. One newspaper article illustrates how the norms have changed for female college students since 1918.

> With today's college coeds clamoring for "no curfew" privileges and the women's liberation movement gaining momentum across the country, rules and regulations set for the women students in 1918 have been long forgotten.
>
> Found recently among the personal effects of a deceased alumnae of North Texas Normal College—now North Texas State University—was a yellowed page listing restrictions for coeds in 1918.
>
> Listed among the "things no girl can afford to do" were:
>
> "To indulge in gossip, coarse language or slang.
>
> "To chew gum in public.
>
> "To permit any sort of personal liberties from young men.
>
> "To loiter in front of young men's boarding houses or to appear to seek the society of young men on the streets or in business houses.
>
> "To spend her vacant periods entertaining young men in corridors, vacant classrooms, or on the campus.
>
> "To sit in the dark with a young man.
>
> "To receive attentions from young men not properly introduced and vouched for.
>
> "To walk in out-of-the-way places or go on picnics or automobile rides unchaperoned.
>
> "To wear negligee costumes on the street or to go downtown in middy blouses or bareheaded.
>
> "To injure her health by failure to wear such clothing as will protect her against the weather.
>
> "To make herself conspicuous by the use of too much paint and powder or by wearing clothes and jewelry too elaborate for the school room."
>
> Welcome to 1970, college coeds.[5]

CULTURAL RELATIVISM AND ETHNOCENTRISM

Someone has said, "Each man is in some respects like all other men, like some other men, and like no other man." This statement reminds us that there are certain universals about human behavior, that groups or societies differ concerning specific patterns of behavior, and that individuals differ in the particular society in which they live.

Universals have to do with certain broad and general levels of behavior. They are related frequently to biological needs like the need for food, clothing, and shelter. In fact, as a biological organism, man shares the need for light, food, and water with all other living organisms. All humans must, therefore, satisfy certain common life demands and confront certain common problems in living.

But some universals are social in nature. For example, all societies need a language and no matter what a person's nationality or cultural origins, he has all the psychic and physical powers to speak any other society's language. All human languages share similarities in phonic principles, general constructions, and usage patterns. Additionally, every society has some type of family in which the human infant begins learning the rules of life in his society.

But societies *differ from one another.* Although each society has some type of family, not all have the same practices. In one society marriage is between one man and one woman (monogamy), in another it may be between one man and two or more women (polygyny), and in another it may be between one woman and two or more men (polyandry).

Customs, beliefs, traditions, values, and norms differ from one society to another. What is considered useless or even immoral in one group may be considered moral, even necessary, in another. In some societies, the embryo of a chicken is considered a delicacy. Where this dish is eaten it is called "scrambled eggs." Eskimoes eat raw liver, and some tribes of Indians eat ants. Japanese eat fish heads and people in southern Louisiana eat crawfish. Some people in the southern United States eat the intestines of swine (they call them "chitlins") while people in other regions would not consider ingesting that part of a pig. Still others will eat no pork at all. In some societies women must keep their breasts covered, while in others the face must be kept hidden.

An anthropologist, doing work among the cattle-raising Guafiro Indians in Colombia, reports the following:

> I remember when once I spoke with an Indian woman of high social class about marriage, and the Indian custom of giving money and cattle to buy the wife. I had not yet come fully to understand the Indian custom, and while the woman spoke of her price I felt terribly sad that a Colombian woman could be sold like a cow. Suddenly she asked, "and you? How much did you cost your husband?" I smugly replied, "Nothing. We aren't sold." Then the picture changed completely. "Oh, what a horrible thing." And she lost all respect for me, and would have nothing further to do with me, because no one had given anything for me.[6]

This anecdote points out two facts. First, norms and values differ from one society to another. Culture is a very variable and relative thing. Second, each person has a tendency to think of the norms and values of his society as superior. That is, each person is *ethnocentric*. Ethnocentrism, which means literally "people centered," refers to the tendency to evaluate other cultures, groups, or societies by one's own standards. From a societal point of view, ethnocentrism has certain advantages. The view that your society's way of doing things is best makes for cultural stability and integration. Patriotism and the loyalty it insures help hold a nation together and creates a kind of national solidarity. Both the good and the bad effects of school spirit, fraternity and sorority competition, and denominational differences are all made possible by ethnocentrism.

Ralph Linton's description of the "One Hundred Per Cent American" is one view of ethnocentrism:

There can be no question about the average American's Americanism or his desire to preserve this precious heritage at all costs. Nevertheless, some insidious foreign ideas have already wormed their way into his civilization without his realizing what was going one. Thus dawn finds the unsuspecting patriot garbed in pajamas, a garment of Indian origin; and lying in a bed built on a pattern which originated in either Persia or Asia Minor. He is muffled to the ears in un-American materials: cotton, first domesticated in India; linen, domesticated in the Near East; wool from an animal native to Asia Minor; or silk whose uses were first discovered by the Chinese. All these substances have been transformed into clothes by methods invented in Southwestern Asia. If the weather is cold enough, he may even be sleeping under an eider-down quilt invented in Scandinavia.

On awakening he glances at the clock, a medieval European invention, uses one potent Latin word in abbreviated form, rises in haste, and goes to the bathroom. Here, if he stops to think about it, he must feel himself in the presence of a great American institution; he will have heard stories of both the quality and frequency of foreign plumbing and will know that in no other country does the average man perform his ablutions in the midst of such spendor. But the insidious foreign influence pursues him even here. Glass was invented by the ancient Egyptians, the use of glazed tiles for floors and walls in the Near East, porcelain in China, and the art of enameling on metal by Mediterranean artisans of the Bronze Age. Even his bathtub and toilet are but slightly modified copies of Roman originals. The only purely American contribution to the ensemble is the steam radiator.

In this bathroom the American washes with soap invented by the ancient Gauls. Next, he cleans his teeth, a subversive European practice which did not invade America until the latter part of the eighteenth century. He then shaves, a masochistic rite first developed by the heathen priests of ancient Egypt and Sumer. The process is made less of a penance by the fact that his razor is of steel, and iron-carbon alloy discovered in either India or Turkestan. Lastly, he dries himself on a Turkish towel.

Returning to the bedroom, the unconscious victim of un-American practices removes his clothes from a chair, invented in the Near East, and proceeds to dress. He puts on close-fitting tailored garments whose form derives from the skin clothing of the ancient nomads of the Asiatic steppes and fastens them with buttons whose prototypes appeared in Europe at the close of the Stone Age. This costume is appropriate enough for outdoor exercise in a cold climate, but is quite unsuited to American summers, steam-heated houses, and Pullmans. Nevertheless, foreign ideas and habits hold the unfortunate man in thrall even when common sense tells him that the authentically American costume of gee string and moccasins would be far more comfortable. He puts on his feet stiff coverings made from hide prepared by a process invented in ancient Egypt and cut to a pattern which can be traced back to ancient Greece, and makes sure they are properly polished, also a Greek idea. Lastly he ties about his neck a strip of bright-colored cloth which is a vestigial survival of the shoulder shawls worn by seventeenth-century Croats. He gives himself a final appraisal in the mirror, an old Mediterranean invention, and goes downstairs to breakfast.

Here a whole new series of foreign things confronts him. His food and drink are placed before him in pottery vessels, the popular name of which—china —is sufficient evidence of their origin. His fork is a medieval Italian invention and his spoon a copy of a Roman original. He will usually begin the meal with coffee, an Abyssinian plant first discovered by the Arabs. The American is quite likely to need it to dispel the morning-after effects of over-indulgence in fermented drinks, invented in the Near East; or distilled ones, invented by the alchemists of Medieval Europe. Whereas the Arabs took their coffee straight, he will probably sweeten it with sugar, discovered in India, and dilute it with cream; both the domestication of cattle and the technique of milking having originated in Asia Minor.

If our patriot is old-fashioned enough to adhere to the so-called American breakfast, his coffee will be accompanied by an orange, domesticated in the Mediterranean region, a cantaloupe domesticated in Persia, or grapes, domesticated in Asia Minor. He will follow this with a bowl of cereal made from grain domesticated in the Near East and prepared by methods also invented there. From this he will go on to waffles, a Scandinavian invention, with plenty of butter, originally a Near-Eastern cosmetic. As a side dish he may have the egg of a bird domesticated in Southeastern Asia or strips of the flesh of an animal domesticated in the same region, which have been salted and smoked by a process invented in Northern Europe.

Breakfast over, he places upon his head a molded piece of felt, invented by the nomads of Eastern Asia, and, if it looks like rain, puts on outer shoes of rubber, discovered by the ancient Mexicans, and takes an umbrella, invented in India. He then sprints for his train—the train, not the sprinting, being an English invention. At the station he pauses for a moment to buy a newspaper, paying for it with coins invented in ancient Lydia. Once on board he settles back to inhale the fumes of a cigarette invented in Mexico, or a cigar invented in Brazil. Meanwhile, he reads the news of the day, imprinted in characters invented by the ancient Semites by a process invented in Germany upon a material invented in China. As he scans the latest editorial pointing out the dire results to our institutions of accepting foreign ideas, he will not fail to thank a Hebrew God in an Indo-European language that he is a one-hundred per cent (decimal system invented by the Greeks) American (from Americus Vespucci, Italian geographer).[7]

SUMMARY

Man is capable of symbolizing, which means that his behavior has meaning. He not only acts and interacts with others, his action is full of meaning. From the time he is a child, man *learns* what the symbols mean and how to interact symbolically. The patterns of human behavior and the meaning of that behavior is called his culture. (Culture also includes man's material symbols: buildings, desks, pencils, etc.) Because man depends upon learning, he has lost virtually all instincts.

Culture, which is passed from one generation to the next, provides man with both norms and values. The norms and values provide the ideal, or a kind of blueprint, for human behavior. These blueprints (or the way one *ought* to act) are influenced by the personality of the actor, the situation in which he interacts, his perception of the norms, his definition of the situation, and the existence of social controls in the actual behavioral decisions of the individual.

Actual patterns of behavior vary from one society to another. Cultural relativism is the term by which cultural variations are described. The tendency for each society to judge the behavior of people in other societies by its own standards is called ethnocentrism. Usually people in one society (or group in a society) judge the other's methods as inferior to their own way of doing things.

Notes

1. Leslie A. White, *The Science of Culture* (New York: Farrar, Straus and Giroux, 1949).

2. E. B. Tylor, *Primitive Culture* (London: John Murray, Publishers, 1871), p. 1.

3. Leslie White, "Ethnological Theory," in *Philosophy for the Future: The Quest of Modern Materialism,* ed. R. W. Sellers, et. al. (New York: Macmillan, 1949), p. 363.

4. Gunnar Myrdal, *An American Dilemma: The Negro Problems and American Democracy* (New York: Harper & Brothers, 1944).

5. "Today's College Coeds Have Come A Long Way," *Denton* (Texas) *Record-Chronicle,* 27 July 1970.

6. See George M. Foster, *Traditional Cultures and the Impact of Technological Change* (New York: Harper and Row, 1962), p. 69.

7. Ralph Linton, "One Hundred Per Cent American," *The American Mercury* 40 (April 1937): 427–29.

Thinking
Sociologically

1.   Select a group of friends (perhaps other members of your sociology class) to play a culture game. Have two persons act as two friends greeting one another in as normal a manner as possible. (Perhaps each person in the group should have a turn playing the part as one of the persons.) Each person should then make a list of the symbols involved in the exchange. First, notice the words that are spoken. See how many words are used that have one meaning for that situation and an entirely different meaning in other contexts. (For example, "hi" is a symbol meaning hello and is used as a friendly greeting. Spelled differently, but pronounced the same, it means something entirely different.) Look for body gestures such as use of hands, facial expressions, body movements. Do we signal our pleasure to see one another, the depth of our interest in the conversation, and the termination of the exchange by body symbols? Discuss the lists of word and body symbols which are used in this daily type of interaction.

2.   When is the last time you saw two ladies holding hands in public? Have you ever seen two men hold hands? Our culture prohibits this kind of behavior, especially for men, although in other societies such behavior is considered normal. Make a list of ways and circumstances in which touching between members of the same sex is allowed in our society. One factor is age. For example, a grown man can hold hands with a young boy. Another has to do with specific circumstances—for example, two football players may embrace after one has scored a touchdown. What factors explain these phenomena of behavior?

3.   "America, love it or leave it" signs are one form of ethnocentrism that expresses, for some, a sense of patriotism. For others, "America, change it or lose it" is also a form of patriotic pride based upon ethnocentrism. How can these opposing views both be ethnocentric?

Ethnocentrism has advantages in keeping groups together. Community fund raising (e.g., the United Fund) is sometimes based upon comparisons with other cities. This appeal to civic pride is based upon ethnocentrism. In view of this fact, how would you consider school spirit? List ways in which school spirit encourages involvement in school activities.

Chapter 4

Cognitive
Objectives

The purpose of this chapter is twofold: (1) to show what personality is and (2) to show how personality development is dependent upon social interaction. As you read this chapter, look for the following points of importance:

1. *The meaning of the term personality*
2. *How the self-image or self-identity is developed and how it changes*
3. *Freud's major contribution to a sociological understanding of personality*
   a. *What is the id, ego, and superego?*
   b. *What are the five phases of personality development?*
   c. *What are the major criticisms of Freud's theory of personality development?*
4. *The socio-psychological theory of personality development and how biological, psychogenetic, and socialization factors combine to form personality*
5. *The five major agents of socialization*
6. *The importance of Cooley's concept, "looking glass self"*
7. *How George H. Mead built upon the concepts of Cooley*
   a. *What is symbolic interaction?*
   b. *To what do the terms "significant others" and "the generalized other" refer?*
8. *Why modern man may have difficulty developing a clear self-image*

The Path That Leads to You

We have been talking about the cultural influence upon the behavior of human beings. Our culture provides us with behavioral expectations which guide the way we act and supply a meaning for behavior. But when a person gets ready to do something he does not stop and say, "Now, what does society expect me to do?" Cultural determinants of behavior work in a much more subconscious way than that. Norms and values are *internalized.* That is, they become much like a reflex action that we do without thinking about it. Consider, for a moment, such a simple thing as eating. Most people in our society eat three meals a day. (There are, of course, exceptions to this general rule.) Physically, the human body could be sustained by two meals or several small snacks (some societies handle eating in such a manner). So accustomed to a midday meal have we become, however, that our bodies experience hunger at about noon. Most behavior is conditioned in such a manner. The rules are so much a part of us that we are unaware of them.

What is the process by which a society insures the internalizing of the rules? What mechanisms exist in a society by which this process is carried out? The best way for us to answer these questions is to look closely at the concept of the social self or personality.

63

WHAT IS A PERSONALITY?

John B. is quiet and shy. If he is in a group, he usually says very little. He smiles when someone else says something funny, but he never tells a joke. People like John, and he has lots of friends.

Bill R. is the life of the party. He's always talking, and he usually says something funny. People really like him. He goes out of his way to help other people, and is always friendly.

Marvin C. doesn't get along well with most people. He is always complaining or criticizing, and he has many unpredictable moods. He usually has one close friend, but not for very long, and others tend to stay away from him.

Carol M. laughs a lot and makes good grades. She is very popular, and gets elected to many things on campus. She is always willing to do her part in any project.

Beverly T. always seems to glow. She is dependable and always friendly. She is the type of person people look for when they want to talk.

Each of these persons is unique. Certain traits seem to be characteristic of each one and when we think of that person, we visualize these traits. And each of those persons has a "self-image" or "self-concept" which means that when he thinks of himself, he also visualizes certain traits. He characterizes himself as witty, charming, outgoing, shy, cowardly, strong, weak, assured, fearful, or any one of a number of combinations of these and other traits. The word we use to describe the characteristic traits of each person is personality.

The word personality comes from the same Latin source from which we get words like "person" and "personal." That word is *persona,* and it originally referred to a mask which an actor would use in changing parts on the stage. When he put on a new *persona* (mask) he became a new (or different) person. This use of *persona* gives us a clue to the meaning of personality. Those ways of behavior, thoughts, feelings, and techniques of solving the problems of life which appear to be characteristic of a person may be said to be his personality.

A person's personality is a part of his self-image. The way people picture themselves will determine to a great extent the kind of behavior which is characteristic of them. (It should be said that this self-image is largely subconscious. That is, we are not usually consciously

aware of what we *really* think of ourselves.) A person who visualizes himself as capable and friendly will act confident and be friendly. On the other hand, a person who imagines himself to be inferior (or not very capable in a given situation) may act timid or retiring (or may strenuously attempt to act superior to compensate for self-doubt.)

Personality, then, is the characteristic behavior of a person or the group of behavioral traits that we associate with the uniqueness of the person. It is the mask one wears or the usual part the individual plays in life. Personality is based upon the largely subconscious self-image. Both personality and self-image form the social self.

WHERE DOES THE SOCIAL SELF COME FROM?

Everybody has a personality. Is one born with it or does personality develop as a result of life's experiences? Can personality change, and, if so, how? We will begin answering these questions by looking at the theory of personality development advanced by Sigmund Freud, the founder of psychoanalysis.[1] We begin with Freud's ideas for two reasons: (1) His concepts of personality development are popularly known. His ideas have gained a wide acceptance among the general population due to popular magazine articles, books, and the mass media. These concepts have had a far-reaching effect upon parental attitudes toward children, child-rearing practices, popular conceptions of mental illness, and the actual treatment of the mentally ill. (2) Freud's ideas, although challenged by some and rejected by others, serve as a good springboard into a more sociological understanding of the social self.

The Three Parts of Personality

Freud said that the personality consists of three separate but inter-related parts:

The Id—The id is man's primitive, raw, core of unconsciousness. It has no sense of morality (good or bad) and here resides the *libido* (life force) which drives the individual in search of pleasure. This urge to pleasure is largely sexual in nature but includes all feelings which motivate a person to desire pleasurable contact with others and even with himself.

The Ego—The constant pleasure seeking of the id must be reconciled with the "reality principle." People cannot go around expressing their sexual urges or aggressive tendencies without regard to the demands

of societal living. The ego, which is the rational and conscious portion of personality, has the function of placing limits on the id. The ego must find socially acceptable outlets for the impulses of the id. In other words, the ego learns the rules for acceptable ways of expressing sex and aggression and channels the desires of the id into these avenues. One of the most frequently used methods the ego finds to control the id is *repression,* which means that these undesirable impulses are pushed back into the subconscious.

The Superego—The superego may be thought of as roughly equivalent to what we call the conscience. Here resides the demands of society for the proper expression of the desires of the id. The superego is stern, and concerned only with what is defined as right. It observes the ego and threatens it with punishment if it does not properly control the id. Its most severe punishment is a sense of guilt.

Stages of Personality Development

Thus, according to Freud, the personality may be viewed as having three parts. The id, which seeks only sensual satisfaction; the superego, unbending in its rigid demands; and the ego, which must reconcile the demands of the authoritative superego and the sensuality of the id.

Freud said that the id functions from birth, but the ego and superego develop during certain stages of life. In the *oral* stage, the infant achieves pleasure from sucking. It is in this stage that the ego begins to develop. The infant establishes relationships with the mother, begins to perceive itself as separate from other people and objects, and learns that certain activities will suffice to get its needs satisfied. The *anal* stage sees the further development of the ego. The child, through toilet training, experiences the first conscious effort to control the unruly id. If the child cooperates with his parents' wishes in the use of the toilet, they grant love and approval. The ego begins to perceive the social meaning of purely biological processes.

The *phallic* stage comes next. It begins at approximately two and one-half years and extends to about six years of age. Freud developed theories about the *Oedipus complex* (it is called the *Electra complex* for girls), which he believed appears during this stage. The boy wishes to possess the mother and destroy the father and the girl wants to possess the father and destroy the mother. The superego begins its development in the repression of these desires for incest (sex relations between blood relatives) and parricide (murder of a parent). The superego calls for identification with the parent of the same sex, and emotional maturity depends upon the successful working out of the Oedipus complex. (Freud saw the actual process of overcoming the Oedipus complex as taking years after the phallic stage had been completed. Thus, popular "cocktail psychoanalysis" ascribes many adult emotional problems to the fact that "He still hates his father," etc.).

The phallic stage draws to a close at about age six and the personality is formed by this age. If the child is arrested at any stage by incorrect handling, according to Freud, he or she bears the emotional scars for life. Everything from fingernail biting, to fear of large crowds, to aversion of authority, to homosexuality may be seen as the result of traumas or anxieties which stem from what has happened to the child during these three stages. He may be rescued from the problems of a malformed personality only by psychoanalysis in which the analyst and patient work back into the patient's childhood background and isolate an event or series of events which have scarred the personality of the individual.

Freud described two subsequent stages of pre-adult development. The *latency* stage extends from the close of the phallic stage to the beginning of puberty (the time at which sexual desires become conscious). During the latency period, sexual desires are dormant and the individual explores the surrounding social and spacial world. Physical maturation brings a reawakening of the sex impulses at the beginning of the *genital* phase. Sexual maturity, if achieved at all, means that the individual learns to accept the sex drives as normal (in which case one is not burdened with an overbearing superego) and to satisfy the drives in a socially approved manner (in which case the id is properly managed).

Freud's theories, while having wide acceptance, are not without certain logical and scientific shortcomings. His observations of human behavior came from his experiences with people who came to him with certain problems. They were middle- and upper-class Europeans whose background was largely marked with a strong Victorian background. What this means is that this theory may not be applicable to other cultures where sex is not looked upon in such a negative fashion.

Others have suggested that Freud overemphasized the infantile origins of human personality. Freud said that personality is fixed at approximately age six and refused to accept any explanation of adult behavior that was not tied firmly to childhood experiences. According to some other theories, personality development is a life-long process and childhood experiences, although important, are not as determinitive as Freud suggested.

Finally, there is no way to put Freud's ideas to a scientific test. His theory remains essentially that—a theory.

Freud's greatest contribution to our understanding of personality development was his insistence that personality is socially created. He emphasized that the social self is the product of experiences of interaction with others. We turn now to survey the process of interaction by which personality is formed.

SOCIAL-PSYCHOLOGICAL THEORIES OF PERSONALITY DEVELOPMENT

Personality, we have seen, is the manner of behaving (including thought and feeling) which appears to be characteristic of a person. It is those traits which one possesses normally. It is the way the person reacts to a situation while "doing what comes naturally." Recent research and thinking indicate that personality stems from a combination of three factors.

Biological Factors

John Locke, about four hundred years ago, spoke of an infant as "tabula rasa." He meant that the individual is like a blank sheet of paper at birth, and the experiences of life are the scribblings upon that page. But an individual at birth is only a *partially* blank sheet of paper. The way the genes combine at the moment of conception determines the sex of the individual, a great deal about his physical appearance and abilities (general body build, eye color, potential baldness or gray hair, how fast he will be able to run, how far he will be able to throw a ball), and much about intelligence. Biology seems to play the part of setting potentials and establishing limitations. Athletic skills are a good example of this fact. No amount of practice or training can enable someone without natural talent to run a hundred yards in nine seconds. The potential for this kind of speed is set at birth. However, training and practice are needed to develop the potential that is present. The same kind of limitations appear to be present in intelligence. Gene combinations set the limits of intellectual ability, and not everyone can learn calculus. Biological factors influence the size of the page and the kind of scribblings which may be put on it.

Psychogenic Factors

These factors have to do with the tremendous consequences for personality development of the very early care of the infant. It seems that the nature of these early experiences may set the tone of the life style which the individual will follow in later life. How the parents care for the infant, whether they are warm and loving or cold and uncaring, seems to give a kind of mental set which conditions his response to the environment. A person's general outlook on life (like hostility, withdrawal, acceptance, optimism, or initiative) seems to be based in these early experiences in infancy.

The infant establishes behavior which is effective in assuring that his wants are attended to, like crying when hungry or wet. The child notes that these signals result in a full stomach or dry diapers. When, however, wails or smiles bring no result or an uncaring cold response, the infant is discouraged from developing those mental and emotional ties with the outer world. The child begins to feel like the adolescent or adult who tells a joke that fails to amuse, or who extends a loving gesture that is rebuffed. Such experiences are indeed painful and if repeated often enough result in withdrawal, loss of the desire to communicate with others, and unwillingness to be self-expressive. Psychogenic factors set general moods and establish overall patterns of our response to our social environment.

Socialization

We have already defined socialization as the process whereby the individual acquires the skills, attitudes, and values necessary for successful participation in society. Socialization is the method by which the individual receives his social inheritance or the manner by which culture is passed on. Eli Chinoy says that it is the process which transforms "raw human material" into a social being.[2] Socialization begins in infancy and continues to a greater or lesser degree until death.

In infancy the individual begins to learn a language. The child is also introduced to symbolic gestures (nonverbal language) and begins to attach meaning to these. (For example, when the father extends both arms, opened wide, to his child, he is communicating nonverbally. This is a gesture which means, "I love you, come here and let me touch you.") The growing child begins to learn the meaning of the words "mine" and "yours" and the necessity of disciplining and controlling his desires. (The child is told "You do not take a toy that someone else is playing with.") Still later the child begins to gain knowledge necessary to employ skills intelligently and in the correct situation. He learns of the gods and spirits (according to the religion of his culture) and the appropriate rituals and ceremonies to please the supernatural powers. He learns to read, add, and subtract, or how to make bows and arrows and track game. Those values and skills necessary for survival (both socially and physically) in one's environment are transmitted to the individual in the process of socialization.

Learning, which is the individual's response to socialization, takes place in at least one of four ways: (1) overt communication, (2) human example, (3) trial and error, (4) logical process of thinking. You probably learned to drive a car by following the instructions which someone gave to you (responding to overt communication). You may have learned to mow the grass by watching someone else do it (following human example). Most people learn to ride a bicycle by simply getting on, falling off, and getting back on again (trial and error). When you learn "the history of the United States from 1850 to the present" by reading your history textbook, you are using rationality or natural processes of thought. The actual experience of learning is usually a combination of two or more of these kinds of activities.

It should be noted at this point that something more than mere learning is taking place in the process of socialization. The individual being socialized is *personalizing* or *inculcating* these skills and knowledge into his own self-conception. The norms, beliefs, values, and attitudes are internalized. The person is not like a vase which has its own shape and is simply filled to the brim. In this case, what is poured in determines how the container will look. What this means is that the individual has similarities to others because man is *social;* the human being is the product of interaction with others. And man is social because man has absorbed a culture that enables him to survive and live successfully in a society. Interaction with others makes a person what he is and gives meaning to human existence. The individual, prior to or separate from the socialization process, is pre-social (some even say pre-human). The process of socialization makes the individual human.

THE AGENTS OF SOCIALIZATION

Every society sets up regularized mechanisms which insure and carry out the socializing process. These mechanisms, of course, differ from society to society. Each society develops its own methods of transmitting the culture from one generation to the next. In our society there are five major agencies of socialization: the family, peer group, school, mass media, and organized religion.

The Family

The first agent of socialization is the family. The earliest and closest ties, as already noted, occur in the family setting. Most of us start our life in the context of a group including at least a mother, a father, and siblings (brothers and sisters). Here the child begins to experience the barrage of statements which form the socialization process.

"Don't run in the house."

"Don't talk with your mouth full."

"You shouldn't take things which don't belong to you."

"Brush your teeth;" "Say, thank you;" "Be nice;" "Don't yell at your mother;" "Do your homework."

These statements are, of course, designed to communicate specific information at a specific time. But anyone can see that they are based upon certain values: discipline is good; obedience is necessary; creativity and competition are necessary and useful.

In the family, patterns of sexuality are also learned. We tell a male child, "Boys don't play with dolls." In our culture, males are also taught that, while girls can show emotion, boys are to be fearless, protective, strong, and capable. Girls, on the other hand, are prepared for their supposed future role of wife and homemaker. Toys scattered about a home on Christmas morning reveal how consistent we are in teaching children the proper roles associated with their sex. After all, very few people would give a four-year-old boy a baby doll and imitation tableware. And how many little girls discover that Santa left them a pair of guns and holsters?

The attitude of parents or siblings have a profound effect on the developing personality of the child. Pessimism or optimism, extroversion or introversion, warmth or coldness, trust or suspicion—these all help shape the general outlook of the child.

Along with these factors, things like the educational achievement of the parents, their ethnic and religious background, their ages, and their occupational and economic status are important in determining the kind of interaction which occurs in the family. The number of children in the family also affects the process of socialization.

The Peer Group

A second agent of socialization is the peer group. Friendship groups usually consisting of persons of the same sex and approximately the same age are known as peer groups. (Adults have peer groups just like children do, although we usually think of peer groups in connection with children around eight to sixteen years old) These groups are more egalitarian and permissive than the family, and group members explore topics which are tabooed in the family. They exist ostensibly for the purpose of the fun in interaction. But they function significantly in the transmission of behavioral patterns. In the play groups of children, there is rude rejection of one who breaks the rules or dresses differently, which is an effective means of social control and the developing of the discipline necessary for obeying the norms of the group.

Another significant function of the peer group is support of the individual in making the transmission from the family to the outer world. Peer groups serve as transition groups from a family orientation to the greater society.

The School

The school is another agent of socialization. The educational system in our society shares a large responsibility for the socializing of the young. Our technological way of life demands specialists in many varied professions and our democratic system must have a well-informed, literate electorate. As our nation has grown more and more toward an urban, mass society based upon an industrial economy, the schools have had to assume a greater responsibility in imparting to the young the skills necessary to survive.

Not only does the school teach the three Rs it also transmits the major cultural values of the society. For the most part, the schools are based upon middle-class values and staffed by middle-class personnel. The values transmitted to the young are, therefore, those of middle-class society and may, in some cases, be different from the values which the child confronts in his family and peer group. Patriotism, ambition, competitiveness, concern for others, achievement, honesty, punctuality, neatness, diligence (all commonly believed to be necessary elements in the American way of life) are internalized by the child when the school system is successful in its job. The school is charged with transmitting morals and manners and making good citizens as much as it is responsible for teaching history and math and producing good accountants.

The Mass Media

The mass media combine to form the fourth agent of socialization. In recent years television, movies, radio, newspapers, and magazines have had an increasing impact as socializing agents in our society. They help the adolescent define his role, and, mediated by the peer group, assert strong pressure on the youth to conform. The behavior of well-known people, what they wear and what they think, become role models for the adolescent. The advertising industry likewise has a socializing effect. Using popular values to sell its wares, advertising helps convey these values to the young. Consider the typical advertisement for a mouthwash. Two young men are out on the golf course and one says, "I haven't seen you with Sally Mae lately. What's happened?" The other responds unhappily, "I don't know. One date, and she won't see me anymore." Sympathetically, the other replies, "Say, man, what you need is Lustavoris!" And he reaches into his golf bag and pulls out a bottle of the product, which he just happens to have with him. Later, at a party, the same two guys are happily talking and this time a girl is in the picture. One says, "Well, looks like you and Sally Mae are getting along all right." The other responds with a big smile, "Yeah, thanks to you . . . and Lustavoris." What is being sold is success with the opposite sex, not a mouthwash.

Organized Religion

Finally, organized religion is an important agent of socialization. Most religious institutions reinforce the basic cultural values and transmit them to its adherents. Leaving aside the denominational differences in doctrine and emphasis, organized religion as a whole advocates concern for others, achievement, patriotism, honesty, order, discipline, politeness, and other middle-class values. In sermon, liturgy, music, and ritual these basic values are reiterated.

Conflicting Socialization

Perhaps we should conclude this discussion of the five major agencies of socialization by making reference to the concept of *conflicting*

socialization. In a heterogenous (composed of unrelated or unlike elements or parts) society such as ours, it is almost inevitable that people become subjected to conflicting influences. What the child sees and hears in the home may not be what the child experiences in a peer group. The child may hear humility exalted in Sunday school and see on television the worship of the strong and crafty. His parents may be unwilling to discuss sex, but it is not a taboo subject in school or among his peers. Additionally, any young person may pick up copies of popular magazines which come weekly or monthly into many homes and read many things not commonly discussed other places.

Conflicting socialization is by no means limited to childhood experiences. Adults are frequently subjected to influences that demand mutually opposing types of behavior. A father may be expected to be authoritarian at home. Among his family members he is a pillar of strength, consistent in decisions and behavior, stable, and faithful. On the other hand, his job may be such that he must be submissive, willing to take orders, and able to adjust to instability and change. In the home, therefore, the father is expected not to submit to life as it happens. He must control events and plan for the security of his family's future. At the office he must be able to accept change easily, and realize he cannot control it. Much the same may be said of the wife's role in the home and as a "working mother."

Conflicting socialization is apt to be a part of the average college student's life also. Frequently the student is introduced to highly liberal and controversial ideas in the classroom. The Christmas vacation may find that same student embroiled in discussions at home where these ideas are resisted vehemently by his parents. The concept of the "generation gap" may, in part, be conceived as the result of conflicting socialization in which the peer group and the school place stress on one set of norms and values and the home emphasizes another.

What has been said so far is that personality is dependent on three elements: (1) certain biological factors which set potentials for individual development; (2) psychogenic factors, or very early experiences of interaction which work as general influences in determining temperment; and (3) learning, or the socialization process whereby cultural values and norms are transmitted to the individual. The major agents in our society which perform the work of socialization are the family, peer groups, the school, the mass media, and organized religion. These agents, however, do not always work in harmony due to the heterogenous nature of our society. The individual may be expected to internalize norms and values which are mutually exclusive. This latter situation is known as conflicting socialization.

It is time now to look carefully at the process of socialization. How exactly does interaction with the group affect personality?

THE PROCESS OF SOCIALIZATION

In the chapter on culture, it was said that man has a symbolizing brain. This fact means that man can think abstractly. He can visualize an object and then, using proper materials, can create what he has imagined. Man's symbolizing brain also allows him to understand meaning. An event is more than a physical occurrence. An event, like the birth of a child or the death of a parent, has meaning which man understands. (Man's culture assigns the meaning. Death, for example, symbolizes in our society an event to be mourned. In other societies, death signals a festive, happy occasion.)

Another advantage of man's symbolizing brain, and most important for personality development, is that man can be self-transcendent. This means that human beings can "stand off" and take themselves as an object. (Object here refers to a person with meaning.) We can imagine how we look to other people. Man then can observe himself as a meaningful object in a world of meaningful objects. Without this ability to be self-transcendent, Socrates' advice "know thyself" would be meaningless.

Charles Horton Cooley referred to man's ability to see himself as others see him when he introduced the concept of "looking glass self."[3] This concept, Cooley said, includes three things:

1) The imagination of our appearance (the total impact of our dress, speech, and behavior) to the other person.
2) The imagination of the other person's judgment of that appearance.
3) Some sort of self-feeling such as pride or mortification, satisfaction or dissatisfaction, security or anxiety.

Cooley said that through this process, a self-concept is created. In other words, through interaction with others and through our imagination of their evaluation of us (it does not necessarily have to be

correct imagination), we develop a concept of ourselves. We internalize what we feel are others' impressions of us and thus incorporate these impressions into our own personality or self-identity.

George Herbert Mead built on the concepts of Cooley.[4] Mead viewed human activity as *symbolic interaction.* That is, people are able to take each other into account in their behavior (interaction) because there is a shared understanding of the meaning of activity (symbolic). Gestures (nonverbal language) and words have meanings which serve as cues to the persons who are interacting. I am aware of myself and know the meaning attached to my action, and I am aware of you, and (because we share symbols) I can interpret or "get the meaning" of your behavior.

According to Mead, the self, or my awareness of myself as a meaningful object, develops from infancy. The infant has no self-conception. Then, through interaction with others, the child finds he has a name, becomes acquainted with the boundaries of his body, and begins to realize a separate identity. The child begins to use the pronouns "me" and "you," and later "I." The child becomes aware of himself and others, acquires a language (both gestures and words), and increasingly participates in symbolic interaction. (At first the mother may have to say, "That is not your toy, do not take it." Later, a shake of her head and a slight frown serve as sufficient cues to communicate her meaning.) The child learns that to win approval and get the desired responses, he must learn to "put himself in the position of others." Mead spoke of this as "role-taking." Here the child is explicitly seeing himself as others see him. The child now can be aware of himself and think expressly of needs and wants: hunger, pain, fear, happiness, ideas, wishes. And he can put himself in the position of significant others (mother, father, etc.) and visualize their feelings and thoughts about him.

Later, as the process of socialization continues, the child makes an important transition. The roles and attitudes of others becomes generalized and less dependent on specific persons. The child thinks at first, "It is not right to do this because Mother says so." Later he feels that he ought or ought not to behave in a specific way not because mother will be pleased or displeased, but because he wants to avoid self-blame or wishes to enhance self-esteem. He has internalized the rules; they are part of him. This latter stage Mead referred to as behavior oriented toward the "generalized other."

Cooley's "looking glass self" and Mead's concept of symbolic interaction mean precisely this for personality development: the individual puts himself in the place of the others with whom he interacts and perceives their evaluation of him. He internalizes these impressions of other's judgment of him and his behavior, and this becomes a self-concept or identity. Thus his self-image is a product of the perceptions of others' view of himself and his behavior. This self-image is created by interaction in which the individual engages beginning in infancy and lasting throughout life.

THE IDENTITY CRISIS

Most of our action may be viewed as an attempt to gain a favorable response from those with whom we interact, especially from those who represent (to us) an important reference group. Conformity in dress, speech habits, and general behavior patterns arise from our desire to get this positive response. Such a response is necessary to a positive self-image. Eric Berne, in his book *Games People Play,* and Erving Goffman, in *The Presentation of Self in Everyday Life,* show how we attempt to "put the best foot forward" in an effort to gain acceptance and esteem from those with whom we interact. The high school student who is so meticulous in dressing correctly (correctly may be defined as blue jeans, tee shirts, and sandals) is conforming to a specific reference group to elicit a positive response. The piano student who asks his teacher "How am I doing?" is asking for an evaluation with which he or she may identify (and is hoping for the teacher to say he is doing amazingly well). Our identity depends upon the evaluation others make of our behavior, and we attempt to control that evaluation so that it will enhance a feeling of self-worth.

Many people in our society have difficulty in developing a clear "self-image." This nation has moved rapidly from an agrarian, small-community type of society to an industrial, urban, differentiated society. In the former type, social relations are based on clearly defined and explicit norms and roles. In an industrial society, norms and roles may be ambiguous. Rapid social change may make the rules unclear. To the extent that this is true of our society, individuals do not, therefore, know what is expected of them. They are unclear as to what the expectations are, and cannot, therefore, clearly perceive how others are evaluating them. The result is difficulty in answering the question "Who am I?" They cannot seem to "find themselves." If, for example, there is confusion about motherhood in this society (Should a mother work? What about breast feeding? Should a mother rigidly toilet train a child? What about corporal punishment?), the young woman who plays this role does not know for sure what to do. Further, she does not know if she has done it correctly. In other words, she does not know how she's doing as a mother and in this role has no clear self-image or identity. When this condition is true of most roles people are asked to play, large numbers of people experience the anxiety of loss of identity. The result is a state of confusion, uncertainty, and bewilderment for the individual and inevitable conflict and disorganization in the society.

When norms become unclear, new groups may arise to fill the vacuum and supply rules for appropriate, meaningful behavior.

SUMMARY

The purpose of this chapter was twofold: (1) to show what personality is and (2) to show how personality development is dependent upon social interaction. Personality was defined as the configuration of behavioral patterns, thoughts, and attitudes which appear to be characteristic of the person. One's self-image gives rise to the personality.

The theories of Sigmund Freud were briefly presented. Freud said that the personality consists of the id, ego, and superego and that these three elements develop through the oral, anal, phallic, latent, and genital stages (especially the first three). Freud's greatest contribution to sociology was his emphasis on the social development of personality.

Building on Freud's ideas, it was noted that biology, psychogenic factors, and socialization appear to be the three important elements in personality growth. The biological makeup of the individual sets limitations and establishes potentials for individual development. Psychogenic factors, or early experiences of interaction, serve to determine the general outlook or temperament of the individual. Socialization refers to the learning experiences of the person in which the rules for behavior, attitudes, and values of one's culture are imported to the individual.

The process of socialization, as it relates to personality development, was described using the ideas of Charles H. Cooley and George H. Mead. These writers, noting man's ability to be self-transcendent, pointed out that the self or self-concept is one's internalized perception of the evaluations of others toward himself. When norms become unclear, interacting individuals have no way of knowing what others expect of him and, therefore, has no measurement of others' view of his behavior. An identity crisis results from such a situation.

Notes

1. Sigmund Freud, *An Outline of Psychoanalysis* (London: The Hogarth Press, 1949).

2. Eli Chinoy, *Society,* 2d ed. (New York: Random House, 1967), p. 15.

3. Charles Horton Cooley, *Human Nature and the Social Order* (New York: Charles Scribner and Sons, 1903).

4. George H. Mead, *Mind, Self and Society,* ed. Charles W. Morris (Chicago: The University of Chicago Press, 1934).

5. Eric Berne, *Games People Play: The Psychology of Human Relationships* (New York: Grove Press, 1969).

6. Erving Goffman, *The Presentation of Self in Everyday Life* (Garden City, N.Y.: Doubleday, 1959).

Thinking
Sociologically

1.   Make a list of adjectives which you feel really describe you by filling in the blank in the following sentence: "I am a _____ person." Try to be careful not to list things you *wish* were true of yourself. Remember that many parts of your self-concept cannot be raised to a conscious level. This list represents what you think about yourself. Try to analyze each of these adjectives and see if perhaps they are a reflection of what others appear to think you are.

2.   Select one attribute listed above which you consider most characteristic of yourself. Make a list of ways in which your behavior is affected because you think of yourself as possessing that attribute.

3.   Break up into small groups in your class and allow each person to discuss one experience which he has had in joining a new group (e.g., when you joined a club, started to college, went into the armed services, got married, etc.). For discussion, consider whether there was a process of socialization which occurred that taught you the norms, skills, and attitudes necessary for successful participation in the group. Were there embarrassments or perhaps some form of punishment that you experienced because you did not know or obey the rules? How effective were these sanctions in insuring that you either left the group or learned and obeyed the rules?

PART THREE

Stratification
and
Race Relations

Chapter 5

Cognitive
Objectives

The subject of chapter five is social stratification. The chapter represents an effort to present the socilogical understanding of social class, the class structure in American society, and the concept of social mobility in the United States. The following is a list of important points contained in this chapter.

1. *The meaning of the terms "social class" and "stratification"*
2. *The factors which are most important in this society in assigning social class ranks to its members*
3. *The differences in a caste system of stratification and a social class system*
4. *Those ways in which the Russian system of stratification compare with that of American society*
5. *The meaning of the term "social mobility"*
   a. *What is the most important factor in the rising standard of living in the United States?*
   b. *Why is this factor so important in the rising affluence of this society?*
   c. *What are four characteristics of the poor in modern American society?*
6. *The meaning of the term "underclass"*
7. *Who is Willy Brown and why is he important in a study of social stratification?*

The Missing Rungs in the Invisible Ladder

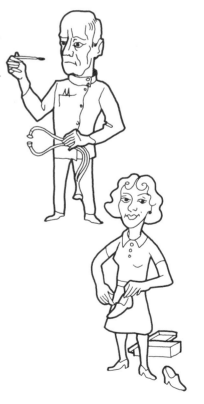

William Jones is a medical doctor; Joan White is a saleswoman in a downtown department store; Sam Smith is a janitor in a large factory. The occupational categories of each of these persons tells us a lot about their educational achievements, their income, their place of residence, and their general style of life. We may say which one *probably* has a greater income, more education, or lives in a "better" section of town than the other, and that the general style of life for one is *probably* considerably different than the others. When we make these generalizations, we are in essence considering what sociologists call class or social stratification.

THE DEFINITION

Robin Williams says that social stratification may be defined as "the ranking of individuals on a scale of superiority–inferiority–equality, according to some accepted basis of evaluation."[1] This definition points up at least four factors about stratification.

(1) It is a systematic method of ranking people. Some qualities are judged to be of greater value than others. Persons who exhibit characteristics associated with these qualities are ranked higher than persons who do not possess (or possess less of) these qualities. Sociologists do not do the ranking; the people of the society assign the ranks. Sociologists merely seek to discover the characteristics of the various strata

83

and the standards used by the society to determine the ranks of its members.

(2) The system of ranking must be widespread among a large number of people. In the case of national stratification, those standards used for ranking must be known and accepted by a majority of the total society. The standards may differ from national standards in subcultures, but must be shared by the members of the subculture. (For example, a boys' gang may use successful theft as a standard for highest ranking. Prestige and social position would be meted out in this group on the basis of the numbers of successful thefts.)

(3) The system of ranking must be durable over a relatively long period of time.

(4) Those persons designated as superior enjoy rights and privileges which are denied to those judged inferior. These prerogatives are in the form of life chances and are differentially dispensed according to rank.

STANDARDS FOR RANKING

What this means is that individuals and categories of individuals in a society or subculture are rated on a scale ranging from high to low or superior to inferior according to some widely accepted standards for ranking. Using these standards for ranking which are shared by members of a society, people are stratified into classifications or social classes.

Max Weber, a German sociologist writing in the early 1900s, has outlined the major components used in modern Western civilization as standards for ranking.[2] These three factors appear to be the basis of stratification in the United States.

Class

Class is a term used to describe a person's "life chances in the market place." It simply refers to money (or the lack of it). Thus a class is a number of persons who share a common position in the economic order.

This term is usually associated with Karl Marx (1818–1883) who divided classes into two levels. The *proletariat* are owners of mere labor power or, more simply, the workers. These are persons with little money or with "poor life chances in the market place." The *bourgeois* are owners of capital. These are persons who control the money since they own the means of production (factories, land, equipment, etc.).

Others, before Marx, had noted differences in economic opportunity. Aristotle spoke of three classes, "One is very rich, another very poor and a third is an average." Adam Smith (in *The Wealth of Nations* written in 1776) recognized that income stems from three sources: the rent of land, the wages of labor, and the profit of stock. Thus some, he said, live by rent, some by wages, and others by profit.

Class (notice that this is not the same as the term *social class*) is used to refer to the levels of economic well-being of categories of persons.

Status

Status is used to describe the relative prestige accorded to a person in his society. We commonly use the word in exactly this manner. For example, we speak about "status symbols" or people who are "status conscious." And we mean, by these terms, that certain persons seek to acquire items which will confer prestige or honor upon themselves. However, according to sociologists, everybody has a status. That is, everybody has more or less prestige, and they are grouped into categories according to ancestry, educational attainment, race, and style of life.

Status, then, has to do with a person's neighborhood, his clothing, his leisure activities, and his associational ties (who associates with whom). Even language may be used to determine the level of prestige a person may legitimately claim. Eliza Doolittle, in the movie *My Fair Lady,* spoke a kind of English which barred her from high status groups in England. Professor Higgins, who spoke proper English, taught Miss Doolittle the "correct" speech patterns. He also supplied her with proper clothing, new associational ties, and better manners. After these changes had been accomplished, Miss Doolittle could successfully make her way among the most prestigious persons of her society. Eliza had moved from low status to a position of high status. It should be noted that if Eliza continued to participate in circles of high status in her society, the process of resocialization would become more complete. Her attitudes, values, interests (as well as speech patterns and clothing) would take on more of the characteristics of her new status group.

Status is divided into two types: ascribed and achieved. *Ascribed status* refers to those attributes with which we are born or which are automatically assigned with the passage of time. Our sex, race, age category, and ancestry (all of which confer or fail to confer elements of prestige) are ascribed statuses. *Achieved status,* on the other hand, refers to attributes for which some type of accomplishment or stroke of good fortune are necessary. Our educational accomplishment (or

lack of it) is an example of achieved status. Sometimes the accomplishment of an achieved status is partially dependent upon an ascribed status. For example, a doctor's son (ascribed status) enjoys a decided advantage for becoming a doctor (achieved status) over a laborer's son. Conversely, a laborer's son is much more likely to become a laborer than is the son of a lawyer.

There is, of course, a close tie between one's class (his economics) and his status, but the tie is never complete. For example, one may have great wealth but little prestige. Plumbers, in our society, usually make more money than high school teachers, but we continue to assign higher status to the teachers than we do to the plumbers. The well-established "old families" of certain communities may have less wealth than, let us say, the executives of new industries that have come into the town. But the more wealthy "newcomers" are frequently excluded from the top of prestige levels. Money, it seems, is helpful in making a claim for high status, but it is not the only variable to be considered.

Power

Power refers to the capacity to control the action of others. Ordinarily, power is associated with a position which one holds in a group and not with the individual. In the classroom, for instance, the teacher has the capacity to control the action of the others (he says when the tests will be, he lectures, he dismisses the class, etc.) not necessarily because he has a dominant, winning personality, but because he occupies the position of teacher. Those people who can take command and have others follow them due to the overwhelming power of their personality are said to have *charismatic* power (see pages 144–45). For the most part, however, those who possess power—such as foremen, priests, policemen, political leaders—ordinarily exercise control over others by virtue of their positions in a specific group, not because of a winning personality.

Power is not always open nor is it always legitimate. There is the obscure power of political bosses or business leaders who get their will carried out behind the scenes where the general populace never sees their use of power. These powerful persons put pressure to bear at important points to control the behavior of others. To do so, they may work through elected political officials, newspapers, private conferences, or economic threat or reward. There is also the illegitimate power of gangsters who may control others by threat of force.

Power, like class and status, is relative. The point is, however, that a person's capacity to control the action of others, which is almost always associated with the positions which he occupies (especially his occupational position), is used to group him into some category of relative superiority–inferiority.

Summary

Social class is defined as a system used to rank individuals on a scale of superiority–inferiority–equality, according to some accepted basis of evaluation. It is, in essence, as Harold Hodges says, "a distinct reality which embraces the fact that people live, eat, play, mate, dress, work, and think at contrasting and dissimilar levels. These levels— social classes—are the blended products of shared and analogous occupational orientations, educational backgrounds, economic wherewithal, and life experiences."[3] In general our society uses three standards as accepted basis of evaluation: class—the individual's economic situation; status—his prestige level based on his ancestry, his educational achievements, his race, and his style of life; and power— his capacity to control the actions of others. A person's class, status, and power determine, therefore, what his social class is. This helps us understand why people pursue economic gain (class), protect and aspire to prestige and reputation (status), and seek control over others and freedom from control for themselves (power).

HOW OTHER SOCIETIES DO IT

Looking briefly at the stratification systems of two other societies may help us understand how social stratification works in the United States.

The Indian Caste System

The word "caste" is probably Portuguese in origin. The Portuguese came to India in the sixteenth century and applied their word *casta,* which means race or lineage, to the different types of Indians whom they encountered. From this source the word caste arose and was used to describe a system of social stratification which was centuries old.

The caste system of stratifying people in a society is characterized by four important elements.

(1)   There is a rigid order or ranking of categories, and there exists clearcut differences between the various levels.

(2)   One's position in the order is ascribed at birth and fixed for life. The only exception is that an individual may lose status and go downward.

(3)   Individual mobility upward in the ranks is non-existent.

(4)   Relationships among castes are fixed permanently by well-known rules.

Indian society contains four castes: the priests (Brahmins), the warriors (Kshatriya), the merchants (Vaisya), and the workers and peasants (Sudra). There also exists a category of persons who have no caste. They are the outcasts or "untouchables" or, more politely, *harigan* or "Children of God." This whole hierarchy is set up according to occupational lines. The four castes are subdivided into about ten thousand other castes which are likewise occupational in character. Generally, it may be said that the more menial and unpleasant the occupation, the lower the caste. This hierarchy of occupations with their rigid rules for behavior within the caste and equally rigid rules for interaction among the castes provides the fundamental social organization for India. The pervasive effect of the caste system on the lives of individuals and the manner in which the caste system influences the total Indian society may be seen in the following facts:

1. Each individual's caste membership is inherited from his parents and fixed for life. No upward mobility is possible. The individual's occupation is determined by his caste membership and is transmitted from father to son. The lower caste person is forced to perform less desirable tasks and the *dharma* (the right way of doing things and, therefore, the path to salvation) requires the person to stick to the traditional calling of his caste. Failure to follow *dharma* leads to expulsion from the caste to the level of outcast.

2. Relationships between castes is firmly fixed by rules regulating behavior. For example, social intimacy is not permitted between members of different castes, especially eating and drinking. Also, no member of any other caste may touch an untouchable (even his shadow may not fall upon a higher caste member.) To do so is to become ceremonially unclean and that necessitates extensive rituals to obtain absolution.

3. Marriage between members of different castes is prohibited. There have been, however, some examples of higher caste men marrying lower caste women.

The caste system in India is approximately three thousand years old. It has existed in essentially the same form during its entire history. What keeps it going? In the first place, it is tied to Hinduism. Its rules are incorporated into the sacred writings of this religion. Beyond that, the religious belief in reincarnation has an important effect upon the stability of the system. The belief is that faithful fulfillment of caste duty is the only way to insure not being born into a lower form when one is reincarnated. Indeed, to be a good caste member in this life is to be reincarnated into a higher caste. Finally, efforts to change the caste system have been met with resistance from higher castes who possess both economic and political power. Their resistance to change stems from the simple fact that they have the most to lose and the least to gain by a restructuring of the accepted methods of social stratification.

When India achieved its independence in 1947, the caste system was made illegal. Both Gandhi and Nehru worked diligently to break up the caste system and make life more bearable for the lower castes and the untouchables. Their efforts have been largely ineffectual.

The social situation in India is not unlike that observed in the United States. Laws are framed in favor of equality, but practices and rituals of discrimination remain. In some areas the untouchable may have opportunities for advancement (especially if his assigned occupation is functionally necessary) while in other areas he is "kept in his place" by tradition, etiquette of caste, and violence, if necessary. Accepted patterns of behavior die slowly, it seems.

The Case of a Classless Society: The Soviet Union

Alex Inkles notes:

> Many radical religious and political philosophies treat all such [status] rankings as invidious, and indeed evil. They urge the establishment of a world in which these distinctions no longer exist, and instead all men are *valued* as equal. Most sociologists are dubious of the possibility of creating such a society, and the unhappy fate of most utopian communities makes this skepticism warranted. There is good reason to assume that ranking people is inherent in man, and that no society will ever be without it.[4]

The Soviet Union is an example of a society which sought to destroy its system of stratification and to establish a classless society. When the Communists took over in 1917, they abolished by law all divisions of citizens, all class distinctions, and the rights and privileges which go along with various rankings of people. Soviet rulers pushed toward this goal by confiscating all private property, equalizing taxes, and redefining the roles of party leaders, trade unions, and other recently established organizations and associations. A sincere effort was made to develop an egalitarian society.

By 1931, however, the Soviet government was confronted by a serious crises precipitated by the shortage of skilled labor, a high turnover of personnel in factories, and the unclear position of managers, technicians, and other highly skilled workers. A nation seeking to industrialize must have a steady output of occupational specialists to man the jobs created by increasing industrial development. Measures were needed to create incentives for acquiring these skills. Increasing industrial production, the goal of the first five year plan which began in 1928, was the objective of these measures. Workers had to accept the authority and responsibility necessary for increased industrial output.

Stalin began to initiate a program which increased incentive by re-establishing social class differences. Piece rates (payment on the basis of the amount of work done) were instituted in both industry and on the farm. Such a practice created the possibility of the more highly skilled experiencing a greater income than the less motivated and unskilled. Professionals and technicians, among whom payment by piece rates is impossible, were paid higher salaries and given special fringe benefits.

Justification for these practices was made by the idea that a transition stage was necessary before true communism could be achieved. Such remains the official communist line: differences exist, but no classes; all are but one group, a toiling intelligentsia, and everyone works for the good of all.

Inkles, based on studies done in the late 1940s, divided Soviet society into three specific classes. In each he found a set of sub-classes.[5]

The Intelligentsia

The Ruling Elite—This group is small in number and consists of high party, governmental, economic and military officials, prominent scientists, and selected writers and authors.

The Superior Intelligentsia—This group is composed of the intermediary ranks of those constituting the ruling elite plus certain technical specialists.

The General Intelligentsia—Professionals, middle ranks of the bureaucracy, managers of small enterprises, junior military men, and technicians compose this category.

The White Collar Group—Among those categorized as white collar are the petty bureaucrats, accountants, clerks, and office workers.

The Working Class

The Aristocracy of Workers—Here are found the most highly skilled and most productive of the workers.

Rank and File Workers—These are workers who possess lesser skills than the aristocracy.

Disadvantaged Workers—(According to Inkles, about one-fourth of the labor force fall into this category.) These are persons whose lack of skill or productivity keeps them at the bottom of the wage scale.

The Peasants

The Well-to-Do—Because of advantages due to soil fertility, crop adaptation, locality, etc., some persons among the peasants may be classified as rather well off.

The Average Peasant—This group ranges from those of average circumstances to those who live in abject poverty.

Inkles points out that each class and subclass differs in life style. Some differences have to do with income, and things like chauffeurs, cars, housing, and dress. Some persons have country homes, vacation retreats, and receive special awards and other types of recognition. Social classes (including class, status, and power) appear to be a reality even in a "classless" society.

THE CLASS STRUCTURE IN THE UNITED STATES

There has been, in the past, a stubborn resistance to the concept of social class boundaries in the United States. Americans, in general, have associated this idea with the radical politics of Karl Marx and Communism. Beyond that, there is the widespread and persistent belief in the possibility of "Abraham Lincoln success stories" (from the log cabin to the White House). According to this view, the social class ladder is open to any who are willing to work, and a person's position in life is dependent upon his willingness to exercise the discipline, control, and ingenuity necessary to make a success of himself. That belief is a vital part of the American dream, and it excludes the notion that someone may be limited in climbing the success ladder by social class boundaries. Along with this, many Americans believe that ours is primarily a "middle class" society. The results of a 1940 Gallup poll point this out.[6] In response to the question, "To what social class in this country do you think you belong—the middle class, the upper, or the lower?" a nationwide sample of Americans responded:

Upper	6%
Middle	88%
Lower	6%

Richard Centers, in 1945, asked a national sample to respond to the same question with four categories instead of Gallup's three. He added the category of "the working class."[7] His results:

Upper	3%
Middle	43%
Working	51%
Lower	1%
Don't know	1%
Don't believe in classes	1%

It should be pointed out that recent governmental interest in poverty and race along with the attention given by the mass media to the persistence of ghetto life for millions of Americans has helped erase the concept of America as a predominantly middle-class society. Americans have been given the opportunity to see the differences between suburbia and the inner city. Perhaps we are not as ignorant of social class differentials and inequalities of opportunity as we once were.

How Many Classes?

Robert and Helen Lynd, in their studies of Muncie, Indiana in the twenties and thirties, discovered a two-class system.[8] They spoke of the working class and the business class. For them, occupation was the most important determinant of social class. People were divided into the two categories based on whether they worked with people (business class) or worked with things (working class).

Perhaps the most popular approach to the study of stratification is the three-class system. This theory envisions three strata: the upper class, the middle class, and the lower class. The upper class is composed of the relatively few people who hold the highest positions in society. The national elite, consisting of the most powerful politicians, the most publicized entertainers, the very rich, and the top industrial and military leaders, are found in this strata. The middle class consists of persons of lesser means and status. This category runs the gamut from highly paid professionals, to clerks, to small business owners and managers, and includes even the better paid blue-collar workers. Finally, the lower class is composed of the semi-skilled, the unskilled, the poor, and the uneducated. These are the persons who exist on the bare minimum when compared to the accepted standards of the given society. This approach to social stratification, while very popular, is criticized chiefly because it does not draw a sharp dividing line between individuals, especially in the middle class. Richard Centers' study (discussed above) in the mid-forties was designed to demonstrate this very fact.

A six-class theory of stratification was suggested by W. Lloyd Warner.[9] Based upon his research conducted in Newburyport, Massachusetts, he discovered the existence of six classes. He divided the upper class into the upper-upper and lower-upper, the middle class into the upper-middle and lower-middle, and the lower class into the upper-lower and the lower-lower. Warner developed his Index of Status Characteristics in this study. He discovered that a combination of specific characteristics are indicators of the social class level of the individual. The four characteristics he found to be most important were: occupation, source of income, house type, and dwelling area. Of these four, Warner suggested that occupation was most important and dwelling area least significant in determination of class. Using these characteristics, Warner found that the people of his study area clustered into the six groupings which he described as status groups or "orders of people who are believed to be, and are accordingly ranked by the members of the community, in socially superior and inferior positions."[10]

A word of caution is necessary at this point. Discussions of social class sometimes leave the impression that there are strict lines of demarcation between social classes. Ranks, according to this view, are discreet categories which are marked off from one another in some significant and observable fashion. The cutoff points of the groupings are clear and easily discovered. Much closer to reality is the idea of a social class continuum which stretches from high to low. People tend to cluster at various points along the continuum, but distinct groups with clear-cut differences do not exist. This view asserts that boundaries between social classes are blurred and the ranks along the continuum tend to fade into one another. A person's economic position, his prestige level, and power is always relative to others in his community and society. What this means is that stratification is a ladder with innumerable rungs and people are categorized into various rankings along this continuum.

Climbing the Ladder

College diploma, better jobs, more money, bigger houses, better neighborhoods, bigger cars, swimming pool. Boy, I'm climbing the ladder of social mobility!

Social mobility is the term used by sociologists to describe the process whereby the individual moves either up or down the class hierarchy. Most attention is paid to upward social mobility. Increased income, greater prestige, a better house in a better community, and a more comfortable life style are factors associated with upward social mobility.

Theoretically, class lines are open in the United States. Any individual may achieve a change in his social class level. Social mobility is visible, desired, and approved in this society, while in a nation based upon a caste system, social mobility is unknown.

Social mobility is an integral part of the American dream. America is viewed (by many Americans and Europeans) as the land of opportunity. In the popular ideology, social mobility is held out as a reality. Americans *expect* to be able to "climb the ladder." The emphasis on public education, an important avenue of social mobility, gives evidence of this fact.

Reality, however, is sometimes different from dreams and such is the case at this point. Workers pulled from the Eastern European countries in the latter part of the nineteenth and early part of the twentieth century by dreams of material improvement found themselves stacked in cities and involved in terrible working conditions (which Upton Sinclair called *The Jungle*). Children and grandchildren of these immigrants did, however, improve their lot. Today, blacks and Mexican Americans find themselves caught in a racial system that is caste-like in nature. Avenues of mobility (such as education, housing, employment) are effectively closed for minority individuals. The frustration of blacks which erupted violently during the 1960s is based upon their recognition that social mobility is only for whites in America.

Still, to some extent the ladder of success has been a reality in American. The growing industrial economy has opened doors of opportunity by creating new jobs and making a demand for more workers with greater specialized training. The rural to urban migration in the United States has been based upon industry's need for more workers. And when the rural areas and the natural increase in the urban areas could not produce the needed numbers of factory workers, we imported them from Europe by immigration. (Our ability to supply the labor market began to catch up with industry's demand in the mid-1920s, and laws were then passed making it more difficult to migrate to the United States). The effect of industrialization was an increase in the standard of living for the majority of Americans.

Industrial growth has created the possibility for economic growth in other ways. New types of vocational categories were given impetus: transportation, communication, and personal and professional services. White collar workers, for the first time, outnumbered the skilled, semi-skilled, and unskilled workers in 1956. By the mid-1960s there were five professional, managerial, and clerical employees for each four blue-collar workers. Many people in the United States, because of a growing industrial economy which opened up new forms of technological and commercial employment, experienced an upgrading in standards of living and the possibility of social mobility.

But the gains achieved by industrialization came at a rather expensive cost. (1) Assembly line production changed the nature and meaning of work. (2) Machines, including computers, threaten man's place in the work force. (3) Not all Americans have enjoyed the fruits of a rising standard of living. The first two of these possible detrimental effects of industrialization will be discussed in a later chapter. We will now turn our attention to the effect of the unequal gain in standards of living.

The View from the Bottom

In 1969, 11.4 percent of the families in the United States had incomes below $4,000. The income distribution for 1969 is seen in table 1. The median family income was $9,590. (*Median* means exactly half were above this figure, and half were below. It is *not* the same as an average). A comparison of the range of income in 1968 with that of 1947 is interesting. Using the 1968 worth of the dollar as a basis of comparison, the distribution of income in 1947 is shown in table 2. Median family income in 1947 (based on 1968 dollar value) was $4,716. Thus the real income has nearly doubled from 1947 to 1968 according to the median family income.[11]

These figures mean that in 1969 at least 27,769,000 Americans existed on incomes below the subsistence level.[12] Nearly one-fourth of the population lived in families with less than a $5,000 annual income. For them, the American dream of opportunity was not yet a reality.

One irony of the poverty of our nation is that the changes in technology which have produced affluence for many and a rising

TABLE 1   U.S. Income Distribution, 1969

Income (1968 dollars)	Percentage
Under $3,000	26.0
$3,000–4,999	28.1
$5,000–6,999	21.8
$7,000–9,999	14.2
$10,000–14,999 } $15,000 and over}	10.0

TABLE 2   U.S. Income Distribution, 1947

INCOME	PERCENTAGE		
	Total	White	Negro/Other Races
Under $4,000	15.2	13.3	31.4
$4,000–6,999	16.9	16.2	23.9
$7,000–7,999	6.7	6.7	7.1
$8,000–8,999	7.1	7.2	6.3
$9,000–9,999	6.8	6.9	5.3
$10,000–14,999	26.6	27.8	16.8
$15,000 and over	20.6	21.9	9.2

standard of living for most has created a situation of hopelessness for the 27 million at the bottom of the income ladder.

The poor are the unskilled, and industrialization has reduced the need for unskilled (and skilled) labor relative to the supply. We now have machines to dig ditches, plow furrows, spread concrete, unload ships, and to perform many other types of work once done by human muscle. (Computers may one day replace white-collar workers in the same manner that the ditch digging machine reduced the number of blue-collar workers.)

Advanced skill is based upon educational achievement, and the poor are the uneducated. Poor schools, lack of motivation by parents, and a value system that ignores education are responsible for many grammar and high school dropouts among the poor. For the same reasons, with the added factor of high cost, a college education becomes impossible.

Minority status confounds the issue even further. Past discrimination accounts for lack of skill, and present discrimination makes it difficult to reap rewards from the skills which some members of ethnic groups have. Perhaps this helps to explain why blacks, who represent only 10 percent of the population, account for 20 percent of the poor. Such information also helps us to understand why the non-white median income is approximately half that of the white income.

Finally, age is a factor. Older persons of today have not been trained for the occupational skills necessary in our society. Their lack of technical skill plus the natural infirmities of old age make it difficult for them to find acceptable and well-paying jobs. Twenty-five percent of the poor families in the United States have household heads who are sixty-five or older. Yet those over sixty-five represent only 10 percent of the population.

The young are also overly represented among the poor. Lower income families have proportionally larger families which means that the percentage of children among the poor is comparatively greater than among the higher income families. Michael Harrington refers to the poor (in *The Other America*) as the "underclass." They may more appropriately be called an undercaste. That is, they are born into a rigid class where mobility is virtually impossible. Harrington also notes that the poor of today are different from the poor of the twenties and thirties in our nation.[13] The earlier group, primarily migrants from Europe and the Southern farms, could live with their poverty because they were sustained by a hope of better times. For them the American dream of opportunity was a reality; today's poor experience the frustration of hopelessness.

The view from the bottom is aptly described by Robert Conot:

Consider Willy Brown. Willy Brown is the archetype of the Negro born in the Black Belt in the early 1920's. He lived in an unpainted shack with a leaky roof, blistering hot in summer and freezing cold in winter, and infested with insects. Water was hand-drawn from a well. His mother cooked on a wood-burning stove. Electricity was one of the marvels of the city. He had a half dozen brothers and sisters, and they all worked in the fields. School was an uncertain thing that would begin in October after the cotton had been picked and end in March when the fields had to be prepared for planting, interrupted every so often in between by heavy rains that made impassable the road to the one-room schoolhouse, presided over by a half-educated teacher. Willy Brown went to school for eight years, but he never learned more than to read a label on a box or to scrawl his name. His social life centered about the church, but with the church's fundamentalist prohibition on cards, dancing, and the like, social life wasn't synonymous with entertainment. A lot of the girls would get pregnant, but the boys, unless they ran away, would usually marry them. As long as the family stayed on the farm there was a good chance it would remain as a unit. Once a man decided to try his luck in the city, however, the probability was strong that it would begin breaking up.

At the time of Willy Brown's birth, the country was just entering the automobile age. Radio programming was unknown. Electrical appliances were primitive and expensive. Airplanes were a county fair novelty.

A few miles from the shack in which a midwife delivered Willy Brown, a country doctor came to oversee the birth of Tom Smith. Although it was

slightly sounder in construction than the Brown shack, in other ways the Smith house was not much different: it had no electricity, no hot running water, no indoor plumbing. The principal difference between Tom Smith and Willy Brown was not in their economic standing, but in their castes. Tom Smith was white. Being white his education, his medical care, his food, his clothing—though inferior by middle-class standards—were vastly superior to those of Willy Brown.

By the time Willy Brown reached manhood, in 1941, every middle-cass home had a radio, and the radio was bringing on-the-spot accounts of events all over the world to its listeners. In the same home, electricity was perking the coffee, making the toast, and running the vacuum cleaner. It was possible to drive across the country in three days, and in an airplane you could fly in one. Motion pictures were bringing the most exotic locations—however distorted—into neighborhood theaters.

All this bypassed Willy Brown. He had no electricity, so he had no radio. He couldn't read a newspaper, so he knew nothing except what his neighbors, most of them as uninformed as he, told him. He saw automobiles and airplanes but, as far as his ability to relate to them was concerned, they might as well have been battleships. While the progress of the world was continuously accelerating, nothing had changed for him since his birth, and, with some minor exceptions, nothing had changed for his father, or his grandfather before that. Only when Willy's selective service board ordered him to report, and then promptly rejected him—for not only was he, like great numbers of his Negro neighbors, a functional illiterate but he was already suffering from a variety of physical ailments, having never in his life been seen by a doctor—was he stirred briefly from his isolation.

Willy Brown married, and, like his father, he became a sharecropper. The land company that provided him with the shack in which he lived staked him to his first crop of cotton, furnishing him with the necessities of life, from seed to salt pork, and he mortgaged the crop to them in return. Thus began the cycle that would go on year after year. The company paid the rock bottom price for the cotton, and if the market price of cotton rose, which it frequently did, it was the company that benefited, not Willy. He was encouraged to live on credit, so as to remain in the company's servitude. He seldom saw more than $25 in cash in an entire year.

By the time Willy's son was born in 1945 the atomic bomb had exploded over Hiroshima. If Willy heard of it at all, it was only to the extent that a big bomb had ended the war—a war about which he really didn't know anything, and cared very little.

Television, jet propulsion, and a myriad other developments passed by Willy's shack, leaving no impression upon him or his growing family. The fertile mind of man began to supplement that mind with computers, and to build instruments that, with their electronic cunning, eliminated the need for human labor. Willy Brown, although he didn't know it, was becoming obsolete. If he had been a machine, he would have been scrapped.

Since he knew nothing of government, he did not know that the government subsidies, intended to help him, were, instead, going to the land company; which, being paid not to produce cotton, cared less and less about retaining his labor. What he did know was that the earth was crumbling about him. That the machines that were threshing across the land were making it impossible, he had no choice. About the time that men began orbiting the earth in satellites, he decided to pull up stakes and move to one of the cities in the north or west about which he had heard a hundred rumors.

When he arrived, he might as well have been a man dropped into his new environment from the 16th century.

So 35-year-old Willy Brown, who had been no match for the machine in tilling the land, came to the city to compete in the shrinking unskilled jobs market. He didn't know how to go about finding a job. He couldn't express himself. He had no knowledge of the value of money, or how to handle it. The law was incomprehensible; the restraints and restrictions of city living a welter of confusion. Some of the services supposedly tailored to his needs were denied to him because he did not know they existed. Utterly naive, he was prey to every trickster and sharpster, both Negro and white. Hardly able to count, he had no concept of interest; hardly able to write, he did not comprehend the meaning of placing his signature on a piece of paper. For information and help, he was dependent on his neigh-

bors, and how he fared often was in direct proportion to their intelligence and honesty.

If he were able to get a job at all, it was of the most menial and usually transitory nature, providing not even the benefit of unemployment insurance. Left to grab desperately for a living, he and his family were always but one step ahead of hunger—and sometimes overtaken by it. Without hope of improving his position, he grew ever more despondent and frustrated. In due time he learned that the nation, while considering him a bum, would, with its social conscience, not let his wife and children starve.

So he gave up on a responsibility that seemed hopeless, and deeded his wife and family to the nation.

During the somnolent 1930's, the life of Tom Smith had continued to parallel that of Willy Brown, albeit on a higher level. Although Tom's teachers at the rural elementary school and small-town high school left much to be desired, the facilities were adequate, there was a free milk-for-lunch program, and Tom was checked by a doctor at least once a year. The school year was nine months long, and by the time he graduated at the age of 19, he had a better education than either his mother or father.

Two years later he was drafted into the army. Three-fourths of the next three years he spent in Europe. When he returned, the G.I. Bill enabled him to enroll in college. He majored in pharmacy and, though not particularly brilliant, managed to pull through. By the time Willy Brown gave up and decided to move to the city, the Smith farm, also, had withered away, but Tom Smith was the proprietor of a small drug store which netted him $12,000 a year. He lived in a three-bedroom house with two television sets, and two cars in the garage. His children—who, in the seventh grade, were in many ways more sophisticated than he had been in the eleventh—were receiving an education that put his own to shame.

Willy Brown's children could have received an equal education in the city, except for the fact that they were utterly unprepared for it. They were like hungry people summoned to a mountain of flour and told to help themselves. The offer of the flour only increased their bitterness and frustration, for they lacked any kind of bag or basket in which to carry it, and had no oven in which to bake it into bread at home.

Willy's eldest son was 15 when the family came to the city. At the age of 15 his education wasn't much better than his father's had been—at the age of 15 his father had been through with school, and was working on the farm. Willy's son for all practical purposes was through with school also, for, from a scholastic standpoint, he belonged in the third grade, and schools don't enroll 15-year-olds in the third grade.

The ninth grade, in which he was put, was beyond his comprehension, so he was soon getting his education on the streets. On the streets it didn't take him long to pick up a rudimentary sophistication—he learned about the cops, and how one could make a fast buck, and how there weren't any rules when it came to Mr. Charley, because Mr. Charley had been waging war on the soul folk for hundreds of years. When he was 18 years old he got a girl pregnant, and if he had been living on the farm that meant they would have gotten married. But in the city, without a job, you'd have to be stupid to take on that kind of responsibility—he'd learned from his father what happens to a man when he tries—so he decided to let the BPA take care of the child.

Weaned on television, the children of the Willy Browns are bombarded with admonitions to enjoy the material goods of an affluent society. By the time they reach puberty the realization is forced upon them that those admonitions are not directed at the people among whom they live. At the threshold of adulthood they begin to view television as a glass door. Through it they can see white America, but for them the door will never open. Every day they are tantalized. Every day they become more frustrated.

At the threshold of adulthood they are thoroughly embittered. Isolated from contact with white Americans, their bias against the Caucasian becomes as thoroughly ingrained—and sometimes more venomous—than the Southern redneck's against them. As the principal manifestation of their oppressor, the white police officer becomes their logical target.

In the rural Black Belt, Willy Brown's anger was kept damped by a mantle of fear, but in the urban Black Reservation Willy Brown's son derives a sense of power from living in an all-Negro community, and from the militant Nationalist psychology that black is good and white is evil. He sees no reason why he must continue to abide by or to obey the white man's laws.[14]

SUMMARY

Stratification, we have said, is the ranking of individuals on a scale of inferiority–superiority on the basis of some accepted basis of evaluation. Individuals in our society are ranked according to their economic wherewithal (class), their prestige level (status), and their capacity to have others obey their will (power). Our system of stratification is open (that is, people may be socially mobile). Comparisons were made between the class system in our country, the Soviet Union's "classless" society, and the caste system of India.

The persistent belief in the "Abraham Lincoln success story," along with the identification of the idea of classes with the theories of communism, have contributed to the unwillingness of Americans to recognize a class structure in this nation. While theoretically class lines are open and industrialization has created a rising standard of living for most Americans, there remain real distinctions of reward and life style for the various strata comprising our society. Rigid boundaries, like those in a caste system, do not exist in the United States. Social classes tend to blend into one another as they form a continuum for which indentifiable cutoff points are difficult to discover. The differentials in opportunity and rewards which are characteristic of our class system appear to be like a river which gradually grows wider, deeper, and flows more strongly along its course. Those at the bottom of the class structure experience the narrow and sparse distribution of life chances and privileges. As one progresses up the rankings, these rewards gradually become more widely distributed.

Notes

1. Robin Williams, Jr., *American Society* (New York: Knopf, 1960), p. 89.

2. H. H. Gerth and C. Wright Mills, *From Max Weber: Essays from Sociology* (New York: Oxford, 1946), chapter VII.

3. Harold M. Hodges, Jr., *Social Stratification: Class in America* (Cambridge, Mass.: Schenkman, 1964), p. 13.

4. Alex Inkles, *What is Sociology?* (Englewood Cliffs, N.J.: Prentice-Hall, 1964), p. 83.

5.   Alex Inkles, "Social Stratification and Mobility in the Soviet Union, 1940–1950," *American Sociological Review 15* (August 1950): 466.

6.   George Gallup and S. F. Roe, *The Pulse of Democracy* (New York: Simon and Schuster, 1940), p. 169.

7.   Richard Centers, *The Psychology of Social Classes* (Princeton, N.J.: Princeton University Press, 1949), p. 77.

8.   Robert S. Lynd and Helen Merrell Lynd, *Middletown: A Study in American Culture* (New York: Harcourt, Brace and World, 1929).

9.   W. L. Warner and Paul Lunt, *The Social Life of a Modern Community* (New Haven: Yale University Press, 1941).

10.   Ibid., p. 82.

11.   *Current Population Reports,* Series P-60 #66, December 23, 1969, p. 1.

12.   *Current Population Reports,* Series P-23 #28, August 12, 1969, p. 3.

13.   Michael Harrington, *The Other America: Poverty in the United States* (Baltimore: Penguin Books, 1962).

14.   Robert Conot, *Rivers of Blood, Years of Darkness* (New York: Bantam Books, 1967), pp. 433–37.

Thinking
Sociologically

1.   Next time you attend a movie notice the symbols used to indicate the various social class levels of the personalities involved in the plot. Notice things like occupation, life style, type of house, clothing, and language. Look for evidences of ascribed status and achieved status. When the plot calls for differentiation in status, you will find that the movie will make use of popular standards of stratification. Can you see evidences in these films of the concepts of class, status, and power? Take a specific television program which involves a male star. What would happen to the plot and what would happen to the props that were necessary for the story if the main occupation of this male star were lowered in status? What differences in symbols would become necessary?

2.   Drive through a low-income area of your town and make a list of things that you see. Try to describe each item on your list; for example, "very old car that looks like it won't run," etc. Then drive through an upper-income area and make a similar list. Compare the lists. What does the comparison tell you about the use of status as a component of social stratification? Additionally, what are the relevant social factors associated with these two divergent life styles?

3.   Consider the following story:
Three couples had been invited to the home of a fourth couple for dinner one evening. All four men were successful executives in related businesses. Their wives were also well-educated, and their homes were expensive and tastefully done in furnishings. When dinner was served, all four couples went into the dining room and sat down at the exquisitely prepared table. The hostess, however, remembered a final touch which demanded that she leave the table for a moment. The men all stood up as she left the table and stood again when she returned to be seated with them. In a moment the maid came into the room to begin serving. No one stood, and no one nodded or spoke to her. Except for her work in serving the meal, she was completely ignored.

What does this story say to you about class, status, and power?

Chapter 6

Cognitive
Objectives

The sociological analysis of interrelations between ethnic groups and the dominant group in society is the subject of this chapter. As you read these pages, you should look for the following type of information:

1. *The definitions of "minority," "race," "social race," "ethnic group"*
2. *The concept of America as a "melting pot"*
   a. *What are the four phases of immigration into the United States?*
   b. *What does the urban migration of blacks have to do with the melting pot concept?*
   c. *What effect did the urban migration of blacks have on the black community in the United States?*
3. *The six major patterns of race relations between minority groups and the dominant segment of a society*
4. *The concepts of "prejudice" and "discrimination" and how they are related*
5. *Patterns of discrimination*
   a. *How is discrimination practiced in employment?*
   b. *What effect does this discrimination have on the minority group?*
6. *The patterns of minority response to prejudice and discrimination*
   a. *What are the tactics of submission and how do they differ?*
   b. *What are the tactics of resistance and how do they differ?*

Red and Yellow, Black and White

Probably no subject on the domestic scene in the United States has generated so much national soul searching as the relationships with racial and ethnic groups. The mass media, political campaigns, local and national conferences, the halls of Congress, and the chambers of the Supreme Court have increasingly echoed with the issues involved in the "racial crisis." The public has had its attention focused on the relationship of the races through riots, demonstrations, sit-ins, boycotts, marches, bloodshed, assassinations, and other confrontations. The inequities in privilege and opportunity which are traced along the lines of demarcation between red and yellow, black and white have filled stacks of congressional paper and miles of newsprint. Racial and ethnic differences do exist among the people who make up the population of this nation.

I'm Homo Sapiens

Sociologists are interested in the patterns of behavior that are associated with relationships among these racial and ethnic groups. We will now explore some of the more important aspects of the sociological analysis of race relations.

WHAT IS A MINORITY?

Perhaps the best way to begin an analysis of race relations is to answer the question, what is a racial or ethnic group? Or, what is a race?

All human beings are members of the same species (*Homo sapiens*). This single category exists, however, in a number of varieties which

are separated on the basis of biological differences, cultural differences, or both. Among the more visible evidence of biological differences are skin color, shape of head, facial characteristics, and hair texture. Populations exist which share similar traits with references to these physical characteristics and through the bearing of children the traits are passed from one generation to the next thus preserving the biological differences between the varieties. Anthropologists sometimes refer to these populations and their physical differences as "genetic pools." Most frequently they are called "races."

It is necessary, however, to speak of "social races." Cultural, rather than biological, differences are frequently used to divide people into races. Different languages, modes of dress, customs, or religions become important in defining social races. People believe that racial differences do exist, and as W. I. Thomas pointed out "If men define a situation as real, it is real in its consequences." Thus, groups are singled out in societies and subjected to various degrees of differential treatment. They are identified as a distinct race because they (or their ancestors) practice a different set of customs or merely because their ancestors emigrated from a different country.

Racial distinctions may continue even when physical distinctions do not exist and when most cultural differences have been overcome. For example, although it may be virtually impossible to tell the difference, biologically or culturally, between an American of Jewish ancestry and one of German ancestry, the two groups are often called different "races."

Cultural beliefs and practices may help to continue cultural differences among races. Despite the fact that social scientists have demonstrated that no "race" is inherently more intelligent, musical, athletic, inventive, or creative than any other race, behavioral differences do occur because of discriminatory cultural practices. For example, white children usually score higher than black children on traditional intelligence tests. Black children are not intellectually inferior, however, but are the victims of what is called *relative cultural deprivation*. Their social environment frequently does not give them the educational opportunities that other groups take for granted. Cultural differences thus contribute to continued social distinction between the white and black "races."

When we speak of race relations or racial and ethnic groups, we have in mind categories of people who are socially defined as different. Perhaps the more fitting term to use in referring to these "racial groups" would be "minorities." The anthropologists Wagley and Harris outlined five characteristics of a minority. They are the following:

1. A minority is a subordinate segment of a society.

2. The minority has special physical or cultural traits which are held in low esteem by the dominant segment of a society.

3. Minorities must be aware of their subordinate position. They are bound together by the special traits which their members share and by the disabilities which these traits bring.

4. Membership in a minority is acquired by birth.

5. The minority members, by choice or necessity, tend to marry within the group.[1]

Thus on the basis of "race" (biological traits like skin color, facial characteristics, hair texture) and/or on the basis of cultural traits (like religion, custom, language) groups within a population are set apart, considered inferior, and treated subordinately. Those groups who experience such treatment may be termed "minorities."

A minority may or may not be a *numerical* minority. A group may exhibit all five criteria listed above and yet outnumber the so-called dominant group. In American society, women are a numerical majority, but many would say they meet all the criteria for a minority (except the fifth one). The blacks of the Union of South Africa are a minority in that white-dominated society, yet they constitute two-thirds of the population. The same is true in many areas of the United States. Negroes in many Southern counties are the numerical majority but remain the "minority." Also, cultural differences between ethnic groups may have completely disappeared, but the social definition of "race" remains along with minority status. Jews in Germany during the Nazi domination were forced by law to wear a Star of David to identify them as Jews. Without the identifying symbol, it was almost impossible to separate them from the rest of the German citizens. Though they looked and acted like the rest of the German population, German Jews were considered a minority and were assigned to a subordinate position in that society.

MELTING POT OR SALAD BOWL?

The United States has been referred to as a melting pot. It has been the scene of a great "experiment in assimilation." Over the last four hundred years, people and cultures of diverse background have been mixed together on a scale which is unprecedented in human history.

The early settlers during the colonial period were largely Protestant Anglo-Saxons. Immigration (and the western expansion of the young nation) introduced a Catholic Latin-based culture and an Eastern European culture containing both Jewish and Russian Orthodox beliefs. There were four periods of immigration into the United States.

1780–1830—English and Scots
1830–1880—English, Irish, Germans, and Scandinavians
1880–1920—Central, Eastern, and Southern Europeans
1921 to the present—the period of numerical restrictions

During the first three periods, literally millions of "foreigners" arrived on the shores of this nation. In 1820, the first year that the census recorded the number of immigrants, 8,385 came into the United States. From this small group, the numbers swelled accordingly:

1821–1840	742,562
1840–1850	2.8 million
1880–1890	3.75 million
1900–1914	Approximately 1 million a year

The greatest number of immigrants for any single year occurred in 1907 when 1,285,349 arrived.

For the most part, new arrivals stopped in the seaport cities of the Northeast. Their strange languages and customs created cultural barriers which brought about ethnic colonies in these cities. Little Italys, Chinatowns, etc., sprang up as the new immigrants sought out others with similar cultural backgrounds. Racially identifiable areas still exist today that have their origin in these immigration patterns.

While these millions of new citizens were arriving, especially from 1900 on, internal migration of blacks was occurring. Southern blacks were moving North, and they too were stopping in the large cities. In 1860, 94.9 percent of the blacks in the United States lived in the South. By 1960 the number had reduced to 54 percent.

Blacks were being displaced by the urban migration of poor whites in the South. Insects and other factors had dethroned King Cotton, and this reduced the need for rural workers in the South. World War I created the demand for labor in the North. All these factors worked together both to push the black man from the South and to pull him to the North.

Blacks, like the immigrants from Europe and Asia, settled in the cities. Even those blacks who remained in the South moved to urban areas. Seventy-three percent of all blacks lived in rural areas in 1910. By 1960 73 percent had moved to urban areas. In fact, in 1960 six cities contained 20 percent of all blacks in the United States, and 51 percent of them lived in cities with a population larger than fifty thousand.

When the black moved to the urban centers of this nation, he took with him his rural background, his lack of education, his lack of technological skill, and his legacy of slavery. Above all he took his blackness which made him visible and served as a reminder to him and all others of his minority status. Claude Brown, in his powerful and concise book, *Manchild in the Promised Land,* describes the essence of the black's urban and northward migration.

Going to New York was good-bye to the cotton fields, good-bye to "Massa Charlie," good-bye to the chain gang, and, most of all, good-bye to those sunup-to-sundown working hours. One no longer had to wait to get to heaven to lay his burden down; burdens could be lain down in New York.

So they came from all parts of the South, like all the black chillun o' God following the sound of Gabriel's horn on that long-overdue Judgment Day. The Georgians came as soon as they were able to pick train fare off the peach trees. They came from South Carolina where the cotton stalks were bare. The North Carolinians came with tabacco tar beneath their fingernails.

They felt as the Pilgrims must have felt when they were coming to America. But these descendants of Ham must have been twice as happy as the Pilgrims, because they had been catching twice the hell. Even while planning the trip, they sang spirituals as "Jesus Take My Hand" and "I'm On My Way" and chanted, "Hallelujah, I'm on my way to the promised land!"

It seems that Cousin Willie, in his lying haste had neglected to tell the folks down home about one of the most important aspects of the promised land: it was a slum ghetto. There was a tremendous difference in the way life was lived up North. There were too many people full of hate and bitterness crowded into a dirty, stinky, uncared for closet-size section of a great city.

Before the soreness of the cotton fields had left Mama's back, her knees were getting sore from scrubbing "Goldberg's" floor. Nevertheless, she was better off; she had gone from the fire into the frying pan.

The children of these disillusioned colored pioneers inherited the total lot of their parents—the disappointments, the anger. To add to their misery, they had little hope of deliverance. For where does one run to when he's already in the promised land?[2]

This land became the meeting place for peoples of varied cultural and biological backgrounds. Millions came from foreign lands. While they were arriving in American cities, internal migration patterns witnessed the movement of large numbers of blacks, burdened with their legacy of slavery and rural habits, northward and into urban areas. Add to this picture the American Indians who were here when the explorers came and the Mexicans who were included by the western expansion of the nation and you begin to understand the complexities of the mixing of cultures which has occurred in the United States.

To refer to this mixing of cultures as a melting pot is, however, somewhat misleading. The analogy connotes a thorough mixing and fusion, which is contrary to the facts. More appropriately, America should be called a salad bowl. The peoples of differing background have been tossed together and some cultural exchange and fusion has taken place. But the complete melting away of differences has not occurred. This is due, in part, to the dominant group's unwillingness both to forget differences and to stop assigning minorities to a particular status.

PATTERNS OF RACE RELATIONS

Interaction among members of a minority group and the dominant group is guided, like all interaction, by norms which have been worked out by the society and are learned by each new generation. The interaction of individuals falls within the basic framework of the structured relations between the races. Brewton Berry, in his book *Race and Ethnic Relations,* has identified six rather distinct patterns which societies have developed for the general structuring of relationships between races.[3]

Annihilation

History records ample evidence that frequently one "race" has sought simply to annihilate another race. The Old Testament tells of the Hebrews' conquest of the promised land and their (unsuccessful) attempts to wipe out the ethnic groups who peopled the land.

A more modern attempt at annhilation occurred during the Second World War. The Nazis, who dominated Europe, systematically and deliberately sought to exterminate all European Jews. About 60 percent of the 9.6 million Jews were put to death. The justification for this mass execution was that Jews were an inferior race and that their presence had already significantly affected European culture in a negative fashion. Thus genocide was required.

Expulsion

Sometimes the more powerful will seek the forceful eviction of the less powerful group. Henry VIII drove the Gypsies from England, the Moors were expelled from Spain, and the Acadians were taken from Nova Scotia to southern Louisiana. Here in the United States the American Indian was driven from his homeland into reservations by the Federal government. For example, over ten thousand Cherokees were moved overland along the Trail of Tears from their home in Georgia to Oklahoma territory.

Assimilation

Two groups of unlike peoples may solve their problems of dissimilarity by merging their two cultures. Intermarriage and cultural borrowing eventually results in the loss of separate identities. Many ethnic groups immigrating to the United States underwent this process of assimilation. In some cases, second, third, and subsequent generations have completely lost the cultural uniqueness of the first generation migrants. They have become "Americanized."

The children of recent immigrants quickly learn the patterns of behavior characteristic of the dominant group.

Segregation

At times the legal structure has been used to subordinate the minority group. Those considered members of the minority have been forced to have separate residential areas, churches, schools, and even occupations. They were separated from the dominant group in use of public facilities and intermarriage was prohibited. This pattern of race relations is all too familiar to the American scene.

Stratification

Here the more dominant group, while not requiring physical segregation, merely assigns an inferior position to the subordinate group. The inferior group is denied an equal distribution of privilege and opportu-

nity. Poor schooling, justice which is not impartial, and occupational deprivation are mechanisms used to keep the inferior "in their place." Slavery is, of course, the most extreme example of stratification in race relations.

Pluralism

Racial pluralism refers to a situation where races or ethnic groups retain their identity and at the same time continue to interact with one another in the absence of conflict. Assimilation, in which the identity of the minority is lost, never occurs. Pluralism is the goal of many civil rights organizations in our society today. While they do not wish to lose their cultural identity, they do want equal opportunities in all areas. Hawaii is perhaps the best example of several races living together in a pluralistic set of arrangements. And yet in Hawaii social conflict is not entirely absent. There, as on the mainland, occupational and housing discrimination is still present.

These patterns are, of course, attached to the norms and values of a society. This means that they are learned and expected ways of behaving. Individuals in both the dominant and subordinate positions must be taught how they are to behave toward each other. Individuals also must be taught to identify themselves with their respective group and how to identify members of the other group. That patterns of race relations are a part of the normative structure of a society means, also, that they change very slowly. In 1954, the Supreme Court ruled (in the case of *Brown* v. *Board of Education of Topeka*) that separate can never be equal. Legally that decision meant the death of segregation. However, norms die slowly sometimes, and in many areas of this land segregation remains the expected behavior. Integration has been little more than token and while minorities in this nation have been granted their civil right to equal opportunity, little has really changed. We can only hope that the future will lead to more pluralism in the United States and less segregation and racial stratification.

PREJUDICE AND DISCRIMINATION

The word prejudice means pre-judgment, that is, an opinion that is based upon inaccurate or at least unsupported evidence. It is, as Gordon Allport suggests, "thinking ill of others without sufficient warrant."[4]

Prejudice includes an *affective* element, which means that it involves an emotion toward others, usually a negative feeling. Prejudice is also *cognitive*. That is, it contains beliefs about what others are like.

The cognitive aspect (beliefs about the other) both reinforces the affective element (negative emotion) and is in turn reinforced by the same affective factor. Prejudice, therefore, is a prejudgment of inferiority which includes a built in set of negative emotions toward and beliefs about the other.

Discrimination is differential treatment. When, for example, a qualified person is not given a job because of his skin color (and not on the basis of his training, experience, or skill), this is discrimination. When a family is denied residence in a suburban neighborhood because they are Jewish in ancestry, discrimination is at work. The same may be said when a woman is paid less for a task which she performs as well as a man. Therefore, when differential treatment occurs on the basis of unequal criteria (he is black, they are Jewish, or she is a woman), discrimination may be said to exist.

Prejudice and discrimination usually occur together, although not always so. A prejudiced person may be prohibited by law from displaying discriminative behavior. For example, the owner of a restaurant may not want to serve blacks because of personal prejudice. However, the law may force the restaurant owner to do so. In this case, the prejudiced person cannot discriminate. On the other hand, discriminating behavior may not be based upon prejudice. A real estate salesman may not show a piece of property to a black family, not because he personally is prejudiced against blacks, but because his business would suffer should he sell a home in an all-white neighborhood to blacks. Thus, in a society in which the social structure is racist, i.e., where power and economics are structurally discriminatory, individuals act out discriminating behavior on the basis of "shared behavioral expectations."

People internalize culturally approved attitudes as well as behavior. Prejudice, which is an attitude, is learned. A person does not inherit a prejudicial attitude, and neither is it automatically acquired. As indicated earlier, a person must *learn* to view himself and his group as different from others, to identify the others, and to classify the others as inferior or at least substantially different and "not one of us." Patterns of behavior which are discriminatory are also learned. Discrimination is simply an expected way of behaving. One of the writers once attended an outdoor party at which there were about forty guests. The host and hostess, a rather affluent and well-educated young couple, were perfect examples of congeniality until it was discovered that the date of one of the male guests was a fair-skinned mulatto who classified herself as a black. (One of her grandparents had been a black.) The background of the young couple hosting the party was such that they resented a black being present. And, although they had accepted the presence of the young lady up until that time, they asked her to leave. The norms which governed the relationship between whites and blacks that they had learned precluded social intercourse among the races and the host and hostess responded according to their background.

Not all cultural traits of minorities are rejected.

Discrimination is not caused by prejudice; the two reinforce one another. Patterns of discrimination insure the low status of the minority group, and this has a tendency to justify the negative feelings and beliefs of the dominant group. On the other hand, the prejudiced opinions of the dominant group help to keep the rules of discrimination intact. For example, the popular stereotype of the black includes the idea that they are poor because they are lazy and will not work (this is prejudice). On the basis of this inaccurate and unsupported opinion, the black is denied membership in labor unions, finds it difficult (because of lack of education) to obtain a white-collar job, and is forced to accept only low paying, temporary jobs (this is discrimination). The discriminating behavior contributes to poverty and poverty supports the popular stereotype. The whole process becomes a vicious cycle.

THE MANY FACES OF DISCRIMINATION

Patterns of discrimination are the mechanisms by which the dominant group withholds equal opportunity from the minority. These activities insure the subordinate position of the minority and are the methods by which the majority maintains its advantages. Discrimination can and does have many faces.

Employment

Occupation in an industrial society such as ours is an important means to social mobility. A person's occupation has a lot to do with the kind of clothes he wears, the section of the city he lives in, and the kind of luxuries he buys. It sets the tone for a person's whole style of life. To discriminate against a group by relegating them to low-paying and non-prestigious jobs and by denying them access to higher status and better-paying jobs is to deny them the opportunity to improve their lot in life. This denial of equal economic opportunity helps to destroy the incentive of members of the minority group. Why be ambitious? Why attempt to get a better education? Why try to get ahead? These questions have meaning for those who are the victims of economic discrimination.

That economic discrimination does exist in the United States is clearly revealed by considering a few simple facts.

The median family income for whites in 1968 was $8,937; for blacks it was $5,360. Almost 42 percent of the white families in the United States made ten thousand dollars or better in 1968. Only 19 percent of the black families fell above the ten thousand dollar income that same year.

Education

Educational discrimination is primarily of two varieties. First, a qualitatively inferior education is often offered to minorities due to segregated schools. In the South, segregation in schools remains the official, even if illegal, policy. In other areas of the nation, racially identifiable schools are just as much a reality because of residential patterns. That is, neighborhood schools become predominantly black because the area in which they are located is predominantly black. In many cases discipline, equipment, and teachers in these schools are substandard. The result is an inferior education.

The second variety of educational discrimination may be traced to the whole framework in which the minority exists. Educational incentive is reduced as indicated above. Home conditions of the deprived are not conducive to study, and even if they were, children of the minorities are not encouraged to take advantage of educational opportunity. The inferior educational background of the parent precludes assisting the child at home. Encyclopedias and other types of equipment designed to assist the youngster in learning are not a part of the home scene. The middle-class teacher and middle-class oriented textbooks often fail to take into account very important cultural differences between backgrounds. One simple example is language. Children of minority areas speak (and hear spoken away from school) a nonstandard dialect. (In some cases they may have been reared

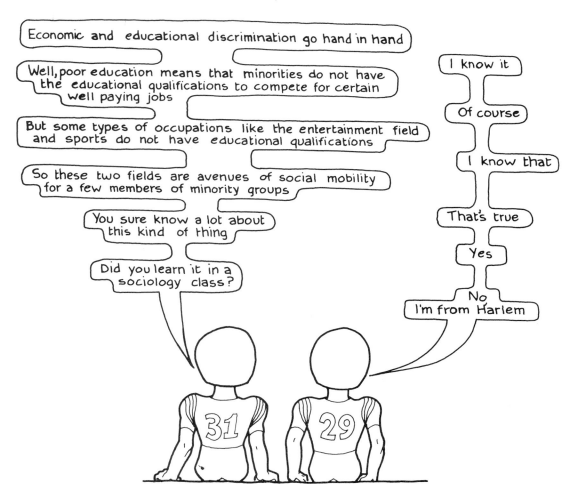

speaking Spanish or some other foreign language.) In school the books they are expected to read and the words they are expected to spell are written in standard English, which sounds as foreign to those raised on dialect as Latin would to middle-class children. To read they must first translate, and to spell they must unlearn the phonic system to which they are accustomed.

This constellation of factors forces upon the minority child a host of educational disadvantages. Many never recover from them.

Housing

Discrimination in housing is illegal. Nonetheless it remains a reality because of support from realtors, home financing institutions, property owners associations, and white homeowners and residents. Where blacks have broken the lines of resistance and moved into white middle-class neighborhoods, the whites have fled to the suburban ring. This flight has been precipitated as the basis of the whites' unwillingness to share a residence area with blacks. The neighborhood is a place, presumably, where roughly the same kind of people live together. It is a social setting for family life and the context in which much socialization takes place. People in a neighborhood share churches, schools, and parks. Beyond that, a place of residence is a significant aspect of status. Evidently, whites remain unwilling, in general, to allow blacks into their neighborhood. The result has been the perpetuation of black neighborhoods and the ghetto.

Politics

Discrimination in politics has taken the form of denial of the vote, poll taxes which put a financial premium on voting, literacy requirements, and tests of familarity with the Constitution and the American system of government. The first of the practices was explicitly discriminatory; the designated minority simply was not allowed to vote. The second method (poll taxes) discouraged all the poor (whether minority or not) from voting. The third and fourth, while not explicitly discriminatory, could be manipulated in such a manner as to exclude the minority.

The denial of political rights is, in effect, the denial of political power. Disenfranchisement of the minority obviated the possibility of the election of officials sympathetic to the grievances of the minority. When, however, they are granted the freedom to vote they may hold the balance of power and in close elections determine which candidate wins. In those areas where they are the majority in number, they can, if mobilized, exercise genuine political power. Through the use of this political power they can work toward the elimination of other forms of discrimination—jobs, housing, education.

THE RESPONSES OF THE MINORITY

Minority groups, we have said, are categories of persons who are different from the dominant society as measured by physical appearance and/or cultural patterns of behavior. They are set apart by the majority and experience less privilege and opportunity than does the dominant group. How do the minorities respond to this differential treatment? Several patterns of response emerge which may be divided into two classifications.[5]

The Tactics of Submissiveness

Minorities may accept the social definitions of their differentness and accordingly work out a set of relationships based on their low or at least different status.

They may *withdraw* from the dominant group. Religious groups like the old order Amish, a fundamentalist Christian sect, frequently withdraw and segregate themselves from society. They establish their own churches, schools, recreational activities, and social agencies designed to separate themselves into a geographical and social colony. They may dress differently so as to heighten their separateness from the general society. In the case of the Amish, they own no automobiles, perferring horse and buggies, and have no electricity in their homes. Their moral code as well as many other rules of behavior are drawn from a literal interpretation of the Bible. The withdrawal of the minority is self-segregation and structures are set up which are designed deliberately to reduce the contact of the minority (especially the young) with the dominant society.

A second tactic of submissiveness may be called *submissive manipulation.* Psychologically, members of the minority may take on an "Uncle Tom" attitude toward the dominant group. Flattery, dogged loyalty, being a "good nigger," and submissively staying in "one's place" become mechanisms used by the minority to gain the favor of the dominant group. Using these tactics the minority accepts the discrimination and unequal distribution of rewards. Members of the dominant group convince themselves that discrimination does not exist since they are always "kind to Negroes."

Many ghetto blacks today tend to view middle-class blacks with suspicion, and often assume that they cooperate and interact with whites merely to gain their favor. Presumably the middle-class blacks accept tokenism, and they and a few others enjoy the rewards of the white world and forget about their own brothers who are still experiencing the deprivation of discrimination. These latter-day Uncle Toms, to the extent that they do exist, continue to practice submissive manipulation and are the brunt of much black hatred. The animosity which disadvantaged blacks feel for the Uncle Toms is revealed in the descriptive term they apply to them. They are called "Oreo cookies" —white inside and black outside. Spanish Americans who practice submissive manipulation are called "coconuts"—white inside and brown outside.

The Tactics of Resistance

Minorities may resent the prejudice and discrimination which is directed toward them and orient their behavior toward the removal of the barriers that separate them from the fruits of their society.

Many members of minorities have experienced *intergenerational social mobility.* First and second generation immigrants to this country have sent their children to American schools which resulted in greater education, better occupation, and the "Americanization" of the children. Many members of some minorities were able to move out of the old neighborhood and into suburbia. The barriers of strange customs in behavior, dress, and language were lost and these persons were able to take their place in the dominant society.

Members of other minority groups were not so fortunate. They are marked by biological differences, especially skin color and facial characteristics, which have barred them from equal access to educational and occupational mobility and have resulted in the continued experience of attitudes of prejudice and practices of discrimination. The frustrations which they have felt in such circumstances has created several varieties of the tactics of resistance.

They turned sometimes to *riot and violence.* Most violent encounters between the minority groups and the majority have been precipitated by the majority. Lynchings, pillaging, and other scare tactics of groups like the Ku Klux Klan were mechanisms used to insure that the black would stay in his place. These violent controls placed upon the black man had their origin in the violence inherent in the slave system and the relations between the white masters and the black slave. Until recently, racial warfare in this nation has been initiated by the white man and directed toward the personal injury or death of the racial minority, especially the black. These patterns of violence have been termed *white-dominated, person-oriented riots.*[6] During the sixties a new phenomenon in racial violence emerged. Riots were initiated by the blacks and directed toward destruction of property rather than persons. These patterns of violence are called *Negro-dominated, property-oriented riots.* In 1964, Harlem, Rochester, Jersey City, Paterson-Elizabeth, Chicago, and Philadelphia were the scene of major incidents of such riots. The next year saw five such riots, the most prominent of which was the Watts riot of August 11–18. In 1966 there were twenty major outbreaks of racial violence, and in 1967 there were seventy-six such riots including Newark (July 12–16) and Detriot (July 23–31). By the end of 1967, twenty eight states and the District of Columbia had experienced a "long, hot summer."[7] These outbrusts of violence, looting and burning were led by the black community and aimed at the destruction of property. They appear to have been unorganized emotional explosions based upon the frustrations, anxieties, and hopelessness experienced by large numbers of urban blacks.

Non-violence represents an organized tactic of resistance. It is associated primarily with the name of Dr. Martin Luther King, Jr. who rose to national fame in the mid-fifties in connection with a successful bus boycott led by blacks in Montgomery, Alabama. King's philosophy was deeply religious and based upon the tenet that "turning the other cheek" is an effective method of correcting the injustices confronted by racial minorities. He emphasized that his program is not the cowardly approach nor mere passivity; it is direct resistance. While imprisoned in Birmingham, Alabama, King wrote an impassioned justification for his non-violent direct action. Laws, he said, may be unjust as well as just. Those who by conscience believe a law to be unjust are morally responsible to resist such a law. They do so by knowingly and openly breaking the law, without resorting to violence. Then they willingly accept the punishment meted out to the offenders of the unjust law. The public conscience is aroused by the injustice of punishmant caused by an unjust law.

Further, mass demonstration, marches, kneel-ins, sit-ins, and other activities are designed to dramatize an issue by creating disturbance and disharmony. Such non-violent actions will create enough of a crisis to produce negotiations which will resolve the injustice experienced by the minority.[8] Laws such as those which force minorities to go to segregated schools and customs which force minorities to sit in the back of a bus are directly challenged by tactics of non-violence. The injustices are resolved and new patterns of interaction are thereby worked out.

During the mid-sixties, still another tactic of resistance emerged. This approach, termed *black power,* is associated with the name of Stokely Carmichael and is set forth clearly in a book (appropriately entitled *Black Power*) written by Carmichael and Charles Hamilton.[9] Basically it is an appeal to blacks to close ranks and present a unified front to the dominant society. This unity is to be based upon a strong political and economic organization and is built on a pride in the African heritage and culture of the black man. The theme "black is beautiful" is dominant in this movement. The pride in blackness creates a self-identification which allows the black community to press for self-determination and autonomy in business, government, and other fields.

Integration is rejected by black power advocates on the basis that it forces the black man to conform to white middle-class attitudes and life styles, and to abandon the unique culture and heritage of the Negro. Black power instead seeks a situation in which the black maintains, or at least works out his own uniqueness while being an accepted part of American society.

Violence may be a part of black power. This is true because gains made through the present political system are too slow and too uncertain. Blacks must no longer be subjected to a colonial status oppressed by white supremacy. The political system is dominated by the whites and has been employed by whites as a tool to suppress the black and deny him any real gains. Progress of the black man to date, as viewed by Black Power advocates, has been based upon the blacks' willingness to accommodate themselves to a racist system. Token gains are all the black has achieved. No longer will the black be satisfied with this subservient position. He asserts his blackness, taking pride in it, and demands the social justice and equality due him as a citizen and as a human being, now.

SUMMARY

This chapter represents an effort to trace the more important aspects of pattern of interaction between minority groups and the dominant society, or what is usually referred to as race relations. A minority was defined as a group within a population that is set apart on the basis of biological or cultural traits, considered inferior to the dominant group, and treated subordinately. America became a "salad bowl" of minorities due to the mass immigration of people from Europe and Asia and the western movement of the United States into lands populated by Indians and Spanish Americans. The American Negro, who migrated to cities and fled northward and westward, added to the complicated patterns of minority relations in this society after the turn of the century.

The historical patterns of race relations was presented next. Relationships between the dominant group and the minority have followed at least one of the following possible patterns: annihilation, expulsion, assimilation, segregation, stratification, or pluralism.

Prejudice was then distinguished from discrimination and the various forms of discrimination were discussed. The minority is subjected to discrimination in employment, education, housing, and politics. In this section, the methods by which prejudice implements discrimination and discrimination, in turn, implements prejudice were discussed. Further, it was noted that both prejudice and discrimination are parts of the norms of a society and as such are learned patterns of behavior.

Finally, the possible responses of the minority to their minority status was presented. They may employ the tactics of submissiveness and either withdraw from the dominant group or seek to manipulate the majority by "Uncle Tomish" obedience. Or, based upon a dissatisfaction with their low status, the minority may turn to the tactics of resistance. Working within the structures of social mobility, members of the minority may climb the social ladders of educational achievement or occupational advancement and thereby remove themselves from the "inferior" position the minority occupies. Others, being denied for one reason or another the opportunities for social improvement, may turn to riot or violence, to the tactics of non-violence, or to movements like black power.

Notes

1. Charles Wagley and Marvin Harris, *Minorities in the New World* (New York: Columbia University Press, 1958), pp. 4–11.

2. Claude Brown, *Manchild in the Promised Land* (New York: Macmillan, 1965), pp. 7–8.

3. Brewton Berry, *Race and Ethnic Relations,* 3d. ed. (Boston: Houghton Mifflin, 1965).

4. Gordon Allport, *The Nature of Prejudice* (Reading, Mass.: Addison-Wesley Publishing, 1954), p. 6.

5. Louis Masotti et al., *A Time to Burn* (Chicago: Rand McNally, 1969).

6. Ibid., pp. 111–14.

7. "Major Riots, Civil Criminal Disorders," prepared for Permanent Subcommittee on Investigations of the Government Operations Committee, U.S. Senate.

8. Martin Luther King, Jr., *Letter from Birmingham City Jail* (Philadelphia: American Friends Service Committee, 1963).

9. Stokely Carmichael and Charles Hamilton, *Black Power* (New York: Random House, 1967).

Thinking
Sociologically

1.   Go back to pages 97–102 and read again the story of Willy Brown. Can you see more evidence of prejudice than you do of discrimination? How was the life of Willy Brown affected by the patterns of discrimination which he experienced in Alabama? Were the patterns of discrimination different in the city? Which "pattern of response" was characteristic of Willy? Which was characteristic of his son?

2.   A minority, it was said, has physical or cultural traits which are held in low esteem by the dominant segment of a society. Divide the class into groups. Each group is to select a single minority and make a list of the physical and cultural traits which are judged inferior by segments of American society. Some minorities which may be considered are (1) blacks, (2) Mexican Americans, (3) the aged, (4) homosexuals, (5) women, (6) Puerto Ricans, (7) Chinese, etc. In class discussion of the lists do you discover similarities in the traits considered inferior? How do members of various minorities tend to respond to the differential treatment which they may receive due to these traits?

3.   Consider these questions:
Does the present emphasis of the youth culture on "doing your own thing," brotherhood, accepting other people as they are, and human understanding look like pluralism? Or is it another way of conformity which really emphasizes segregation or at least a new mode of assimilation?

PART FOUR

Social Change, Collective Behavior, and Deviance

Chapter 7

Cognitive
Objectives

This chapter is about social change. In it, society is viewed as a process which is growing, changing, and always in flux. It is like a human body. That is, society is an ever-changing living organism. But despite its constant change, there is a basic framework which remains much the same. The twenty-year-old man is not anatomically the exact replica of the ten-year-old he once was. Yet he is the same person. As you read the chapter, look for the following points:

1. *The difference in describing social changes and conceptualizing social change as a sociological subject*
2. *Characteristics of the three levels of change. How do they differ and which may properly be called social change?*
3. *The manner in which short-term, regular cycles of social change help to control deviancy*
4. *How impersonal forces affect the structure of society*
5. *The definition of social change*
6. *The five forces of social change*
7. *The role of the individual in social change. What is an innovator? An advocate? An adapter?*
8. *Why some innovations are resisted*

The Winds of Change

When the sociologist speaks of social change, he has in mind alterations in some aspect of the usual way of life within a total society or some significate percentage of the society. The change may occur in behavior, attitudes, values, expectations, or any combination of these four elements. The sociological curiosity wants to know what changes occurred between point A and point B of a society's existence. Further, the social observer wants to know what caused the changes and what were the results of the change in other areas of social life and individual behavior.

For example, in our own time civilization has caught up with certain pre-civilized peoples. Social change which occurred over several thousand years is some societies is telescoped into a couple of decades in these pre-civilized societies. In an article entitled "Out of the Stone Age," *Newsweek* reported on the arduous experience of the Masai in East Africa.

For 58 colonial years, British administrators in East Africa looked on the fierce, nomadic Masai tribe as a living embodiment of noble savagery. Barefoot, bejeweled, wearing red ochre in their hair and off-the-shoulder shuka robes that left one buttock exposed, the Masai moran (warriors) roamed the arid plains near Mt. Kilimanjaro, tending their treasured cattle. "The Masai," a British officer wrote a half-century ago, "resemble the lion and the leopard—beautiful beasts of prey that please the artistic sense but are never of any use and are often a serious danger." But times—and administrations—change. Today, the independent governments of Tan-

129

zania and Kenya, where Masai lands are located, view the half-naked hunter-herdsmen as embarrassing reminders of their own backward past—and they are taking steps to drive the Masai out of the Stone Age and into the present.[1]

The governments of Tanzania and Kenya have employed several tactics to effect social change in the proud Masai. The picture of a stalwart Masai warrior has been replaced on the nation's one hundred shilling note by a cornfield, symbolizing agricultural productivity. A two-month jail sentence has been effected to punish anyone entering the capital district "with his private parts exposed." Concerted effort has been exerted to settle the wandering Masai tribes into permanent communities and to make them abandon their traditional cattle herding methods for more modern and productive techniques. Both governments need more beef for domestic consumption as well as for

Social change represents widespread alterations in patterns of behavior.

export. Technical assistance is offered in ridding cattle of disease, constructing new water holes, and improving stock. Kenya offers title to land which individuals will settle on. "Time may be running out for the Masai" as civilization overtakes them and completely manages their societies.[2]

The change from pre-civilized man to the American suburbanite is almost an unimaginable leap. The many changes involved in the transition make up the slow and not necessarily progressive history of societal change. Unlike the Masai experience, the American transition has occurred in multitudinous changes which built upon one another, each standing on the shoulders of the former, in spurts, in regression, in catastrophic events, in small inventions, in new starts, in rediscoveries, and new beginnings. Total societal change comes about by social changes that occur in the processes of society. The impact of the change on related parts of social life is the subject of this chapter.

WHAT'S NEW?

It is not difficult to give examples of the rapidity of changes which appear to be occurring everywhere in American society. Alvin Toffler *(Future Shock)* made the point that impermanence is an integral part of contemporary American society. Throw-away bottles and clothes are matched by throw-away people (e.g., divorce). Trade-ins on automobiles, dishwashers, and even Barbie dolls emphasize the non-permanent aspects of the things we own. Few Americans expect to finish payments on the house they buy on installments. The rest live in apartments. Advertising alerts us to the prestige involved in discarding the used in favor of the new. In such a manner, we are socialized to the reality of impermanence. Toffler feels that the average American may be overstimulated with the ever-increasing rate of change. In an atmosphere of geographical mobility and temporary possessions, the average American may be unable to put down roots which are necessary for a stable personality and individual well-being.

Toffler's descriptive account of changes, however, helps little in conceptualizing social change. What he did is bring to the surface the sense of hurry and external stimuli characteristic of what has been called "the rat race." But *what* is changing and what *causes* the changes? What is *not* changing and why do some aspects of culture remain relatively constant? These are important questions which must be solved in order to understand social change.

CHANGE AND NONCHANGE

Change may be viewed as occurring at three overlapping levels: personal life changes, short term cycles, and social change.

Personal Life Changes

Every individual experiences changes based upon the normal life cycle of physical and social maturation. The first day of school for a child is an example of this type of change. The growing child takes on a set of new roles which makes new demands upon him and offers him new privileges. In most societies major transition points in the individual's life are marked by some induction ceremony known as a *rite of passage.* In a public manner, the individual's assumption of the expectations and rights of the new social roles are acknowledged. Such rites of passage in our society include baptism, confirmation, bar mitzvah, graduation ceremonies, weddings, retirement, and a host of other traditions that have to do with special groups and clubs.

The progressive movement through the normal pathways of growing up and growing old in a society do not, however, constitute social change. Normal structures are set up in a relatively stable society to accomodate the usual maturing process of the people who make up the society. These rituals help to stabilize change and enable the individual to cope with new expectations that accompany the process of growing up. The normal life cycle represents individual change which may or may not be traumatic for the person involved. Such change does *not,* however, represent what sociologists call social change.

Short Term Cycles

In every society there exists changes in patterns of behavior of large numbers of people that may be called "short term cycles or fluctuations." Wilbert Moore defines this kind of change in the following manner: "By small scale changes we shall mean changes in the characteristics of social structure that, though comprised within the general system identifiable as a society, do not have immediate and major consequences for the generalized structure (society) as such."[3] Societies, like individuals, may have periodic *rites of passage* which allow change-of-pace activities for the total society. Holidays, for example, release individuals from normal expectations and allow tension release. Some festive activities occasion the temporary waiving of normative restraints and allow for *controlled deviance* and may, says Moore, reduce nonconformity. Halloween, for example, allows some types of minor mischief and may, in so doing, allow individuals to blow off steam. Reducing pent-up emotions in this socially approved manner may keep the individual from breaking rules in "normal" situations. Harvest celebrations and religious holidays create a spirit of brotherliness and goodwill which reduces the strain of a highly competitive society and provides an integrative function by emphasizing communal values.

These normal fluctuations in the routine of societal life represent an extremely predictable type of social change. One knows the "norms" for behavior at Christmas time, for example, and we may generally predict how most people are going to act in given situations during this time. Not so easy to predict is another type of short term cycle of social change that will be further discussed in chapter 8—crazes,

new styles of clothing, and the "in" language of a given group. These are instances of social change which appear to come and go at whim. For example, who can predict what terms will become part of the "in" language? It has included such terms as "What's up, doc?" "heavy," "right on," and "cool." Girls have been chicks, and guys have been dudes. "Freaking out," "stoned" and "dig" have also been a part of accepted speech. Such language styles are totally unpredictable.

Fluctuations in behavior at this level represent social changes which are normal aspects of the orderly activity of the society. As the weekend reduces the monotony of work for most Americans, so normal social life is punctuated with periodic occasions and fads which reduce the routine and give an opportunity for the expression of change. As such, they help to stabilize a society.

Social Change

The third and last level of change may be termed structural change. Unlike "small scale change," it may alter in a permanent fashion the structure of the society. This level of change has to do with long term trends as well as spasmodic, catastrophic events (e.g., revolutions) which radically alter the behavior of individuals within the society. Think, for example, of the difference in social life today generated by the social acceptance of the automobile as a means of transportation. Dating patterns, as a single instance, show how a long term trend based upon a technological invention can alter permanently the structure of a society. In horse and buggy days, "courting" occurred in the "sitting room" of the young lady's home. At best, the young man sat with his girl on the front porch while her father listened attentively to make sure that the swing did not stop. Today the automobile has changed that pattern. Much of the freedom and mobility of young people in dating relationships today has stemmed from acceptance of the automobile as a part of American social life.

TRENDS AND SOCIAL CHANGE

Some of the trends which are both causes and effects of structural social change are urbanization, industrialization, population growth, educational changes, and ideological fluctuations. These trends, some of which represent the aggregate effect of small scale changes, move at differing rates of speed and sometimes in contrasting directions. For example, the sudden jump in birth rate (population trend) following the Second World War called for the training of more school teachers. Colleges and universities geared themselves to produce more elementary and secondary teachers (economic development). The gradual decline in birth rate since the mid-fifties has resulted in a situation in which approximately twice as many college graduates with teaching certificates are being produced each year as are needed to fill teaching positions. These social changes, themselves results of other social changes, call for the establishment of new trends to reduce the tension and social strain they have created.

Such an analysis of social change calls to mind the ideas of Karl Marx, who saw history as the record of the conflict between impersonal trends and consequent developments in the social structure. Marx saw this conflict displayed in the tension between classes. The "haves" (the bourgeoisie) and the "have nots" (the proletariat) are products of the structural forces which come from social changes. Marx saw inevitable strains existing in the different rates of change, the contrasting directions of trends, and the tendency of the society to "right" itself by making further changes. His predicted outcome of these societal changes may not have been correct (i.e., that the inevitable solution to these struggles lies in the classless society of communism). He appears, however, to have had a clear grasp of the manner by which societies change.

Social change occurs in many forms. As Wilbert Moore put it, "The course of change may be gradual or rapid, peaceful or violent, continuous or spasmodic, orderly or erratic."[4] Changes in social arrangements do occur. What are the mechanisms which trigger these changes? Let us take a look at these spurs to social change.

THE FORCES OF CHANGE

When a sociologist speaks of social change he is referring to patterns of behavior. A new way of doing something is accepted by a large part of a society when individuals who make up that society behave in the new way. Let's take a hypothetical example. Suppose a minority group is relegated to specific jobs, to certain levels of education, and to a certain form of social intercourse with the dominant group. Tactics of segregation and subjugation are practiced to insure a continuation of these social arrangements. Then specific things happen to the structure of the society which make these arrangements less functional for the dominant group. Opportunities for advanced education equal to that of the dominant segment of the society are opened to the minority. New vocational opportunities are made available. New status equal to that of the majority is gradually available to the members of the minority group. Such a state of changed affairs amounts to new patterns of behavior among both the dominant and once subordinate groups. What has changed is the way of doing things based upon new expectations (norms), values, and attitudes. The fact is that individuals act differently and their changed behavior, taken in concert, reflects social change.

Thus individuals change their behavior because the new way appears to them more rational or functional or expedient. The new pattern seems to fit into their needs more adequately than a former way of accomplishing the same goals. The new way seems "right." The acceptance of one new way of accomplishing a task may necessitate several other changes in the individual's way of life. The effect of large numbers of people accepting new individual behavior is social change. The question at this point is: Which elements of society most often offer the individual new alternatives?

Technology

Technological advance in the form of new inventions is a major stimulus to social change. Industrial development in Western civilization, which has a history extending back to the crusades in Europe, has been based upon man's curiosity and his desire to conquer his environment. Man seeks several goals: using more of his environment more efficiently, accomplishing specific goals having to do with sustaining life, and, in the more recent past, developing time-saving and labor-saving devices for an easier life. These issues have been major driving forces behind technological development.

The mule, once an integral part of the agricultural system of this nation, may one day be no more than an oddity seen in zoos.

Inventions such as the steam engine, the assembly line, and the computer have had the effect of reducing the number of persons needed to do manual labor. Industry has gradually reduced the hours needed for factory work. Today some businesses are experimenting with a four-day week. The result has been an increase in the leisure time available to the average American.

The rapid increase in leisure time has led to several innovative changes in patterns of behavior in our society. Mass entertainment, organized sports, and such things as camping are among some of these explosive changes. Camping, in turn, has created a new attitude toward state and national parks in keeping with the new emphasis on protecting the environment. The desire for natural beauty and the tragedy of abuse by overuse and carelessness has made ecology a new national movement. Additionally, the cordiality and informality of camping experiences has helped to offset the lack of neighborliness and feelings of estrangement which may be characteristic of the urban setting most people leave behind when they leave for a weekend of camping. At least one social observer has said, "Families who find themselves neighbors on a campground become acquainted immediately, are eager to help each other, become close friends within a day or two, and then just as suddenly are gone off to new 'instant friendships.' . . . Americans seem to be developing shallow roots that can sink quickly in strange grounds, knowing that they will take hold. While the faces of the people differ, the values and norms remain the same."[5]

Technological developments have also increased the ability of industry to mass produce products for widespread general consumption. Only one person can own the original of a piece of art. But today prints of the original are available for millions of people. Household gadgets and ornaments of sometimes dubious quality and comparatively inexpensive prices are available for the general populace. Candles are an example. In the days of handmade candles, a few candlemakers produced a limited number of candles at a slow but steady rate. Assembly line and machine production provides a virtually unlimited supply of an almost unimaginable variety of inexpensive candles to decorate the average home.

Poverty and the degree of affluence of the individual is associated with these developments in technology. The ability to consume conspiciously the products which applied science has created is one measure of an individual's economic worth, and results in his being ranked on an economic scale. The more one may consume, the higher the status. Poverty is, therefore, measured in economic terms dependent upon the power of the person (or family) to consume the products which industry can produce.

Family structure has felt the impact of technological changes. Modern technology made superfluous the need for child labor, and this resulted in longer periods of schooling for children. Since youngsters were no longer needed to work the fields, mines, and factories, "baby sitting" services were arranged through the social invention of the public school. The increase in working mothers since the Second World War has extended the need for such services into the preschool years of childhood and has resulted in a proliferation of nursery schools, day care centers, and kindergartens. The need to fill after-school hours and summers has resulted in a host or organizations designed to occupy the time of youngsters. Such things as Boy and Girl Scouts, Little League, clubs, recreational facilities, church choirs and other religious organizations, and summer camps have arisen to fill this gap.

Children may see little of either parent, as compared with nineteenth-century practices. Some observers speak of the "vanishing father" syndrome: a situation in which the children do not see the father at work, and seldom see him at home. As a result, the authority characteristic of a father in a more patriarchial society is lessened. Whether these changes are positive or negative in their effect is perhaps a matter of opinion. The fact remains that the modern, urban, nuclear family of today is vastly different from its counterpart in this nation fifty years ago.

Inventions based upon man's dissatisfaction with present solutions to problems are results of social changes and are prime causes of further social changes. The replacement of man's muscle with a machine and the substitution of a machine for the human mind has had radical effects upon social organization. Progress in medicine (sanitation, birth control, organ transplants), communications (radio and television), transportation (automobiles, airplanes, rockets), and power (electricity, gas, solar energy) has made man's life today different from any previous generation. New patterns of behavior, with a variety of duties and privileges, have arisen to accomodate and exploit these changes.

Education

A second major stimulus to social change is education. Americans place high value upon education as the best hope for meaningful change. Most suggested solutions to social problems contain (at least implicity) a belief that education of the people involved is a useful tool in effecting a remedy. Education has been held out as a promise for social mobility. Everybody has heard of someone who started "on the farm" or "in the slums" (interpreted as the bottom of the social scale), worked his or her way through college, and became a "success." Education remains an important source of socialization into dominant values, attitudes, and skills as discussed in chapter 4. As such, formal school prepares the individual for the world of work and gives him many of the social skills necessary for being successful in our society. To the degree that the school successfully accomplishes these ends, it serves as a perpetuation of the status quo and may resist social change.

The public school is also an area in which information on new fads and fashions is disseminated. The uniforms and vernacular of the youth culture, as well as its heroes and idols, are perpetuated by the peer groups developed in school. Communication of attitudes, values, and skills (i.e., the socialization process) is facilitated by the opportunities for communication which abound during the school hours. The newest in clothing, speech, or attitude may be seen on television or at the movies, but it must be authenticated by one's peer group. The school affords an efficient method for the peer group to do its socializing work.

Government

A third major force creating social change is the government. Like the schools which may serve as arenas to conserve the status quo as well as agents of change and innovation, the government with its legal and bureaucratic structures and its plodding nature may act as a resister to change. Passing laws by a majority vote of a legislative body is more difficult than having laws created by a single person (e.g., a dictator or a tribal chief).

Despite the sluggishness of government and its tendency to maintain stability, government may exert considerable stimulus for change by enacting far-reaching programs that alter patterns of behavior. In American government, this is especially true at the federal level. Such legislative programs as income tax, social security, welfare, relief for natural disaster, tariffs, control of monopoly, interstate transportation, control of mass communication, draft conditions, and defense programs seem to illustrate the power of government in initiating change. Government at the federal level also facilitates the coordination and diffusion of innovative ideas. Government, through federally-sponsored research, may even help to bring new ideas to the surface.

Civil rights legislation in the areas of employment opportunity, educational facilities, and housing is probably the best example of governmental activity in social change. Beginning with the post-World War II experiment in integrating the military, the federal government has acted as a spur to reduce segregation and its resulting

Congress just passed a law that says couples must have a license to have a baby

Why?

Population control, I guess

Means fewer consumers

Yeah, and voters

and taxpayers

Boy, one thing really brings about a lot of changes doesn't it?

discrimination. The 1954 landmark decision of the Supreme Court in the case of *Brown* v. *The Board of Education of Topeka* stated that "separate cannot be equal" and that segregation of blacks from whites is unconstitutional. Federal troops were sent to Little Rock in 1956 to insure desegregation of the high school. Two years later, Congress passed its first civil rights law in sixty years.

Stimulated by the non-violence movement of Martin Luther King, Jr. and the black power movement of Stokely Carmichael and H. Rapp Brown, as well as the NAACP, CORE, and other black organizations, the sixties saw the enactment of much civil rights legislation.[6] These laws have had some negative effects. They have stiffened resistance in some areas of the white community and they have also further frustrated the black community by not rapidly fulfilling their rising expectations. Nonetheless, the enactment of the laws and their firm enforcement has stimulated a gradual change in American folkways and mores. Perhaps the attitudes and values as well as the behavior of the American populace is moving more toward our formally stated ideals. There can be little doubt that federal activity has pushed the American public closer to conformity with these ideals. In the words of Martin Luther King, Jr.: ". . . in spite of the difficulties and frustrations of the moment I still have a dream. It is a dream deeply rooted in the American dream. I have a dream that one day this nation will rise up and live out the true meaning of its creed: 'we hold these truths to be self-evident; that all men are created equal.' "[7]

Population

A fourth agent of change is population growth. No simple analysis can explain the complex relationship between population increase and social change. Population growth is itself a result of prior changes, especially technological developments in the area of medicine, sanitation, and food production. These changes have lowered death rates by extending life expectancy and reducing infant mortality. The drastic effect which these factors have on population is seen in the following facts. It took several million years for the world population to reach its present size of 3.6 billion. At the present rate of increase, it will take only thirty years to add an additional three billion. World population reached one billion about 1850. Around 1930, it passed two billion. The 1960 world population was three billion. According to World Health Organization statistics, 3.7 persons are born each second. That fact means that 221 are born per minute, 318,575 per day, and more than 2.2 million per week. At that rate, it requires only three years to add the equivalent of the total United States population to the world population, while the equivalent of the population of England, Wales, Scotland, Ireland, Sweden, and Norway is being added to the world population each year.[8]

The impact of this rapid increase in population is felt in the social changes which sudden and steady growth cause in a society. Cities are mushrooming. Patterns of city growth have changed from relatively small and isolated urban areas to chains of cities which interlock and have no open country between them (called metropolitan communities, strip cities, and megalopolis). The economy struggles to provide jobs for the millions who enter the job market each year. Environmental pollution becomes a widespread problem. Police and fire protection must be provided at an increasing rate. Housing is in short supply. Increased strains on individuals and on social structures demand increasing numbers of mental health facilities, physical health clinics, courts, and jails. Transportation problems grow with crowded freeways, parking garages, and subways.

Concern with the effects of the population explosion has resulted in medical research on birth control and has led to the development of birth control pills, intrauterine devices, and other contraceptive methods. The wide adoption of these contraceptives is an example of social change. Traditional values and attitudes toward the family and its purpose in society are being questioned. The proliferation of such organizations as Zero Population Growth and changes in the attitudes of some religious groups (including adherents of the Roman Catholic Church) result from recognition of the dangers of overpopulation and represent social changes growing out of the population crisis.

Population growth has created a demand for certain products which has resulted in technological changes. Prefabricated houses, subdivisions, mass production of all types of consumer items, and the gigantic advertising industry are among the ways in which technology has responded.

It should be noted that should population trends be radically reversed, a new set of "population" problems will emerge for which new changes must compensate. A population with a low birth rate and a low death rate is a population whose average age increases each year. This fact means that children and young adults are outnumbered by middle-aged and old people. Older citizens and especially the aged pay relatively fewer taxes than do young and middle-aged adults. On an average they do not consume the products of industrialization as do younger citizens. And in the case of the aged, they need more services from governmental agencies. The result is a relatively shrinking tax base, relatively fewer consumers (especially in specific industries), and greater demand for governmental services. A series of innovative social changes must be initiated if and when the U.S. population stabilizes or begins to decline.

Television

The last stimulant to social change to be mentioned here is television. It has been estimated that the average child growing up today in American society will watch a total of seventeen years of television in his life time. That figure represents almost a fifth of his life and almost a third of his waking hours. Despite the poverty of empirical research on the impact of television on social patterns, there can be little doubt that its effect has been significant. Mealtimes and bedtimes are planned around favorite programs. In some instances even sexual activities are secondary to television. Children's programs take the place of baby sitters, and advertisers recognize how these young minds can be influenced about the products of industry.

Television has the potential effect of increasing the individual's awareness beyond his own personal experiences. The life styles of subcultures as well as life in foreign societies are revealed. The horrors of war are watched in living color. Political leaders become known as personalities to be liked or disliked regardless of the principles for which they stand. New fashions are compared to one's own wardrobe and new products for consumption are described in detail.

The growth of television has been little less than phenomenal. It took only fourteen years (from 1946 to 1960) for the ownership of television sets to average one per household in the United States.[9] That in itself is social change. The growth of the television industry has provided new occupations and brought changes in other industries as well. For example, the growth of professional sports, the decline of the neighborhood theatre, modifications in the movie industry, and the growth of the advertising industry have all been affected by television.

Before leaving the subject of agents of social change, one further word is in order. No single force explains social change. All the factors mentioned in this chapter work in concert effecting changes in each other, upon themselves, and on outside elements. Each is itself a result (or even more properly a series of results) of change, as well as a cause of change. These impersonal forces move at varying rates. Within each are other mechanisms that resist change, impede progress, and retard growth. The rapidity of social change, as well as its overall direction, is determined by the functioning of each of these factors and their collective impact upon one another.

THE INDIVIDUAL AND SOCIAL CHANGE

Earlier it was said that social change is a process by which patterns of behavior are changed as individuals adopt new practices, attitudes, or values. The place of the individual in the process of social change is by no means limited to or fully described by this simple statement. Three basic roles for the individual in the process of social change may be distinguished.[10]

The Innovator

People develop methods for solving problems and coping with the environment. These methods, as a part of the cultural heritage of a society, are passed from one generation to the next by the process of socialization. Innovation, on the other hand, may be defined as a new way of accomplishing a goal or the conceptualization of an entirely new goal. The innovation may be the invention of a new tool or the introduction of a new behavior or attitude (a social invention). Innovators are, therefore, individuals who for some reason have the capacity to envision a situation in such a way as to disregard the recognized and commonplace ways of coping with problems.

The innovator must be free from the restrictions of his culture, at least with regard to the specific problem involved. Effective socialization has the result of placing blinders on most individuals. The natural tendency of the well-socialized individual is to view familiar problem-solving devices as the only, or at least the most rational, method of achieving a goal. The innovator may be viewed as a socialization "dropout" in specific areas. This is true because an innovation is usually regarded as deviant by the majority. The innovator's inadequate socialization frees him from the limitation of defining his innovation as deviant. By intent or by accident, he approaches a problem from a new perspective.

Innovations may be new inventions within a given society or may be transmitted from an outside culture. The latter is termed cultural borrowing and takes place when an accepted pattern of behavior and/or accepted artifacts in one culture are lifted and carried into a new setting. Many elements of social change occur when this kind of cultural contact takes place. The "westernizing" of non-western nations is the diffusion of western traits in those nations. Hot tamales, pizza, chopsticks, yoga, judo, karate, and the widespread interest in such things as Zen Buddhism are instances of our own cultural borrowing. The cultivation of corn and smoking tobacco were borrowed from the original Americans (the Indians), while our Christian religion and alphabet were borrowed from the near East (for an illustration of the extent to which we are dependent upon cultural borrowing for many of our practices see pp. 57–59).

The Advocate

A novel way of accomplishing a goal is invented by an innovator or introduced from a foreign culture. The task of the advocate is to insure its widespread acceptance. Sometimes the innovator and the advocate are the same person. This pehnomenon is, however, infrequent since the traits for an oddball innovator and an efficient leader or advocate (sometimes called a change agent) are very dissimilar. The advocate must persuade a large number of "followers" that the innovation provides some functional advantage for them.

Frequently advocates are charismatic leaders. Max Weber defined charisma as "a certain quality of an individual personality by virtue of which he is set apart from ordinary men and treated as endowed with supernatural, superhuman or at least, specifically exceptional powers or qualities."[11] Charisma is the ability to sway other individuals on the basis of the dynamism of one's personality. The term has been applied to such men as Jesus Christ, Martin Luther King, Jr., Ghandi, John Kennedy, Adolf Hitler, Mao Tse-Tung, Franklin D. Roosevelt, and Fidel Castro. The captivating charm of Hitler was described by Albert Speer.

Hitler entered and was tempestuously hailed by his numerous followers among the students. This enthusiasm in itself made a great impression upon me. But his appearance also surprised me. On posters and in caricatures I had seen him in military tunic, with shoulder straps, swastika armband, and hair flapping over his forehead. But here he was wearing a well-fitted blue suit and looking markedly respectable. Everything about him bore out the note of reasonable modesty. Later I learned that he had a great gift for adjusting—to his surroundings.

As the ovation went on for minutes he tried, as if slightly pained, to check it. Then, in a low voice, hesitantly and somewhat shyly, he began a kind of historical lecture rather than a speech. To me there was something engaging about it—all the more so since it ran counter to everything the propaganda of his opponents had led me to expect: a hysterical demagogue, a shrieking and gesticulating fanatic in uniform. He did not allow the bursts of applause to tempt him away from his sober tone.

It seemed as if he were candidly presenting his anxieties about the future. His irony was softened by a somewhat self-conscious humor; his South German charm reminded me agreeably of my native region. A cool Prussian could never have captivated me that way. Hitler's initial shyness soon disappeared; at times now his pitch rose. He spoke urgently and with hypnotic persuasiveness. The mood he cast was much deeper than the speech itself, most of which I did not remember for long.

Moreover, I was carried on the wave of the enthusiasm which, one could almost feel this physically, bore the speaker along from sentence to sentence. It swept away any skepticism, any reservations. Opponents were given no chance to speak. This furthered the illusion, at least momentarily, of unanimity. Finally, Hitler no longer seemed to be speaking to convince; rather, he seemed to feel that he was expressing what the audience, by now transformed into a single mass, expected of him. It was as if it were the most natural thing in the world to lead students and part of the faculty of the two greatest academies in Germany submissively by a leash.[12]

Charismatic leaders advocating a cause for acceptance frequently are confronted with counter movements which find their own charismatic champion. For example, the charisma of Martin Luther King, Jr. and the civil rights movement gave rise to the white backlash which pushed George Wallace into national prominence.

Advocacy for an innovation is frequently done by the impersonal forces of the mass media. Advertising, however, takes advantage of personality power in these attempts to have an innovation accepted. Popular television and movie stars, athletes, beauty queens, astronauts, and even politicians "endorse" a new product or idea. The charisma of the specific individual is employed to gain acceptance and consumption of the advertised product.

Several tactics are necessary for successful advocacy of a new device or behavior pattern. Sometimes the advocate must urge the relinquishing of an old device, behavior pattern, or attitude. New standards may be provided to evaluate the old methods. The advocate may enable the potential adopters of the new practice to think in terms of the values and norms of some group into which they hope to be inducted as members. The advocate may make the potential adopter aspire to the prestige of the new reference group. That is, the adopter is told that he can raise his social rank and receive greater status by adopting the new device.

The Adopter

Adopters are those individuals who take up the innovative practice or ideas. Two types of people appear to be most likely to become adopters: marginal persons and socially mobile individuals. Marginal persons are partly socialized into two cultures or subcultures. Their socialization process is therefore incomplete or inadequate in a special sense. Their perspective lacks the coherence of a single culture with stable norms. Marginality helps free them from the sanctions at work in both cultures or subcultures and innovative practices can be engaged in with relative impunity. Adoption of a trait by marginal persons may, however, stigmatize the trait and retard its further diffusion in one or both subcultures.

Socially mobile individuals are especially receptive to innovative practices and trinkets. This is true since they desire to legitimize their claim to higher status and greater prestige. New practices and devices conspiciously consumed are both the claim for status and the justification for that claim.

Adoption may have a snowballing effect. That is, adopters in a sense become advocates and help spread the diffusion of a trait within a culture. A trait "catches on" and the prevalance of its use becomes a force which stimulates further adoption. In some cases, however, widespread adoption may retard diffusion since adoption removes novelty as a trait becomes commonplace by use. The attention gained by the manipulation of a new device is lost when the device is no longer new. Faddists then must turn to other trinkets or to new ideas.

Adopters, like innovators and advocates, must to a degree be the products of inadequate socialization. They must be able to see the connection between the new attitude or device and some problem in their own life. Additionally, they must be able to reject the familiar methods of meeting the specific goal for which the innovation is designed. In some cases, however, adoption is conforming behavior. Such is especially true for those adopters who take up the innovation in the later stages of its adoption. Early adopters may be viewed as deviants and, depending upon the nature of the changes involved, may be negatively sanctioned for their behavior. Later adopters do not ordinarily run this risk and may simply be conforming to the norms for their reference group. Public cigarette smoking by the female sex is a case in point. Today the female smoker is as comfortable and sophisticated in public as is the male smoker. Her earlier counterpart was, however, not so fortunate in the judgments that might be leveled at her for the same behavior.

Non-adopters, it would seem, are those in whom the socialization process has done its work effectively. Unable to see the morality ("I think it's sinful") or the functionality ("My way is just as efficient") of the innovation, they resist the new practice. Depending on the nature of the change and the personality of the individual, these non-adopters may condemn or even punish others for adopting the innovation. Counter movements may be established to offset the effect of the new trend. Or the non-adopter may accept others' adoption of the innovation, but remain unchanged in his own attitude or behavior. He may simply live out his life without the advantages (or disadvantages) of the change in the way of doing things.

Resistance to an innovation may be based upon the fact that the new trait does not fit into previously held ideas. For example, hybrid corn, though demonstrably superior in yield, was rejected by Mexican American farmers in the Rio Grande Valley because tortillas made from hybrid corn were a different color than those made from the old corn. Among some groups of oriental farmers, modern techniques of farming are rejected because the new techniques interfere with their concepts of nature. The Biaga of central India rejected modern plows in favor of their traditional digging sticks. They believed that the

The varying popularities of different musical styles illustrate the process of adoption.

digging sticks gently helped mother nature bring forth her yield; the plows were like cutting her with a knife.[13] Or, to bring the point closer to home, consider the American aversion to snails as an acceptable food source. Also, many Americans reject artificial prevention of conception because this practice is, in their minds, an interference with nature.

SUMMARY

Change occurs on three overlapping levels. (1) The individual experiences changes in roles as he moves normally through his life cycle. (2) Short term fluctuations or cycles are normal experiences which occur at specific intervals and in an orderly fashion in societal life. (3) Structural social changes may occur in unregulated, spasmodic, catastrophic, or trend-like fashion and can alter permanently some aspect of social behavior in a society. This latter type of change demands compensatory changes in other parts of the social system, which may or may not occur at an appropriate rate of speed. In such a manner, social developments occur, social change takes place, and strains and problems in the structural fabric of the society may appear.

Major forces stimulating social change (and themselves responding to social change) in American society are: (1) technological advance in the form of new inventions and innovative industrial arrangements, (2) education in the form of formal schooling and the existing academic community, (3) governmental activity in implementing new programs and enacting new legislation, (4) population growth with its attendant changes in urban concentration and its resultant social problems, and (5) television due to its capacity for communication of knowledge and information and its potential for increasing the viewer's awareness of his world. These impersonal forces, it was suggested, cause changes within each other, as well as affecting other structures within the society. No single causative agent is sufficient to explain the phenomenon of social change. These forces collide, cooperate, move at varying speeds and sometimes in opposite direction creating challenges in the social environment and creating the need for compensating changes to meet these challenges.

The place of the individual in social change was described in three roles: the innovator, the advocate, and the adopter. Non-adoption and individual resistance was found to occur when innovation in attitudes, ideas, or practice did not fit previously held values or norms.

Notes

1. "Out of the Stone Age," *Newsweek,* 28 August 1972, pp. 35–36.

2. Ibid.

3. Wilbert E. Moore, *Social Change* (Englewood Cliffs, N.J.: Prentice-Hall, 1963), pp. 46–47.

4. Ibid., pp. 33.

5. Melvin L. De Fleur, William V. D'Antonio, and Lois B. De Fleur, *Sociology: Man In Society* (Glenview, Ill.: Scott, Foresman, 1970), p. 202.

6. See Masotti, Hadden, Seminatore and Corsi, *A Time To Burn* (Chicago: Rand McNally, 1969), pp. 30, for a discussion of the civil rights laws enacted during the 1960s.

7. Martin Luther King, Jr,. "I Have a Dream," address at the March on Washington, 1963. Reprinted in *Negro Protest Thought in the Twentieth Century,* ed. Francis L. Broderick and August Meier (New York: Bobbs-Merrill, 1965), p. 403.

8. Shirley Foster Hartley, *Population: Quantity vs. Quality* (Englewood Cliffs, N.J.: Prentice-Hall, 1972), pp. 4, 5.

9. Melvin De Fleur, *Theories of Mass Communication* (New York: Rand McKay, 1966), p. 73.

10. Richard LaPiere, *Social Change* (New York: McGraw Hill, 1965).

11. Max Weber, *Theory of Social and Economic Organization,* trans. A. M. Henderson and Talcott Parsons (New York: The Free Press, 1957), p. 358.

12. Albert Speer, *Inside the Third Reich* (New York: Macmillan, 1970), pp. 18–19.

13. Elwin Varrier, *The Biaga* (London: John Murray, 1939), pp. 106–7.

Thinking Sociologically

1.   Social change alters roles, which all are to play, by reconstructing expectations for appropriate behavior in a given situation. Life styles of large numbers of people are rearranged as the new content of behavior is adapted. The trend toward working wives and career women began after World War II and, more recently, the women's liberation movement has altered both the male and female roles in our society. Actually, say some social observers, the *differences* in male and female roles are becoming reduced and both roles are becoming more similar. To understand the nature of these role changes and new expectations, divide your class into halves. Ask one group to describe the role relationships between a traditional American couple. Assign the other group the task of describing that same relationship between a completely "liberated" couple. Have each group make a list of expectations placed upon each sex. What do these lists tell you about social change?

2.   Some social observers say that due to overpopulation problems, couples may one day be required to secure a license to have a baby. Should this occur, a significant social change would have been accomplished. In your opinion, what present day norms and values would have to be modified to support this one aspect of social change? For example, consider the value of individual freedom in our society. What aspects of this value would undergo modification in order to bring about a mass acceptance of the necessity to be licensed before becoming parents?

3.   Being an innovator is difficult because the socialization process is very efficient in teaching us how to solve problems. Sometimes it is difficult for us even to imagine an alternative way of doing certain things. So accustomed do we become to particular methods of confronting problems that alternative solutions never suggest themselves. For example, divide your class into halves. Assign each half the following problem. Suppose you were the only survivors left in the world after some catastrophe had destroyed civilization. Other than problems of physical survival, what questions of social survival would

emerge in your community? To build a better world (since you are beginning society anew) how would you handle the following problems: (1) the division of work, (2) the role of marriage and the family, (3) the perspective or religion of the society you will build, (4) the control of deviancy, (5) the problems of private possession of property, status symbols, and class distinctions.

After each group has wrestled with these questions, compare suggested solutions. How similar are the proposals of the two groups? In addition, how many "unique" solutions are suggested?

Chapter 8

Cognitive
Objectives

The sociological interest in collectivities and collective behavior is the subject of chapter 8. Fads, fashions, public opinion, panic reaction, revolution, congregation, and crowds are among the types of phenomena which sociologists have in mind when they speak of collective behavior. The following are points which will be stressed in this chapter:

1. *The meaning of the terms "aggregate," "category," and "ethnic group"*
2. *The definition of a collectivity*
3. *The general characteristic of collective behavior*
4. *The contributions of Gustave Le Bon, Herbert Blumer, and Neil Smelser to our understanding of collective behavior*
5. *The various types of collective behavior.*
6. *The difference between a crowd and an audience, the meaning of the terms "public" and "public opinion," how propaganda is used in creating public opinion and swaying a public*
7. *What fads and fashions are*
8. *Why a revolution may be appropriately described as collective behavior*

Fads, Fashions, Fans, and Fanatics

Sociologists, we have said, are interested in human behavior in a *group* context. In chapter 2 a very explicit definition of a group was offered. We said that a group is two or more people interacting to achieve a common goal while guided by socially determined and mediated roles. Sometimes, however, people can "get together" in ways that do not meet this definition. People can be "grouped" in such a way that they do not, sociologically speaking, constitute a group. These types of groupings may be called "collectivities."

For example, there are *aggregates*. These are congregations of people: audiences, assemblies, crowds, and spectators.

Then there are *categories,* which are groupings of individuals who share a common characteristic: all persons in the United States who make $10,000 or more annually, all people 65 years of age or older, all redheads, all juvenile delinquents, etc.

And finally there are *ethnic groups*. An ethnic group is a population who share cultural or physical traits and who protect these traits by the imposition of social or geographical barriers.

A collectivity may be defined as a relatively large number of people who have separately and independently been exposed to a common stimulus, and who have responded to the stimulus with little or no communication or interaction with each other. All the persons who have read Desmond Morris' *The Naked Ape* make up a collectivity. A total community's reaction to a disaster may be viewed as collective behavior. A riot, a revolution, a craze, a fad, or a revival are examples

An audience is an example of an aggregate.

of human beings behaving as collectivities. Sociologists, needless to say, find the subject of collective behavior a very fascinating subject.

Collective behavior is usually characterized by specific elements that set it apart from activity associated with social groups. For the most part, it is relatively unstructured. There appear to be few, if any, rules or procedures to follow. The social group is, as noted earlier, guided in its activities by explicit and implicit rules which more or less determine behavior of group members. Collectivities, on the other hand, operate with fewer rules and, as shoppers at Christmas time in a department store, frequently resemble a stampede.

Second, collective behavior is episodic. For the most part, examples of collective behavior take place in isolated and unrepeated episodes rather than on a routine or regular basis. Flight in panic before a storm or other disaster is, to say the least, not a regular activity in a community.

Third, collective behavior is irrational. It may be based upon hope, wishes, fears, or beliefs. Its relatively unstructured and episodic nature tends to contribute to its irrationality.

Finally, it is unpredictable. The direction of collective behavior, as well as its eventual outcome, cannot be accurately foretold.

Sociological interest in collective behavior began with the work of a Frenchman named Gustave Le Bon (1841–1931).[1] Le Bon emphasized the irrational and unpredictable nature of humans in crowd behavior. The individual, Le Bon said, is caught up in the overwhelming impact of collective emotion. The individual feels the sentiment of an invisible power, contagion is experienced, and suggestibility results in irrational behavior. Thus, the individual in a crowd will often act in impulsive and uninhibited ways which are not characteristic of him outside the excitement of the crowd. He seems to suggest that a "mind of the crowd" exists. This "crowd mind" assumes control and drives otherwise rational and well-meaning individuals to behave in a manner which would be uncharacteristic of them as isolated persons.[1]

COLLECTIVE GROUPINGS AND SOCIAL MOVEMENTS

In 1939, Herbert Blumer published a significant essay which has served as an important statement of guidelines for the study of collective behavior.[2] Blumer distinguished between what he called "elementary collective groupings" and "social movements." The former emerge in response to restlessness when change is experienced. These are not lasting and give way to the more formal "social movements." By social movements, Blumer meant an organized activity which has recognized leaders and seeks to achieve some specifically stated objective. Blumer appeared to be saying that elementary collective groupings are a kind of spontaneous outburst against some situation which is felt to be disagreeable. Sometimes these outbursts are mixed with violence. The "restlessness" gives way to a "social movement" when leadership is selected (or emerges) and goals to be accomplished are stated. Later Blumer added to his earlier article.[3] Social movements are first of all collective efforts to establish a "new order of life." They emerge from a condition of dissatisfaction with the present order of things and are powered by the desire to establish a new and improved social order. Blumer made a distinction between general and specific social movements.

Examples of general social movements are the women's liberation, peace, and youth movements. These social movements represent the emergence of new values which cause persons to look at themselves in some new way. When a woman, for example, begins to view herself as equal to a man, it becomes increasingly difficult to continue playing the subordinate role expected of her. When a significant number of women experience general dissatisfaction with the established role of women in our society, then the emergence of a woman's equality movement is likely.

General social movements are characterized by their generally disorganized, uncoordinated efforts. The objectives of such a movement are vague, and generally often informal. As a result, general social movements tend to show signs of activity in scattered locations and arise in response to a number of situations.

People who feel uneasy about ugly urban surroundings may begin an organized effort to make things more beautiful. Not all, however, are willing to join the movement.

The function of general social movements lies in their awakening effect. Generally they succeed in making others, including the media, aware of the state of general dissatisfaction with the present state of affairs experienced by some. As a result, general social movements give rise to specific social movements.

Specific social movements are reform movements and revolutionary movements. According to Blumer, "a specific social movement is one which has a well defined objective or goal which it seeks to reach. In this effort it develops an organization and structure, making it essentially a society. It also develops a recognized and accepted leadership and a definite membership characterized by a 'we-consciousness.' "[4]

In short, a social movement normally begins in an informal and loosely organized manner without clear objectives. Often it is characterized by impulsive behavior and is "under the dominance of restlessness and collective excitement." As it develops, however, it tends to become better organized with a more specific focus. Blumer described the development of a specific social movement as being accomplished through five stages of development.

Agitation

In the beginning, agitation plays the most important role and sometimes persists in later stages. Its purpose is to arouse people and to recruit people for the movement. It generally seeks to arouse people by sowing the seeds of dissatisfaction which will hopefully jar them loose from their present resigned state to one of openly challenging their position.

Sometimes those content with their present position will become agitated enough to become dissatisfied. Most often, persons are already dissatisfied with their present state and the "agitators" merely offer them the vehicle to manifest their accumulated grievances.

An example of an agitator might be a person who approaches a minority in the United States with a simple message: you are entitled to certain privileges which are being denied to you. If the agitator is able to convince his audience that they should be dissatisfied with their exclusion, and that they should challenge those in power with demands that they receive their due, then the agitator has accomplished his task.

Esprit de Corps

Agitation arouses the people and recruits members, but the development of esprit de corps is essential to give the movement cohesion and solidarity. Thus social movements tend to develop feelings of closeness and intimacy, and members are made to feel special and select.

The feeling of "weness" is important for a movement if it is to grow and reinforce the feelings of dissatisfaction aroused by the agitator. It should be noted that the best manner of developing a rapport between members is to develop a strong sense of "we" versus "they." Thus, all social movements must have enemies who can be identified in some manner. Terms such as "male chauvinist pig," "whitey," and "the establishment," are efforts to define the enemy.

Other methods of developing esprit de corps include informal fellowship and ceremonial behavior. Social movements may have slogans, songs, expressive gestures, uniforms, and secret handshakes to distinguish the "in-group" from the "out-group." The raised fist, the "brother" handshake, the peace sign, the song "We Shall Overcome," the slogans, "Peace Now," "Up Against the Wall," "Huelga," "Sisterhood is Powerful," and "One Way" all represent rallying cries for various movements.

Morale

Morale is based on (1) a conviction of the rectitude of the purpose of the movement; (2) a faith in the ultimate attainment of the movement's goal; and (3) the belief that the movement is charged with a sacred mission. In short, the development of morale is largely akin to the development of a "sectarian attitude and a religious faith." All those things related to the social movement are viewed as good, ethical, moral, and desirable. All things and persons who oppose the movement are viewed as evil, despicable, unethical, and unjust.

Not surprisingly, at this point in their development, all social movements tend to develop sacred literature, myths, and charismatic leaders. The literature may consist of bibles, creeds such as *Das Kapital,* or poems and novels which represent the struggle of the movement. Myths such as those which depict the groups as a chosen people, myths about the utopian world to be, and myths about the evilness of one's opponents are developed. Charismatic leaders are those persons held in awe by members of the movement. They are usually endowed with high intelligence, great leadership abilities, and so forth. Examples such as Marx, Mao, Martin Luther King, and Mary Baker Eddy represent the kinds of leaders essential to a social movement at this stage in its development.

Group Ideology

This pertains to a body of doctrine, beliefs and myths. Usually it consists of (1) a statement of the objective, purpose, and premises of the movement; (2) a body of criticism and condemnation of the existing structure which the movement is attacking and seeking to change; (3) a body of defense doctrine which serves as a justification of the movement and of its objectives; (4) a body of belief dealing with policies, tactics and practical operation of the movement; and (5) the myths of the movement.

Ideology provides the movement with a philosophy. It seeks to give the movement direction and justification, as well as weapons of attack, weapons of defense, and inspiration and hope. Above all, the ideology must appeal to the members of the movement.

Tactics

Three important tactics have already been discussed—gaining members, holding members, and reaching objectives. The formation of operating tactics presents each movement with rather immense difficulties, depending upon the content of the movement, the enemy, and the nature of the problems giving rise to the movement. Methods of reform revolution must be worked out and tactical operations determined.

THE STRUCTURE OF COLLECTIVE BEHAVIOR

Building on the work of Le Bon and Blumer's earlier article, a significant contribution to our understanding of collective behavior was made by Neil Smelser.[5] Smelser argued that while collective behavior is relatively unstructured, it is not as different from other forms of human behavior as some writers imply. He shows that collective behavior does have some structure and some degree of predictability.

Smelser borrowed from economics the concept of the "logic of a value-added approach." This concept is simply that in economic production, each stage in the developmental process adds to the value of the product. Iron ore is mined, smelted, tempered, shaped, combined with other materials, painted, and delivered to the consumer as an automobile. Each stage adds to the value of the product and each one must be accomplished in proper sequence. (That is, you can't paint iron ore and sell it as a six-thousand-dollar automobile.)

Collective behavior, Smelser posited, is a process of stages and at each stage the emotional payload of the total process is heightened. To illustrate, Smelser studied the concept of "panic." Panic was defined as "collective flight based on hysterical belief" and develops through the following stages:

Structural Conductiveness—Panic is based upon an underlying setting which is conducive to strain. There must be limited escape routes, and communication of panicky reactions must be possible.

Strain—Panic participants must define the situation as holding immediate threat. But the exact dimensions of the threat are not known. Individuals will soon begin to experience an uncomfortable feeling of helplessness.

Anxiety—The feeling of helplessness expands into a general apprehension which provides the atmosphere for hysteria.

The Precipitating Factor—This factor transforms the vague anxiety into the fear of a specific threat and "confirms" the suspicions of the anxious individuals.

Mobilization for Flight—Someone or something "pushes the panic button" and triggers action. A "flight model" or some type of "primitive leadership" develops as someone starts to run and others join by following his example.

Counterpanic Forces—Facilities (a new dam or ditch), organization (the normal work of policemen or firemen in the crisis), norms (deepseated patterns of behavior), and values (like faith in a fundamental institution) may reduce the risk and danger of panic. These counterpanic forces may enter at any point in the sequences of stages either to divert panic or to reestablish normal activities during the panic situation.

Not all social scientists accept Smelser's theory of the sequential development of panic or the predictable nature of human behavior in a disaster. Most would agree, nonetheless, that social conditions do play a part in the conditions that build up and eventually emerge as collective behavior. When his theory has been tested by actually observing human reaction to disaster such as storms, war, or floods the following conclusions have been drawn. People in a crisis situation do not flee in wild pandemonium like animals in a stampede. Some people refuse to flee, while others are triggered into flight by the desire to find their family and friends (or perhaps to save personal possessions). People are not rendered helpless by indecision. After the initial shock of the crisis, most citizens take the initiative in rescue and recovery.[6]

It appears that a lifetime of social conditioning is not reversed in crises and human behavior continues to follow expected and rather predictable lines of activity even in reaction to disaster.

TYPES OF COLLECTIVE BEHAVIOR

A collectivity has been defined as a relatively large number of people who respond independently to a stimulus without a great deal of interaction or communication occurring among them. The words "relatively large numbers" and "without a great deal of interaction or communication" are rather unspecific. But the definition was purposely designed this way since collective behavior as a concept includes such a wide range of activities. We will now briefly analyze some of the types of behavior which sociologists see as characteristic of collectivities.

Crowds

A temporary collection of individuals in physical proximity to one another and exerting a mutual influence on one another may be called a crowd. The spectators at a football game may be viewed as an example of a crowd. This is a temporary gathering of individuals who do not know each other. They are all reacting to a common stimulus (the game), but the individual reaction of each person has an effect upon all others (the excitement is contagious). Two hundred students gathered at free speech rally listening and responding to a speech denouncing the industrial-military complex are a crowd. The same collection of students sitting around in the student union would no longer be a crowd. (There is no common stimulus, and there is no mutual influence.) If someone came in with free beer, they would quickly become a crowd.

Sociologists generally speak of two types of crowds. They are the *expressive* and the *acting* crowd. The expressive crowd is a non-hostile collection of people interested in expressing their feelings. A revival meeting with its emotional and evangelistic spirit and its collective excitement is an example of an expressive crowd. An acting crowd, on the other hand, is a number of individuals whose behavior is fanatically focused on the accomplishment of a specific purpose. A mob with its tension, explosiveness, spontaneous leadership, and unconcern with the consequences of its behavior is an example of an acting crowd. Individuals caught up in an acting crowd experience a feeling of collective power and a commitment to a cause which seems to have unqualified approval. The goal of the acting crowd may not be destruction. A high school pep rally prior to a football game may become an acting crowd. The opposing team is burned in effigy, something akin to hysteria breaks out, and individuals (stimulated by the behavior of others) say and do things which in other circumstances would be considered completely inappropriate.

Audience

An audience is much like a crowd. The difference is that in the audience members do not influence each other as much as in a crowd. Also, an audience, unlike a crowd, does not necessarily have to have physical proximity. For example, several million individuals simultaneously watching the six o'clock news constitutes a television audience. All individuals are responding to the same stimulus, but their behavior, unlike the people in a football stadium, has no effect upon other individuals participating in the event. A sedate church service and a collection of people watching a movie are examples of audiences. In these latter examples, some social contagion may exist.

What type of collective behavior is this?

Laughter, dozing, applause, singing, or whispering may exist as the participants influence each other. This influence is much more subdued in these instances than it is at political rally or in other types of crowd behavior.

The Public and Public Opinion

A public may be defined as a human grouping whose members take a specific position on a given issue. When one refers to *the public,* he has in mind citizens in general who share a concern about a specific phase of societal life. The hypothetical "John Q. Public" is the average citizen, relative to a given issue. There are, therefore, many publics —an art public, a sports public, a political public, etc. In the same way, one individual is at the same time a member of many publics. The individual joins and then leaves a public on the basis of his own voluntary will.

Public opinion consists of the positions which are taken by the members of a public regarding a given issue. Social differences are important in understanding the differences in public opinion. Differences in age, sex, occupation, education, social class, race, religion, and the like are significant factors in determining public opinion. Youth, in general, tend to have a more favorable opinion of changes in the social order. Older citizens, as a rule, tend to favor things as they are.

Public opinion may also be swayed by propaganda which, in sociological terms, may be defined as the organized attempt to coerce a public into the acceptance of an idea or course of action. Any contest between individuals or groups for public approval or support will almost inevitably involve measures designed to influence public opinion. Advertisements may be seen as attempts to influence public opinion. Political campaigns and public bond issues make ample use of propaganda, as does psychological warfare.

Propaganda efforts make use of a number of tactics in attempting to sway public opinion. Some of these tactics are the following:

1. The band wagon effect—"Everybody else is switching to it."

2. Appeal to hero-types—"Joe Namath uses Greasy-Deazy hair dressing."

3. Testimonial—"My laundry gets cleanest with Doozy soap."

4. Association with places of comfort and delight, such as the out of doors, rural areas of scenic beauty, or cozy home-like scenes are popular tactics.

5. Identification with the "common" man or average citizen in an antisnobbery manner is a useful tactic. The identification with people of all ages and all wholesome types increases the potential buyer's sense of belonging.

6. Appeals to superiority, such as the politician's insistence that his, rather than his opponent's, record is better.

Propaganda efforts make use of simple language which may be understood by the general populace. Emotional terms are favored over logical terms and slogans, and jingles which are easily remembered are frequently used. "Four More Years," "In your heart, you know he's right," "I like Ike," and "America, Come Home" are examples of slogans. Propaganda techniques are replete with stereotypes. Propagandists may "set up" an enemy who is arbitrarily assigned responsibility for the unpleasant situation or evil circumstances the propagandist proposes to remove. The enemy is stereotyped. For example, the word "communist" may be used as a label in this country to identify the enemy. The logic of this approach is that the public, having accepted the stereotype, will be receptive to the propaganda which contains the stereotype.

Not infrequently the effort to sway public opinion includes:

1. Distortion—In an effort to sway public opinion, propagandists may emphasize some features of a situation and ignore others. The half truth appears logical and is sometimes convincing.

2. Falsification—Fiction may be presented as fact, lies as truth.

3. Repetition—Next time you see a commercial on television, count the number of times the brand name of the product being advertised is spoken and shown. The assumption is that when you go to the grocery store to buy some soap powder, you'll be able to recall the name of the soap and not remember Brand X.

Fads and Fashions

A fad is a cultural pattern that appears suddenly, lasts a brief time, and disappears suddenly. Craze is another term for a fad. Davy Crockett t-shirts, stuffing people in telephone booths, the sudden popularity of certain trinkets and toys (like the hula hoop and the skateboard) may all be listed as examples of fads or crazes. Exactly how or why such behavior starts and "catches on" is impossible to determine.

It can be said that industrialized societies are more conducive to fads than pre-modern societies. In the more primitive communities the emphasis is on the sanctity of tradition and custom rather than individual expression. Also, in these kinds of societies individual attention, even of children, must be given over to life sustenance. There is little time or opportunity to develop interest in activities which are not directly associated with survival. In an urban society, on the other hand, less attention is paid to tradition, the anonymity of the cities encourages people to individual expression, and affluence gives both the time and the opportunity to develop individual interests (in fact, crazes may be one way urban man overcomes his boredom).

Fashion refers to a cultural pattern that endures over a period of time. Thus, the major difference between a fad and a fashion is that change occurs more gradually in fashions than in fads. Fashions have to do with things like clothing styles or architectural design or automobile types. Innovations in fashion ordinarily are associated with persons considered to be authoritative. Prestigious individuals wear a new style of clothing and others are likely to follow suit in an effort to copy the life style and make a claim for prestige.

Revolution

It is necessary to mention briefly the idea of revolution as an example of collective behavior. Much sociological interest has been aroused in the general subjects of riot and revolution due to recent developments of student unrest and political upheaval both in this nation and in others.

James C. Davies made an effort to isolate the social variables which seem to give rise to revolutionary movements. He noted that some thinkers have said that revolutions occur after a period of progressively worsening economic conditions. Following Karl Marx, these writers have said that when conditions become intolerable, people will resist through revolutionary activity. On the other hand, others have pointed out that revolutions occur only as social and economic conditions are improving. People who live in hopeless poverty do not revolt; their interest is in finding food for their next meal.

Davies attempted to combine these two mutually contradictory opinions. He conceived revolution as occurring when a period of economic and social advancement is followed by a short period of sharp reversal. The time of economic improvement increases the expectation of continued ability to satisfy needs. The time of sharp reversal causes anxiety and fear that gains made will be lost. Thus, expectations of need satisfaction increase while past progress appears to be blocked in the future. Frustration develops and revolt occurs.

Taking three revolutions of the past (Dorrs Rebellion in 1842 in the United States, the Russian revolution in 1917, and the Egyptian revolution in 1952), Davies illustrated how his theory works. In each nation a period of economic and social improvement gave way suddenly to a period of reversal which threatened the progress made and frustrated the expectations of need fulfillment of large numbers of people. The gap between what was and what should have been became too large to tolerate and leaders emerged to organize and channel the frustration and anxiety of the people toward revolt which is supposed to lead to reform.

The increased use of violence by minority groups in the United States may be the result of such a "rise and drop" experience. For example, federal legislation, Supreme Court decisions, the "war on poverty," and social concerns like VISTA have resulted in rising expectations for black Americans. Rising aspirations were met with token change and blacks discovered that doors were as tightly locked as ever. The black man was given opportunity to fulfill his rising expectations only on legal paper. In practice, nothing changed. The gap between what he expected and what he was actually getting became intolerable and in his frustration he turned to violence.

Much of what has been said earlier in this chapter is useful in understanding reform movements and revolution. The creation of publics, the use of propaganda to affect public opinion, the contagion of crowd behavior, and the suggestability of people caught up in crowds are all factors which help give rise to and determine the success of revolts. It may even be that the subjects of fads and fashions may be relevant to a discussion of reform movements. Some students may think, "They have had a riot at Yale, but we've not had one here. Let's take over the administration building." Student unrest thus becomes fashionable.

TWO EXAMPLES OF COLLECTIVE BEHAVIOR

Using the principles and theories presented thus far in the chapter, it is interesting to look at two examples of collective behavior.

Social movements, we have said, are examples of collective behavior. Unlike a panic which is short-lived and spontaneous, social movements are slower to develop and usually endure for longer periods. Social movements usually allow individuals with various related grievances to group together under a single banner. These movements may be directed at specific goals like the Vietnam prisoner of war issue. Organizations established to remind the American public of the prisoner of war issue lost their function when the POWs were finally released or exchanged. Other social movements such as the women's liberation movement have more general goals in mind. It would not be expected that advocates of this movement would disband if women gained the right to enter previously all-male clubs or all-male occupations. The movement would still have other concerns.

Women's liberation appeared previously in American history in the form of the women's suffrage movement in the late 1800s. The more recent women's movement dates itself to the writings of Betty Freidan *(The Feminine Mystique)* and is concerned with equal opportunity for women in a male-dominated economic world.

Women's liberation is a movement whose goal is a revolution in the present images of what is expected of males and females by reorganizing sex roles. The immediate goal of the movement is to make females as well as males aware of the extent to which American society is male dominated. They challenge positions, labels, and occupations which are presently male oriented. For example they deplore the fact that one who leads a session is called a chair*man* and suggest that the proper terminology is chairperson since that position may be held by either males or females. In the same manner, they support the right of women to undertake occupations previously held only by males (if qualified to do so), and seek to encourage the economic independence of women both before and after marriage. Recent developments such as the appointment of women to various positions of responsibility and their greater visibility leads us to believe that this movement has been to some extent successful in opening doors for opportunity. It is less certain if sex roles are actually changing.

Another interesting social movement which has been receiving some popular attention is the so-called "Jesus movement" or "Jesus revolution." This social movement is made up primarily of high school and college youth. It is theologically fundamental in outlook, and is nondenominational and nonsectarian. Its ranks are composed of extremely zealous, Bible-reading youngsters who are "high on Jesus," "turned on to God," and "hip to Christian love." They "witness," (i.e., talk to nonbelievers about Jesus) sing, and have their own special symbol (a raised fist with the index finger pointed upward to symbolize that Jesus is the one way to salvation.)

The Jesus movement may be seen as meeting two important needs. It acts as a warning to established religious groups that their brand of religion is found wanting by large numbers of youth and, second, it offers the young person the opportunity to participate in a non-adult and therefore "revolutionary" movement without being truly anti-establishment.

SUMMARY

Sociological interest in "collectivities" and "collective behavior" was the subject of this chapter. A collectivity is a large group of people who respond individually to a common stimulus with little or no interaction or communication. The writings of Gustave Le Bon, Herbert Blumer, and Neil Smelser were briefly presented to show the development of the sociological theory of collective behavior.

Crowds, audiences, publics, fads, fashions, and revolutions were discussed as instances of collective behavior. The partially predictable nature of human behavior in collectivities was shown in discussing these elements of collective behavior. It was noted that social roles and norms which generally guide behavior are not completely destroyed when people are caught up in collective action.

Women's liberation and the Jesus revolution were discussed as two examples of collective behavior of the social movement variety.

Notes

1. Gustave Le Bon, *The Crowd* (London: Allen and Unwin, 1917).

2. Herbert Blumer, "Collective Behavior," in *Principles of Sociology,* ed. Robert E. Park (New York: Barnes and Noble, 1939), pp. 221–82.

3. Herbert Blumer, "Social Movements," in *New Outline of the Principles of Sociology,* ed. A.M. Lu (New York: Barnes and Noble, 1951).

4. Ibid., p. 202.

5. Neil J. Smelser, *Theory of Collective Behavior* (New York: The Free Press, 1963).

6. Enrico L. Quarantelli, "Images of Withdrawal Behavior in Disasters: Some Basic Misconceptions," *Social Problems* 8 (Summer 1960).

7. James C. Davies, "Toward a Theory of Revolution," *American Sociological Review* 27 (February 1962).

Thinking
Sociologically

1. Begin to notice types of propaganda directed toward you as a member of a specific public. Does the mass media utilize special techniques to influence your opinion and attempt to direct your behavior? Make a list of events during the day which are intentional efforts to subject you to propaganda. Don't leave out things like billboards, magazine and newspaper advertisements and articles, and comments by friends. What tactics of propaganda are being used in these events?

2. Agitation is the first stage in what Blumer described as the normal process of a specific social movement. The creation of agitation occurs in statements made by core leadership of a movement and these statements are designed to demonstrate (or even create) a general sense of unrest and dissatisfaction. Develop a list of statements from mass media sources which you consider to be efforts at agitation. Determine for each statement the nature of the unrest or dissatisfaction assumed by the person making the agitation statement. (Consider political rhetoric, merchandise advertisement, and reform movements as sources of these statements.)

3. Fads, it was said, are cultural patterns which appear suddenly, last a brief time, and disappear suddenly. All of us are influenced in our behavior by fads but not infrequently are unaware of their impact upon us. To demonstrate the popularity of fads, have the women in your class make a list of "male" fads while the men will make a list of fads they feel are popular among females. In discussion, compare the two lists. Are there similarities between them? Are there incompatible fads? How correct has each group been in their evaluation of the other sex's fads?

Chapter 9

Cognitive Objectives

Each of us has violated the rules at some time. If caught, we suffered some form of punishment such as embarrassment, a spanking, a traffic ticket, a fine, or a jail sentence. If circumstances were such, however, that we were not caught—does this make us any less guilty? The answer to this question is not a simple one, as we shall see in this chapter, for it depends on one's viewpoint of what causes some individuals to act in a deviant manner while others do not. We shall see why some deviancy appears to be a necessary part of every society. Other important points to look for in this chapter are:

1. *Why deviant behavior is normally described as dysfunctional*
2. *Why sociologists are interested in studying deviance*
3. *Explanations of deviancy*
   a. *deviancy seen as the result of individual sickness*
   b. *deviancy seen as unexpected behavior*
   c. *deviancy seen as behavior learned in groups*
   d. *deviancy seen as the response of society*
4. *How these viewpoints affect the manner in which one tries to solve the problems of deviancy*
5. *How visibility affects one's label*
6. *The consequences of being labeled as deviant*
7. *The need to control deviance*
8. *The difference between primary and secondary deviance*
9. *The positive aspects of deviance*
10. *The need for deviants to test boundaries*

Did Robin Hood Go to Heaven?

In previous chapters, the sociologist has been viewed as being mainly concerned with the social system in terms of the manner in which we learn the proper rules of behavior, how these rules help us to know what to expect from others, and the enforcement methods which insure that those who break the rules are punished. Sociologists, however, are also interested in those who fail to learn the rules of the game, those who break the rules intentionally, and the reaction of society to rulebreakers.

FUNCTIONAL AND DYSFUNCTIONAL BEHAVIOR

Some individuals in society behave in a functional manner, that is, in cooperation with the attainment of societal goals. Hence, a driver who pulls his car over to the curb upon hearing a siren conforms to the laws regulating the right of way and conforms to the expectations of other drivers. In addition, the driver's actions also help in an indirect manner to preserve traditional societal goals which seek to save lives and protect property. A person's behavior may also be dysfunctional or in conflict with the attainment of societal goals. Those who are referred to as nonconformists "weirdos," freaks, and so forth, represent styles of life which often conflict with the conventional. Couples who live together without first legalizing their relationships in the

171

expected manner—by obtaining a certificate of marriage and having some type of wedding—are normally criticized. The reasons have little to do with whether the couple may or may not be happy in such an arrangement, but rather from the fact that this relationship does not fall within the civil laws (e.g., inheritance, child support, divorce) established to protect and define the responsibilities of the individuals involved.

One of the major purposes of this chapter is to illustrate the ways in which seemingly dysfunctional behavior may be considered functional. In fact, all societies require some nonconformist behavior in order to function properly.

SOCIOLOGICAL INTEREST IN DEVIANCE

Sociological interest in unconventional behavior dates back to Durkheim's classic work on the topic of suicide.[1] This sociological interest continues today, illustrated by the courses in "social problems" taught by sociology instructors. A typical outline for a social problems course will include topics such as racism, alienation, prostitution, homosexuality, war, pollution, overpopulation, drug abuse, crime, poverty, civil disorders, divorce, loneliness, and the generation gap, just to name a few. Each of these problems is normally regarded as harmful to the attainment of a "good" society. The purpose of the sociologist is not to judge the morality or immorality of these behaviors, but rather to look at the role they play in a society. Thus, sociologists seek to answer the following questions: Why do some individuals become deviants while others do not? Why is deviance found in all societies? What is the function of deviance?

EXPLANATIONS FOR DEVIANCE

Attempts to explain deviancy have usually relied on four separate viewpoints which may be termed (1) deviancy as the actions of a sick individual, (2) deviancy as extreme behavior, (3) deviancy as learned behavior, and (4) deviancy as actor-audience interaction.

Deviancy and the "Sick" Individual

Central to this viewpoint is the idea that deviancy is the result of a faulty individual personality. Those who hold this point of view ask the question, "What kind of person would be disposed toward criminal behavior?" The answers they seek focus upon hereditary factors or problems in personality development to explain why the person behaves in that manner.

An example of this viewpoint is the psychoanalytic explanation. This is based on the assumption that healthy personality development requires that one successfully pass a series of psychosexual stages. Failure to do so will result in a faulty personality structure. Thus psychopaths who kill without compassion for their victims are explained as persons with a defective conscience (superego, in Freudian terminology). These murderers cannot realize the implications of their actions and thus feel no guilt. The defective conscience presumably resulted during the childhood of this particular individual when he or she failed to develop a strong sense of guilt in regard to breaking rules.[2]

The disadvantage of the "sick" individual perspective is that it implies that deviance serves no useful purpose and that deviance always lies in individual personalities. Emotional disturbance is undoubtedly a major element in some cases of deviancy, but it can not explain all the deviance in a society.

Deviancy as Extreme Behavior

Rules of behavior in every society are essential to ensure that persons can work with others knowing approximately what to expect from them. This, after all, is what a norm is—a shared behavioral expectation. Thus deviance is doing what is unexpected. At the same time, every rule has a toleration gap around it which allows for permissible deviance. Most businesses, schools, and groups expect that some "cutting corners" within the toleration gap will occur.[3] A teacher, for example, who allows four class absences before absenteeism affects a student's grade is allowing for deviation in the expectation of class

attendance. Department stores allow for shoplifting, employee thefts, and accidental breakage in their profit margin. Society is aware that a certain amount of deviance will occur.

If friendship (expected behavior between close acquaintances) can be imagined as a continuum with indifference at one end and overconcern at the opposite end, then a friendly person is one who stays within the tolerance gap and is not too friendly or too unfriendly. Those who ignore you altogether and those who push friendship upon you are both deviant because they represent extreme behavior on the scale. Another example is the cocktail party at which all are expected to indulge in alcoholic beverages. If one refuses to drink, he is likely to be considered a bad sport. Most non-drinkers soon learn that if they go to a cocktail party, they must be willing to hold a glass of tonic water or club soda and to sip it just like the other guests who do drink. Social drinking usually means that it is permissible to become "high" or tipsy but one must not become drunk, lose control, and forget one's manners. The deviants at a cocktail party are defined as those who refuse to drink or who drink too much—the extreme behaviors.

The disadvantage with this view of deviance is that the continuums oversimplify actual behavior. The example above concerning friendliness is not entirely valid since the norm of friendship is in reality toward the friendlier end of the scale. Thus, one is more likely to be considered deviant for being just a bit unfriendly than too friendly. It would also be expected that social class differences would exist in the tolerance gap allowed. A cocktail party at an exclusive country club would differ significantly from a cocktail party for college fraternity members with regard to the tolerance gap for allowable drunkeness. Furthermore, this viewpoint of extreme behavior fails to take into consideration the particular situation. In times of stress, extreme behaviors may become temporarily "normal."

Deviance as Learned Behavior

Both conventional and deviant behavior find support in relationships with others. One is socialized into deviant roles just as one is socialized to accepted behavior. The ideas we believe in, as well as our values and behavior patterns, are derived from interaction in groups with which we have the most contact and with which we strongly identify. Thus we can learn to respect other people's property, or we can also learn the reverse, depending on the group (or subculture) from which we learn our beliefs.

Festinger has noted that all men appear to have a need to verify their beliefs. Thus, when we are uncertain about what is expected or are faced with a confusing issue where the norms are unclear, we seek assistance from others.[4] At the same time, we will tend to value the beliefs of certain persons or groups more than others—often choosing those groups that are in agreement with our beliefs. The result is that the beliefs we hold the strongest are those we share with others who are important to us. If the "significant others" happen to consist of a deviant subculture, than our beliefs will reflect that group's beliefs.

One of the most interesting aspects of the socialization process is that we learn to enjoy being wanted, loved, and appreciated. Because having attention centered on ourselves is so fulfilling, we normally attempt to act in ways which will bring esteem and respect from others. Thus to some extent we are willing to behave and to conform to the expectations of others in exchange for their admiration and attention. Once again, this pattern holds for both conventional and deviant behavior.[5] If our reference group is the athletic set, we are assured that if we practice often, learn the rules of the games, join organized teams, lift weights, and play "fair," others will pay some attention to us and perhaps even like us. On the other hand, if our reference group is a juvenile gang, the willingness to take risks (stealing tape decks in the daytime) and not being afraid to fight are the kinds of behavior which will bring attention and reward and, most often, it is this type of behavior which we will practice.

Most types of behavior require learning techniques from others.

Viewing deviance as learned behavior helps us see deviants acting as members of a group rather than alone. Most human activities require that one person must depend upon others to do their part. We must, however, be able to do something useful for others if we expect them to do their part as well. Thus, a newspaper salesman is dependent on others to investigate the news, write, proofread, and edit the story, do the typesetting, run the presses, package the bundles and transport the papers to the corner where he picks them up. In the same manner, a car thief must have a "fence" to whom he can sell the stolen car. The "fence" in turn must have persons who can change the identification number on the car in order to make its sale appear legal. Since deviant behavior is often group behavior, a system of norms coordinates the activities of those engaged in it. The "code of thieves" which states that a thief must not steal goods obtained by another thief or the loyalty shown by a gangster unwilling to "finger" an accomplice are examples of a system of norms which support organized crime. Thus, working at a conventional job or working at a deviant activity both require interdependence upon others and demand a network of norms which must be learned if the necessary tasks of each person are to be performed.

While this viewpoint widens the scope of study to include the groups a deviant belongs to, it overlooks the fact that society defines the characteristics and circumstances of deviant behavior.

Deviance as Actor-Audience Interaction

Robin Hood is a thief!

Robin Hood is a hero!

Most recently, the study of deviance has moved from a concern with criminals, delinquents, and other rulebreakers, to a broader concern with the response of society to the rulebreaker.[6] Deviance is viewed as an interaction between the person who commits the behavior and those who respond to his actions. In this viewpoint, it is assumed that no behavior is inherently good or bad until it is defined as such by society. Thus, one of the concerns of this perspective is to discover those responsible for labeling deviants.[7]

A deviant suspect confronts the audience when he is caught by law enforcement agents and his behavior is made public (for example, by reporting it in the media). Judgment is passed on the nature of the deviancy of his actions by the courts and the suspect is labeled as a deviant if found guilty and assigned to a special role (criminal). He may be allowed to go free, and so his behavior has not been defined as deviant. An example of the above process is a man who is arrested for hitting another man. The police, as representatives of the community, question the suspect to collect evidence which is presented during the trial to effect a decision as to whether the man acted out of

Labeling can be an informal process.

self-defense or with malice. The result of the public judicial process is that the suspect will be labeled as either an assaulter or as a courageous man. As one can see, the audience—in this case the courts—actually determines whether or not hitting a man is labeled as deviant behavior. Thus, deviancy is not an inherent quality of the act, but a consequence of the response by others to that act. In turn, a deviant is a person to whom the label "deviant" has been successfully applied by others.[8]

The fact that different audiences may be expected to respond in different ways helps us to understand why a particular behavior such as smoking pot may be considered to be both "outrageous" and "heavy," depending on the group. Consider, for example, the exploits of the legendary figure Robin Hood. To the sheriff of Nottingham, Robin Hood was the leader of a band of thieves whose evil deeds made journeys through Sherwood Forest potentially dangerous. On the other hand, according to the legend, Robin Hood was beloved by the common people. To them, Robin Hood was a bold and courageous person who dared to oppose the established order. In addition, he shared with the poor people what he stole from the rich. These two distinctive perspectives of this one person give us some indication of the nature of labeling.

A fact often overlooked is that an act must first of all be visible to an audience before it can be labeled.[9] For example, if no one sees a person robbing a store, and no one reports it later, there will be little chance of that particular thief being labeled deviant.

REHABILITATION OR PUNISHMENT

The manner in which social control agents will try to alleviate the problems of deviance will depend on their perspective of deviance. We will use drug abuse as an example.

If the deviant person is viewed as a "sick" individual, then drug abuse would be approached with a view to characterizing the types of persons most likely to experiment with drugs. Research would try to define the personalities prone to this behavior, or to find some physical characteristic common to all drug addicts. If the results were conclusive, then social agencies concerned with drug abuse would not need to educate *all* young people about drugs, but could focus their attention on those most likely to become addicts.

If the extreme behavior approach is utilized, drug abuse can be viewed as resulting from a dependence upon escape. All people daydream occasionally, but no one is expected to spend most of the day "spaced out." Drugs make it possible for a person to escape as long as his supply holds out. This approach to drug abuse would overlook the "experimenters" and focus upon those who are most alienated from their family and society.[10] Drug abuse is thus viewed as a problem of extreme alienation, dependence upon escape for coping with problems, and the inability to deal successfully with the world. This viewpoint would probably employ a counseling therapy on the grounds that drug usage is a symptom of deeper emotional problems.

If the control agents viewed deviance as learned behavior, drug abuse would be approached from the perspective that the first thing to do for an addict is to isolate that individual from peers and deviant subgroups. Changing the environment, however, is not sufficient until that person can learn to value the accepted behavior of the larger society in the same manner that non-socially approved behaviors are now valued. Thus a change in the environment coupled with a new reinforcement pattern will be the approach most likely utilized.

Finally, viewing deviance as actor-audience interaction would probably result in a perspective that present definitions of drug abuse require reevaluation. Some might argue that the definitions of society toward drug use should be more realistic. Perhaps punishment could be made more appropriate for the severity of drug usage. The legalization of marijuana, for example, if it were ever to occur, would redefine a deviant behavior as acceptable. Research within this viewpoint would possibly emphasize the effects of being identified as part of the drug culture, the response of society to addicts, and the treatment of addicts.

GOOD GUYS AND BAD GUYS

It is possible to imagine four different situations with regard to the behavior of an actor and the manner in which that behavior is perceived by an audience.[11]

1. A person who breaks no rules and is perceived by others as being a law abiding citizen represents the "good guy."

2. A person who breaks the rules and is perceived by others as a rule breaker is the "bad guy."

3. A person who breaks the rules but is not perceived by others as a rule breaker is the "secret bad guy." Interestingly enough, since this person is not presently perceived as deviant, he is treated as if he were a genuine "good guy" and is allowed (until discovered) to take part in normal social activities. An example of this case is the embezzler who steals small amounts from a bank for many years. Until the funds are discovered missing and until the theft is traced to this person, the individual will continue working, maybe even getting periodic raises in salary and other rewards for faithful service. During this time it is also possible for that person to continue as an active member of the community and take part in religious and charitable activities. The situation changes the day the warrant for arrest is signed and from that time on the embezzling bank employee moves into the category of the "bad guy."

4. A person who breaks no rules and is perceived by others as a rule breaker is the "mislabeled bad guy." Many a good mystery story has been written about the accused suspect who is really innocent. This situation can result in tragic consequences. A man who is mistakenly identified as a homosexual because of his mannerisms or interests, for example, cannot expect to maintain his normal life style. If he works with children, he will surely lose his position; his spouse will be embarrassed by the rumors and gossip generated in the neighborhood; friends who have known this individual for years will fail to keep appointments

and generally avoid contact with him. Even if the man is finally cleared of suspicion, the scars left by such an experience will make it difficult for that person to return to a normal routine. Even more tragic, however, is the situation when a mislabeled deviant is unable to prove that it was all a matter of a misunderstanding and mislabeling.

It has been hypothesized that mislabeled deviants are prone toward deviancy. This is sometimes called a self-fulfilling prophesy, i.e., if a person is mislabeled as deviant and if others respond to that "mislabeled bad guy" as if he were a deviant, then it is highly probable that this mislabeled person may take on the role that others seem to be wanting that person to play. For example, if all long-haired youth were labeled as drug users, and if adults treated all these youth as if they were dangerous drug addicts, then some who never thought of "turning on" might experiment in order to fulfill their expected roles.[12]

THE CONSEQUENCES OF DEVIANCE

By now the student should recognize the relativity of deviance. Whether any act will be considered deviant depends when the act takes place, who commits the act, who is harmed by the act, and who perceives the act. Some actions have broad tolerance gaps within which behavior is permissible. Some rulebreaking affects only the actor (such as drug addiction), while some rulebreaking is harmful to others (the drug addict who mugs people on the street to obtain money for drugs). Finally, an act is not deviant until a behavior is perceived and defined as a "rulebreaking behavior."

There are various implications of being caught and labeled as a deviant. First, labeled deviants are assigned to certain roles, such as criminal, bankrobber, kidnapper, swindler, and killer. These labels are made "official," so to speak, by the formal public process of arrest, trial, and imprisonment. It should be noted that newspaper reports and television coverage of trials insure that the public knows that one has been labeled as deviant. It is also interesting to note that there are no comparable ceremonies or rituals to advertise to others that one has "served his time" and now wishes to leave that role of the criminal behind and assume again the behavior associated with the label of "normal" citizen. Shedding a deviant label is not a simple matter.[13]

Labeled deviants are often punished when they attempt to move back into normal roles because this is the manner in which society illustrates to others that "crime does not pay" or that "you reap what you sow." It is not uncommon to hear ex-cons complain that getting a job is made difficult because potential employers still think of them as "jailbirds." Also consider the plight of the high school girl who gets pregnant. Until very recently, as soon as the school authorities became aware of her condition, she was automatically suspended and not allowed to return to normal daytime classes. Furthermore, her actions made her undateable and by implication a bad influence on the "virgin" minds of the other girls. It is thus not difficult to imagine that a young lady who observed one of her friends going through such an experience would very likely be deterred from promiscuous behavior. Deterrence is thus a matter of making a few suffer the consequences to serve as examples for others. This method of social control is as old as antiquity and immediately brings to mind images of men and women bound in stocks in the town square for all to see and to jeer at so that others might be deterred from similar actions. Because, as noted, deviance is defined by the audience, the previous example of the pregnant high school girl need not end in humiliating consequences. In such a situation, it is possible for the girl to move to another part of the country and have her baby and return to her high school or to enroll at another high school distant enough to lose her past. If such were the case, the same girl might find herself involved in familiar activities and being treated as any other high school girl.

While the label "deviant" is avoided by most, it is possible that the deviant label may at times be rewarding for some. Non-conformists, to some extent, employ deviant behavior as a means of attack, defense, or adjustment to the reactions of society. The rowdy, boisterous, and bullying behavior of juvenile gangs is in many cases an attack against

the larger society. It should not surprise us that gang members will take pride in being labeled by others as mean, tough, or dangerous. Those who are willing to accept the label of deviant are allowed greater tolerance in their behaviors. A person who has spent some time in a mental institution or been under psychiatric care would be permitted to act in rather bizarre ways without being punished, as long as his actions do not harm others. On the other hand, the same behaviors performed by unlabeled individuals will not be tolerated and will result in labels such as unstable, strange, and weird, as well.

SOCIAL CONTROL

Some means of social control are informal.

In order to keep things functioning smoothly, deviance must be kept under control. Uncontrolled deviance may have a negative effect upon a group due to the disorganization which unexpected behavior can evoke. Consider the school you attend. It is a delicate organization which requires the cooperation of students, teachers, and administrators. Norms exist which coordinate the activity of all participants. If, as an example, students were allowed to come to class whenever the spirit moved them, rather than at an appointed time, the educational process would be disrupted. Teachers would spend most of their time repeating for those who came in late the ideas already presented to those who came early. If arguments were settled by fist-fighting rather than logical reasoning, most students would find it difficult to concentrate on English literature when one might expect to be beaten up over an interpretation. If students were allowed to miss as many classdays as desired, high absenteeism might undermine the principle that the same materials have been presented to all students, and that a test on the material is the best method of determining how much the student has learned. Finally, uncontrolled deviance would destroy the sense of trust we have in others. If one is uncertain as to whether another will or will not play by the rules, then cooperative efforts and friendships based on mutual understanding between people is not possible. Perhaps it is this aspect of human behavior which makes unfaithfulness—whether committed by a friend, a spouse, or a group—so severely punished by all societies.

PRIMARY AND SECONDARY DEVIANCE

At this point, one-time deviants should be distinguished from life style deviants.[14] The primary or one-time deviant is a person who has broken a rule but whose life style is not based on deviant behavior. An example of the primary deviant is a person taking an examination who accidentally sees the answers on another person's examination and decides to change his own response. Whether this event represents that person's first experience at cheating or not, so long as this act does not change his normal pattern of life, it remains primary deviance. A secondary or life style deviant consistently acts in a manner defined as deviant. A person who cheats in everything he does is an example of secondary deviance. This person's entire life is one of finding new ways of cheating. He will have others do his papers for him, he will cheat in athletics and cards, he will try to get out of doing his part of a project and will take credit for the efforts of others. This person's life is maintained and reinforced by behaviors deemed deviant by society. Members of organized crime, compulsive gamblers, shoplifters, and habitual criminals illustrate the more extreme forms of secondary deviance.

Accidental deviance should also be distinguished from intentional deviance. Accidental deviance resulting from imcomplete socialization is excusable and normally results only in embarrassment. For example, the unsophisticated diner who goes into a Chinese restaurant for the first time and who drinks the water from the fingerbowl or who places the hot steaming napkin on his lap will likely cause other diners to laugh at his actions. The unsophisticated diner will be embarrassed when told that the towel is used to wash one's hands before the meal is served and that the finger bowl is used to clean one's fingers during the meal. Incomplete socialization is for most of us the greatest cause of deviance. "The most embarrassing moment of your life" is usually one resulting from being unaware of or confused about the rules or expectations for a particular situation. Almost all types of deviance which result from incomplete socialization are excusable if they do not harm anyone.

Intentional deviance, on the other hand, is punished severely because it is expected that "one should know better." Examples of this include being caught shoplifting, cheating, or hurting someone. These behaviors result in permanent negative labels, unlike the diner who will be only temporarily labeled as a "country bumpkin" until he acquires the norms of dining.

POSITIVE ASPECTS OF DEVIANCE

Some degree of deviance may be welcomed by an individual, a group, an organization, or a society.[15] Deviation from the normal procedure will in many instances allow for needed advancements toward desired goals. Despite the fact that bureaucracies are set up to insure that certain channels will be used, "cutting through the red tape" literally means circumventing established procedures and is a type of deviance. When a bureaucracy responds quickly to an immediate need, such as allowing a person to begin working before his employment application has received formal approval, the bureaucracy is deviating from "standard operating procedure" but is at the same time meeting a need which benefits both the employee and the company.

Deviance may also allow for the release of frustration and tensions which have been building up over a period of time.[16] Accumulated discontent has been known to be expressed by a boycott, picket lines, demonstrations, or by presenting a long petition expressing one's position. Peaceful demonstrations are also a deviation from the standard procedures of submitting a complaint to the proper authorities (in triplicate) and awaiting approval to appear before these authorities a few weeks later. The demonstration allows groups to express their anger when they feel it and to gain attention from the media. The 1960s was an era of civil rights demonstrations throughout the South. Sit-ins, economic boycott of stores, and parades down the main street of towns were often in the news. Despite the fact that demonstrations are potentially dangerous, some would say that sit-ins and passive resistance are preferable to arson, vandalism, rioting, looting, and the open violence which took place in several major cities in the late 1960s and early 1970s. These deviant activities among civil rights workers in the South often resulted in changes with regard to segregation in a peaceful manner.

What is illustrated in the example above is the fact that deviants help to define the boundaries of behavior. This positive function of deviancy is often overlooked, but one must understand that the only material found in society for drawing the lines between the right and wrong is the behavior of its members. The boundaries of what is acceptable behavior are constantly being tested by the nonconformists in our society. Each time the society moves to punish an individual for stepping over the established boundary, it buttresses the authority of the violated norm and redefines where the boundaries are located for the rest of the group. For example, street demonstrations in recent years have tested the boundaries between a peaceful demonstration a riot. When the police are called in to arrest demonstrators, unacceptable behavior is being defined by the authorities for all to observe. If the police had not been called, then we can extend the boundaries of what is an acceptable demonstration to include the characteristics of that demonstration. The fact that the urban riots resulted in the training of special police units for crowd control should reinforce for each of us the norm that riots resulting in violence, looting, and arson remain unacceptable. In the same way, a woman who keeps taking her hem up half an inch each day will eventually come to test the boundaries of what is an acceptable length for a skirt. Although we would expect different reactions to her depending on whether she is a teenager, a mother, or a stripper, cutting away at the skirt length will eventually lead to a confrontation with the "authorities" who maintain the boundaries. She may be grounded for a period of time, receive ridicule from other wives, or be arrested for indecent exposure. The length of her skirt when the authorities act will serve notice to other women of how much coverage is demanded by the norms. When we compare the mini-skirt with the ankle length dress of the 1800s, we can observe that the boundaries for decency in women's wear have been repeatedly tested and that the boundaries have loosened rather than hardened.

This last example brings up the fact that deviance, by testing the boundaries, also changes the norms. The first women who tested the norms of who could smoke in public probably became the object of various jokes and sanctions. In the nineteenth century, smoking was considered to be proper behavior for gentlemen only. This boundary

What boundaries are being defined here?

was tested repeatedly and greatly loosened to the point that any woman can now smoke in public.

Thus deviance helps to maintain groups and to bring them together.[17] Each time that deviant behavior is opposed, the whole society is strengthened. In uniting together to punish the deviant, the community not only realizes a common opinion that "things have gone far enough," but it also establishes moral rule and normal behavior for all members of society. Normal citizens are reinforced in their conventional behavior by having the boundaries laid out. Thus, we know what is "right" by knowing what behaviors are punished and are, therefore, wrong. It seems a rather strange way to arrive at proper behavior, yet societies usually define what is right as that which is not wrong.

WANTED: DEVIANTS

As one can see by now, deviant behavior in our society plays an important role in defining boundaries and maintaining group cohesion. Thus, the functioning of society requires that a small group of deviants exist within that society to test boundaries. Some deviant behavior is even institutionalized, as illustrated by the gambling casinos in Las Vegas which allow one to indulge in activities elsewhere considered illegal. State regulated off-track betting is an attempt to institutionalize "bookmaking" and to find another source of revenue for the state. Nudist camps allow a state of undress for those who wish a change from the conventional. Finally, war is an example of institutionalized deviance in which a soldier can receive medals for actions which would land him in jail in a normal life situation. Thus to some extent societies learn to absorb some types of deviant behavior into the culture rather than eliminating all deviancy outright. For as long as American society has existed, deviant groups have been present. The hippies of this era have their predecessors in the beatniks, the bohemians, and the gypsies. Deviant political ideologies, such as the American Socialist Party, have their predecessors in the Communist Party, the Populist Party, and the Tories, all of which were radical viewpoints in their time. Other such groups will continue to be a part of American society in the future.

SUMMARY

Sociologists are interested in activities which conflict with social order. Deviancy, although usually regarded as dysfunctional, may be functional as well. Four explanations for deviance were discussed: (1) deviancy as the result of a sick individual (the source of deviancy lies in the personality of the deviant); (2) deviancy as extreme behavior (unexpected behavior is deviant); (3) deviancy as learned behavior (the deviant is viewed as a member of a group); and (4) deviancy as actor-audience interaction (the response of society is the source of deviance).

The manner in which these perspectives might affect approaches toward drug abuse and rehabilitation were discussed. Also discussed was the importance of visibility and the realization that one must be "seen" before one can be labeled as deviant. The process of labeling was discussed and distinctions were made between primary, secondary, accidental, and intentional deviance. The positive aspects of deviance were discussed, such as the manner in which it allows for immediate expression of anger and the fact that its enforcement brings the community together. Some deviants appear to be necessary for a society to function properly. Without deviants to test the boundaries, the limits would be unclear to the remainder of the community members. By establishing the boundaries, the deviant defines proper behavior for others.

Notes

1. Emile Durkheim, *Suicide* (Glencoe, Ill.: The Free Press, 1951).

2. Albert K. Cohen, *Deviance and Control* (Englewood Cliffs, N.J.: Prentice-Hall, 1966).

3. M. Clinard, *Sociology of Deviant Behavior* (New York: Holt, Rinehart, and Winston, 1963).

4. Leon Festinger, "A Theory of Social Comparison Processes," *Human Relations* 7 (1954).

5. Cohen, *Deviance and Control,* Chapter 8.

6. Howard S. Becker, *The Other Side: Perspectives on Deviance* (New York: Free Press of Glencoe, 1964).

7. T. Scheff, *On Being Mentally Ill* (Chicago: Aldine, 1966).

8. Becker, *The Other Side.*

9. E. M. Lemert, *Social Pathology* (New York: McGraw Hill, 1951).

10. M. Clinard, *Anomie and Deviant Behavior* (New York: Free Press of Glencoe, 1964).

11. Becker, *The Other Side.*

12. Scheff, *On Being Mentally Ill.*

13. J. L. Simmons and H. Chambers, "Public Stereotype of Deviants," *Social Problems* 13 (1965): 223–32.

14. Becker, *The Other Side.*

15. Kai T. Erikson, *Wayward Puritans* (New York: John Wiley, 1966).

16. L. H. Coser, "Some Functions of Deviant Behavior and Normative Flexibility," *American Journal of Sociology* 68 (1962): 171–81.

17 R. A. Dentler and L. T. Erikson, "The Function of Deviance in Groups," *Social Problems* 7 (1959): 89–107.

Thinking
Sociologically

1. Walk across the campus, saying hello to everyone who passes by. Give each person a big grin, shake their hand, ask them how they are doing, etc. Note the reactions you will receive. How many people were caught speechless because they didn't expect such friendly behavior? How many didn't want anything to do with you? How many commented on how weird you seemed to be? Was your behavior deviant?

2. Ask a friend who is single if he or she would like to go out on a blind date. Describe the date as nice looking, pleasant, bright, and so forth and watch their reactions—then add on the fact that this blind date was recently released from a mental hospital. What reaction do you observe? Try the same experiment again with another person varying the ending (a blind date who was recently released from jail, who is a known alcoholic, or believed to be a homosexual). Can you tell by the reactions you receive which of the above is considered the "most" deviant?

3. Next time you are asked to participate in a group, try acting deviant by refusing to cooperate, criticizing the ideas suggested, acting cynical, and so forth. Note if the group you are in becomes more cohesive as they band together to reprimand you for your behavior. How long does it take for them to "put you down" and how do they express to you the fact that they are in agreement? The amount of time it takes will give you some idea of your tolerance gap and also of their willingness to allow the boundaries to be tested.

4. Look at two issues of the newspaper and look for examples of labeling. Court decisions are an obvious example but what about gossip columnists, letters to the editor, and society pages?

PART FIVE

The Family, Political Sociology, and the Religious Institution

Chapter 10

Cognitive Objectives

Like the sky which we seldom notice because it is always there, the family is often taken for granted even though it forms the setting for many of our daily activities. The purpose of this chapter is to illustrate the important role of the family in society. As we shall see, without the family institution, it would be impossible for a society to continue "from generation to generation." Some of the important things which this chapter emphasizes are the following:

1. *The major roles which the family plays in society*
2. *How the family assists in creating persons who conform to society's rules*
3. *What a nuclear family is and how it differs from the extended family*
4. *How the family in our society meets the issues of family organization which face all societies*
5. *The changing functions of the family in modern America*
6. *The ways in which society affects the family and ways in which the family affects society*
7. *The major steps in the life cycle and how the family functions in each segment of the life cycle*

A Forest of Family Trees

Each society must find some reliable and consistent manner of perpetuating itself to insure that it will continue after the death of those members presently active in the society. The reproduction of new members, however, is not sufficient to insure continuation of the society. Some provision must be also made for the socialization of each new member into the appropriate attitudes, values, and behavior expected of individuals in that society. Replenishment of its ranks and education of new members are two problems which every society must solve.

There are only two methods by which a society may replenish its members. The first is through the recruitment of new members from other countries, called immigration. This method of population growth involves certain problems. Immigration occurs at uneven rates. The socialization process is, at best, only partially successful since adult immigrants may be expected to remain somewhat torn between the ways of doing things in their home country and the way of life in their new country. A better method of replacing members, and one which all societies use, is to allow for a socially approved reproductory relationship between adults. Then each society sets rules to insure that babies born from these relationships will be cared for and sheltered until able to manage for themselves. We are of course talking about the family. Thus society allows consenting adults to create a household and become parents, and holds these adults responsible for the training and education of their children during the early and impressionable years from infancy to early adolescence.

One of the reasons the family holds a pivotal position in society is this responsibility for the general education of the child (referred to as socialization). The family plays the most important role in the humanizing process since it teaches an infant the language and customs of the society in which he is to live. In the family setting, children become adults.

THE FAMILY'S ROLE IN MODERN SOCIETY

The family functions in at least two important roles in modern society. (1) It produces humans and therefore replenishes a society's population. (2) It helps create individuals who know how to behave as society expects, including getting married, having their own children, and bringing these new social recruits up in a family setting.

The family seems to be a very efficient method of helping to create socially acceptable individuals. Consider one alternative. Family socialization could be replaced by a system designed to police everyone all the time. This arrangement would be both expensive and complex, since someone would have to police the police who police the people. It is more efficient for a society to allow each individual to police himself by socializing that person to conform to the expected behavior of that society. Enforcement agencies are provided, however, to punish an individual who fails to police himself (the rule breaker).

How important is "child socialization" by the parents? Imagine yourself as a member of a group who has just been stranded on an island with little or no hope for rescue. Let us imagine that this group of which you are a member should decide that here is an opportunity to create a new society. If the group decided, for example, upon a society where all persons embrace and kiss each time they met, consider the process required just to change the habits of old members who are accustomed to shaking hands, nodding to one another, and saying "hello." All of the original founders would have to be trained not to hold out their right hand as before, but rather to put both arms out and pucker in the preparation for a hug and a kiss. Those unaccustomed to embracing and kissing other persons' spouses, persons of their own sex, or those unattractive to them would have to learn to overcome these inhibitions. Given the time and cooperation of all members, it is possible to imagine that all would remember to embrace others, but it would require that each person consciously force himself to remember until it became a part of his everyday behavior. However well trained, if these individuals were eventually rescued from the island, there is no doubt that they would be able to return without much difficulty to the previously learned manner of salutation: approaching with a smile, holding out one's hand in expectation of a handshake, and nodding one's head in recognition.

Hugging and kissing as a way of saying hello could be taught to the children in the group in a number of ways. Observing adult behavior would be the most effective method. Parents of the child would model the behavior for their children from the child's earliest age and be constantly available to praise them when they remembered and to scold them if they failed to remember the proper salutation. It may be assumed that children who were taught the embrace/kiss hello would be almost uninhibited and would embrace all others without thinking twice. When it becomes natural to their way of acting, then one can say that these children have learned the proper behavior (folkways) with regard to saying hello. If these children were ever to leave the island, it would be expected that they would feel awkward the first time someone put their hand out to them for a handshake.

It is this process of teaching children the proper behavior which is in general the central responsibility of the family. The family does not, however, accomplish the process of socialization alone. It is assisted by the church, schools, mass media, courts, law enforcement agencies, and government. Socialization does not end as the child grows older, but continues throughout adulthood. As the child matures, contact outside the family increases and the influence of these contacts slowly takes the place of the family as a major socializing agent.

FACING FAMILY ISSUES

The nuclear family is normally composed of two adults of the opposite sex, living together in a socially approved relationship with their own or adopted children. Americans usually equate the nuclear family with family organization, but throughout the world variations exist in family organization. Sometimes the nuclear family is found within a larger family unit composed of grandparents, uncles, aunts, cousins, and grandchildren. This type of organization is referred to as an extended family system and is common in many countries.

Even within American culture there are various types of families. A nuclear family may contain only one adult member as the result of death, divorce, or separation. It is also possible for two adults without children to be a nuclear family. Extended family systems also exist in the United States, especially among first-generation immigrant families and also among experimental family types.

It is essential to recognize that the kind of family one grows up in and the manner in which one goes about choosing a spouse (along with its related activities, such as dating, engagement, weddings, family ties) are not allowed to develop haphazardly. The family is considered to be too important both to the individuals involved and to the society's future to be allowed to develop according to whim.

The norms relating to the family organization which determine the kind of family you grow up in are referred to as the family instutition. Family norms in many societies have been studied and the following questions illustrate the kinds of issues faced by each society and examples of alternative solutions. Some alternatives may appear rather strange to Americans, but each has been utilized successfully by different cultures to meet the needs of that society.

Who Is Eligible to Marry?

In our nation the legal age to marry without parental approval is generally twenty-one years for males and eighteen years for females. In some states, the legal age for marriage is younger. These ages also usually distinguish the adolescent from the "legal" adult. In short, marriage is for "adults" in our society. Other countries allow marriage for females at fourteen or fifteen years old and males at sixteen years old. These societies have differing ideas about what an adult is, and whether one must be an adult to be married.

Laws exist to prohibit some types of persons from getting married, such as the insane, the retarded, and imprisoned criminal. Until the late 1960s, miscegenation laws in the South prohibited interracial marriages. These laws imply that some individuals are considered "unfit" for the important job of establishing a family.

Marriage within one's own immediate family (incest) is almost never allowed, but each society must decide if it will allow marriage only within one's group (endogamy), allow marriage only outside one's own group (exogamy), or allow both. In American society, the type of exogamy where a woman from a lower social status marries a man from a higher social status remains an ideal. Endogamy is most likely to occur where strong pressures exist to marry within one's religious denomination or racial grouping. In the United States, marrying up into a higher social status may be the ideal, but in reality most Americans are generally endogamous, marrying within racial, religious, and social groupings.

How Many Spouses?

A marriage with plural spouses is referred to as a polygamous marriage. If a husband has several wives, the marriage is termed polygyny. If the wife has several husbands, the term is polyandry. Neither is characteristic of the American society, and polygamy is illegal in every state. Some writers have noted that Americans, while not practicing polygamy, do practice "serial monogamy"—having several husbands or wives, but only one at a time. Serial monogamy then refers to the procedure in which persons marry, divorce, remarry, divorce, remarry and so forth.

Where Will Newly Married Couples Live?

If the bride and groom move into the home of the husband's parents, their residence is patrilocal. If they move into the bride's parents' household, the couple is matrilocal. In instances when place of residence does not matter, their residence is termed bilocal. When the newly married couple is expected to begin their own household, the normal custom of American marriages, the residence is then termed neolocal.

Who Should be "Head" of the Family?

If the authority rests in the husband, the family is patriarchal; the term matriarchal is applied to families where the authority is based on the mother's role. The term equalitarian is used to refer to situations in which the husband and wife both hold equal amounts of power and authority. The authority structure in America, generally speaking, remains patriarch, although there appears to be a trend on the part of younger, better-educated couples toward an equalitarian structure.[1]

When you grow up, I want you to be a doctor.

What Is the Attitude of Parents toward Children?

Parents may be permissive and indulgent towards their children or disciplinary and aloof. In the United States, most differences in these attitudes are related to social class.[2] Middle class families show a greater willingness to allow freedom and are less willing to employ physical punishment. Generally, middle-class families have greater expectations for their children than do lower-class families.

These questions and many others are faced by each society. The variations in family organization described by anthropologists in various cultures illustrate the attempts made to arrive at a practical and acceptable manner of meeting the reproductive and socializing needs of each society.

THE FAMILY AND SOCIAL CHANGES

The American family system has been the brunt of considerable criticism by individuals who seek to cleanse, improve, or abandon the family altogether. This criticism has perhaps resulted in some changes in family structure but, in general, the family has managed to withstand all challenges to its existence. The reasons for its persistence are rather easy to see. First, the family meets the sexual needs of adult members of the society. People do not necessarily marry for sexual reasons, but marriage allows for a stable and socially approved sexual relationship. In addition, the family also provides a place of common residence and economic cooperation. Members of a family have a home, a physical and psychological place of protection which is relatively permanent and serves as a place of comfort and refuge. Finally, the family often pools the money earned by each for the mutual benefit of all.

In the past, the family was entirely responsible for religious and formal educational training as well as recreational functions. In modern America, the family has embraced its role as a protective and socializing agent and relinquished its responsibilities in the area of religious training to church organizations. Formal education is now

The family is no longer entirely responsible for providing food.

mainly the responsibility of the school system, and recreation is today more a function of formally organized associations.

The family is often viewed as a passive agent in social change while outside factors such as technology, industry, and government are viewed as active agents of social change. It must be admitted that the family is not as dynamic an instigator of change as are these other social forces.

External forces may determine the family structure, as in the following examples. (1) The kind of economic subsistence is related to the type of family structure. For example, polygyny (plural wives) is most ofen found in underdeveloped cultures characterized by nomadic tribes or dispersed patterns of settlement. (2) Cultures with complex social stratification systems are usually characterized by monogamous family systems. Thus, one would expect to see a trend toward monogamy as countries undergo industrialization.[3] (3) The type of religion has an effect on divorce rates and family size. Thus, predominantly Catholic societies or predominantly family-oriented groups (e.g., Mormons) would be expected to have larger families and lower divorce rates than non-Catholic or non-Mormon societies.

The family also may be viewed as a mini-culture which is affected by and affects the greater society. One can point to several examples of the influence of the family on social processes. First, extended family systems restrict freedom of movement and choice for its members because decisions are supposed to be made on the basis of what is best for the family, not for the individual. Cultures characterized by extended families reduce individual responsibility and may be expected to have limited degrees of social mobility for individuals. Another example is that the status of women will be expected to be higher in cultures which are characterized by monogamous marriages then in cultures characterized by polygyny.

THE FAMILY AND THE INDIVIDUAL LIFE CYCLE

One very specific certainty about the family is that you are always a member of a family, either the one in which you are a son or daughter (family of orientation), or the one where you are the parent (family of procreation). The term "life cycle" is used by sociologists to refer to the life segments a person goes through during his lifetime. The life cycle is normally broken down into infancy and childhood, adolescence, young adulthood, adulthood, and old age. We will discuss each of these, emphasizing the different issues which are significant at each stage of the life cycle.

Infancy and Childhood

The fact that respondents in surveys are always asked about their family attests to the belief held by social scientists that family background affects present and future behavior. Thus, persons brought up in a home not knowing where the next meal is coming from are expected to differ from persons born in a home where money is less of a problem or persons from a home where people are mainly concerned with how to spend the money they have.

Socioeconomic or social class background has been found to be related to childrearing methods. For example, higher social economic classes often show greater affection toward their children. Lower classes are more likely to use physical punishment and have rigid rules of behavior. The upper classes tend to explain to children the reasons for proper behavior, and they have higher educational aspirations for their children.

There are also similarities, however, in childrearing practices among all social classes. For example, socially approved sex roles are taught to boy-children and girl-children. A girl learns what is feminine when she wears her first frilly dress and when she is no longer allowed to play with the boys because they are too rough. Boys are taught to play ball, to be cowboys, and to fight. Thus, early in each person's life, male-children and female-children come to view each other as similar in some ways and different in others. These differences in sex roles result in the double standard—some behavior which is permitted for one sex is not permitted for the other—and the contention that since the sexes are not equal, then one must be inferior to the other. It is not surprising to hear supporters of equality for both sexes advocating changes in sex role training.[4]

It should be noted that sex role training as well as all other types of socialization processes do not discontinue as the child grows older. Parents are the most active socialization agents during early childhood. But as we grow older, other adults, peers, older friends, and the mass media continue the socialization process through adolescence, adulthood, and old age.

In summary, our childhood experiences are to some extent affected by the social class into which we are born. During this period, children learn to be adults. In the traditional nuclear family these processes are repeated time after time and give evidence to the fact that the family institution has developed effective and consistent methods of socialization.

In recent decades, specific types of experimental families have arisen, like the kibbutz and communal living arrangements where the children belong to all members of the group. The kibbutz is character-

Childhood is changing.

ized by common ownership of property except for a few personal belongings, and communal organization of production and consumption.[5] Thus, the community is run as if it were one household. All members are provided for on an equalitarian basis without special privileges. How these children will differ from children born in a traditional nuclear family like that which predominates in American society is not entirely known. We may, however, predict they will be different from children reared in a two-parent home, just as we might expect that children brought up in mother-only and father-only homes will also differ.

Adolescence

During adolescence children become socially aware of their surroundings.[6] At first, one's understanding of people consists of being aware that some people dress better than others, or that all people do not go to the same restaurants, vacation spots, or colleges. Later the adolescent begins to understand the basic idea of stratification—people are ranked according to their economic status and there are a few on top and many below them. Soon the developing individual becomes conscious of the fact that he feels more comfortable with those with whom he shares a certain likeness. Perhaps this is true because he knows what to expect from others who are similar in specific ways. He is likely to seek as friends those who show similar tastes and aspirations. At about the same time girls become interested in boys and soon thereafter, vice versa. The maturing young person also becomes interested in dating at this stage and the tendency is to search out as dating partners those persons who show these basic similarities.

Since dating is a new experience, young people usually do not know what to expect, or what the other person is expecting. The tension resulting from fear of embarrassment or fear of failure usually means that a first date is awkward, rather formal, and frequently superficial. As the adolescent becomes better acquainted with the opposite sex (and with appropriate dating behavior), dating becomes more enjoyable and more informal. In sociological terms, the adolescent becomes socialized into the norms of dating and so dating becomes an enjoyable activity.

Eventually most dating adolescents face the question of premarital sex.[7] At this time, when sexual compatibility and satisfaction are advocated as necessary for a successful marriage, each person must weigh the need for sexual expression against the possibility of arousing feelings of guilt or shame.[8] When one takes into account this society's Judeo-Christian heritage and the norms resulting from that heritage, sexual openness requires that one either ignore the norms (but still receive social disapproval) or feel guilt for having violated the norms.

Thus there are three possible solutions to the question of engaging in premarital sex. Those who decide to engage in premarital sexual activities feel it results in an increased understanding of their partner, which strengthens their relationship. Others believe that sex belongs only in marriage, and point to the fear of social disapproval, especially if a pregnancy should occur. Overall, these persons feel that premarital sex will weaken the relationship between them. A third possibility involves a change in the rules regarding what is proper for premarital behavior. There are signs that the premarital norms in our society have loosened somewhat. Many note that most premarital sexual activity is between partners who eventually marry. Sex in the context of a "meaningful relationship" (not necessarily marriage) is becoming permissible among some groups. Perhaps these norms will change even more in the future.

Eventually most young people choose a marital partner. When people wish to explain how two persons chose one another they often say, "they fell in love." This statement may be true, but it implies that these two persons chose one another from all other people in the world. A person is not, however, entirely free to choose whomever he wishes. In fact there are restrictions on the choice of a mate.

We will call our possible choices "eligibles." We must begin by placing most of those who live outside our immediate geographic area on the list of ineligibles. When we consider the territory we cover each day, it is plain that we have a relatively small area within which we live, go to school, go to church, go to friends' houses, etc. The "perfect" mate might be living one hundred, five hundred, or two thousand miles away but with increasing distance the chances of ever knowing about him or her decreases.[9] Second, out of all the people within our territory of daily encounters, we must of course exclude all persons of the same sex as ourselves, those who are already married, and (usually) those who are engaged and already claimed by others. In our society, women would most likely also exclude those men much younger than themselves while males would most likely exclude women much older than themselves from the list of eligibles.

Choice of date or mate also depends upon our religious commitment, ethnic background, and racial attitudes. It is possible, for example, that Jews might exclude non-Jews, Mexican Americans might exclude non-Mexican Americans, and whites might exclude blacks from the eligibles. Furthermore, you usually exclude those persons who are incompatible with your personal taste.[10]

Obviously, by now the list of remaining eligibles is rather short. The list may get even shorter as we realize that we come into social contact mostly with those who belong to our own social class. Although it is not highly unusual for someone who is poor to date and even marry someone who is well-to-do, it is more likely that we will date and eventually marry someone very close to our own social class because we share similar social lives and because we simply come into contact more frequently with those who are of a similar social class level. Within this remaining group of eligibles, each person searches for that person for whom he feels affection. We usually try to seek out someone who shares similar views and attitudes as ourselves and yet who is dissimilar enough for us to meet our psychological needs.[11] When and if we find a person like this, "we fall in love," and hopefully we convince him or her to do likewise.

In summary, adolescence is a time of awakening. We come to a better understanding of the social world around us, including the opposite sex. We begin dating, awkwardly at first. Increased familiarity soon helps to ease the situation and make it enjoyable. These experiences assist us in finding a person who shares most of our attitudes and yet is different enough to meet our needs.

Many people do not accept traditional roles.

Young Adulthood

This stage is one of decision making. Decisions must be made concerning education and career. One of the major decisions involves marriage. Some persons remain single, and devote their lives to a career which gives them satisfaction. Others choose an alternative form of marriage, such as group marriage or a non-formalized marriage ("living together"). Most, however, look forward to a traditional marriage.

Marriage involves one of the major adjustments most young adults will have to make. Within a relatively short period of time, the new couple will be expected to work out their sexual, psychological, and social problems to the satisfaction of both. Some of the nagging questions each couple must answer are: Should we have children? If so, when and how many? How are household tasks to be shared? How are finances to be handled? How often should we visit our in-laws? How independent can we be of each other? How shall we handle disagreements? Thousands of questions like these must be answered adequately if a marriage is to continue to be satisfying and meaningful for both mates.

Some persons today look upon marriage much the way their parents and grandparents did: a lifetime commitment in which the husband and wife each have a traditional role. Other individuals do not wish to accept the traditional roles of husband and wife, and seek a marriage relationship in which each partner can develop a meaningful self-identity within the context of a fulfilling love relationship and a feeling of responsibility for one another. Each couple must work out their own variation of the marriage relationship.

Marriage in our society appears to be characterized by two rather incompatible ideals. The first is that marriage is a permanent relationship. (Most wedding ceremonies still contain the phrase "till death do us part.") The second is the feeling that marriage should bring a sense of self-fulfillment and happiness to each partner. The result seems to be that few people who marry do so with the intention of setting up a temporary relationship. However, a marriage which fails to adjust quickly and adequately to the satisfaction of both individuals will likely end in divorce.

Adulthood

This stage of the life cycle is the most productive from the point of view of society. As an individual, each adult contributes to the society by working, paying taxes, voting, and buying goods. In addition, as families, adults bear and raise children.

Parenthood requires major adjustments. The husband and wife must take on the additional roles of father and mother. The marriage relationship must expand and become a family relationship. Children become a center of attention, and activities are planned around their needs and wishes.

Since the family has ceased to be an economic unit where all members work together to make the farm or ranch successful, the family has turned its attention to the cultivation of strong relationships with one another. This is known as the family's affective function. Thus, happiness of the marriage and personal fulfillment have also resulted in greater attention given to the social and emotional development of children. Modern American families which remain intact are probably closer in terms of affection, understanding, and enjoyment of each other's company than any family system in history. For this reason, leisure activities such as camping, boating, and family vacations are common family activities.

Old Age

Old age is viewed negatively in our society. In America, which is characterized as a youth-oriented society, the elderly are not normally

Modern families spend much leisure time together.

viewed as contributing members to our society.[12] Most of the elderly are retired, which is viewed by many as the ideal situation. Freed from having to work, they can do whatever they want. In reality, however, most find that being retired means a severe loss of status. When asked, "Where do you work?" or "What do you do?", the elderly person invariably qualifies his answer that he is retired by noting what his job used to be. This points to the fact that there is no prestige in being retired, so one must judge that individual through his occupational status prior to having retired. The loss of occupational status also means the loss of pride in one's work and the end to further opportunities for advancement.

There is a great deal of criticism today against a mandatory retirement age. It is conceded that aging slows down one's reflexes, and that persons in occupations where one's reflexes are essential to the health or welfare of others should be forced to retire when tests show that a person is slowing down. On the other hand, experience gained on some jobs makes an older worker more valuable. The mandatory retirement of these individuals is a waste of potential and experinece which cannot easily be replaced. Critics of a mandatory retirement age believe that persons should retire when they can no longer do their

job effectively rather than when they attain a certain age. Taking physical stamina into consideration, these critics note that special considerations such as shortened working hours and less strenuous activities could be available to the older worker in order to take advantage of his experience while giving him greater opportunities for leisure.

Loneliness is an acute problem for the elderly. Inevitably one of the partners from a marriage will outlive the other partner, involving a difficult adjustment. Some do make these adjustments, and find new interests to occupy their time. Many move into nursing homes, while others move in with their children (if they have any). Each of these alternatives provides a manner by which the elderly may solve the problem of a changed life situation. But each alternative raises knotty problems which are difficult to solve.

Living alone requires some degree of physical well-being. Entering a home for the aged involves money and the sacrifice of some privacy and independence. Those who move in with their children enjoy the company and assistance of their children and grandchildren, but many times also feel as if they are a burden. At times, conflict between the elderly and the family erupts from the lack of freedom for both parties involved. The family must take the elderly person into consideration when planning activities, while the elderly person has little say in making decisions for the family group and is expected to go along with the decisions made by the younger "head of the house."

While remarriage is possible, loyalty to the deceased partner, opposition by their children, and the images that society has about the elderly—including the idea that they are nonsexual and "too old for romance"—decrease the probability that they will seek out a new partner.

When being old means only looking back to earlier times, then death is welcome. Death, of course, ends the life cycle of an individual, but during that lifetime, an animal-like infant has learned a language and culture and passed it on to others. That person grew stronger and wiser. He loved, married, and brought children into the world. A majority of his time was set aside for work, with time allowed for leisure activities. Inevitably the life cycle comes to an end. This process, with each life different from the other, is repeated millions upon millions of times, all within the family system.

SUMMARY

The family plays two important roles in society: it replenishes the population and it socializes the offspring produced. As we have seen, all societies must face the basic questions as to who may or may not marry and what form a marriage should take. Our American pattern of marriage is only one of several alternatives. The modern family in America tends to emphasize its affective function and has relinquished its educational, religious, and some of its recreational functions. The family is affected by the larger society, but the family also affects the societal structure as well. Finally, the major issues and problems which face each individual may be viewed according to the step in the life cycle in which that individual finds himself. Thus, the problems of infancy and childhood differ from the issues faced by the adolescent, young adult, adult, and the aged.

The family institution often escapes notice because we are so totally involved in "family life" all the time. But it remains a pivotal institution because it makes possible the continuation of a fairly stable cultural tradition passed on from one generation to another.

Notes

1.   Robert O. Blood, Jr. and Donald M. Wolfe, *Husbands and Wives: The Dynamics of Married Living* (New York: Free Press, 1960).

2.   August B. Hollingshead, *Elmstown Youth: The Impact of Social Classes on Adolescents* (New York: John Wiley, 1949).

3. Robert F. Winch and Rae L. Blumberg, "Societal Complexity and Familial Organization," in *Selected Studies in Marriage and the Family,* ed. Robert F. Winch and Louis Wolf Goodman (New York: Holt, Rinehart, and Winston, 1968).

4. Betty Friedan, *The Feminine Mystique* (New York: W. W. Norton, 1963).

5. Yonina Talmon, "The Family in a Revolutionary Movement-The Case of the Kibbutz in Israel," in C. M. F. Nimkoff, *Comparative Family Systems* (Boston: Houghton Mifflin, 1965), pp. 259–86.

6. James S. Coleman, *The Adolescent Society* (New York: Free Press, 1961).

7. J. L. Reiss, *Premarital Sexual Standards in America* (New York: Free Press, 1960).

8. Albert Ellis, *The American Sexual Tragedy* (New York: Lyle Stuart, 1962).

9. Alvin M. Katz and Reuben Hill, "Residential Propinquity and Marital Selection," *Marriage and Family Living* 20 (1958) : 27–34.

10. Karl Wallace, "Factors Hindering Mate Selection," *Sociology and Social Research* 64 (1960) : 317–25.

11. Robert F. Winch, *Mate Selection: A Study of Complementary Needs* (New York: Harper and Row, 1958).

12. Elaine Cumming and William E. Henry, *Growing Old: The Process of Disengagement* (New York: Basic Books, 1961).

Thinking
Sociologically

1.   Make a list of the things you normally do with your parents. How many of those things on your list would be considered educational, recreational, economic (money-making), and affective? Are most of your family activities affective?

2.   Try to imagine a society without families. How would the reproductive and educational functions be fulfilled in such a society? Write the make-believe biography of the first two years of a child born in such a society.

3.   Go to an upper-class area of town and observe the children at play. Then observe children at play in a low-income section of town. What differences do you observe? Write a brief description of the differences.

4.   Ask a person over sixty years old to tell about his or her dating experiences and engagement. Compared to your own experiences and those of your friends, how have the norms of courtship changed?

5.   Select eight couples you know, four who are married and four who are about to be married. Determine in what ways they are endogamous and in what ways they are exogamous. Keep in mind factors such as social class, area of residence, and education.
Ask the soon-to-be-married what they expect to be the most difficult adjustment they will have to make after marriage. Ask the married persons what they found to be their most difficult problem of adjustment. What differences do you observe between the already married and those soon to be married? Can you see any differences between the responses of males and females? Are any of these differences based upon the ages of those whom you have interviewed?

6.   What are the common stereotypes of middle-aged persons who have never married? Discuss the reasons for these stereotypes.

Chapter 11

Cognitive Objectives

Due to the daily reporting of events and personalities, the political institution in America is probably the most visible and perhaps the most perplexing of all institutions. Political news is interesting because political activities are a continuous clash between conflicting demands. In this chapter you should look for the following items:

1. *What is beneath the formal structure we call the political institution*
2. *The interests of political sociology*
3. *How political beliefs are learned from childhood through adulthood*
4. *An explanation for political disillusionment*
5. *The difference between the order and process perspective*
6. *The three political ideologies in America*
7. *What a revolutionary is*
8. *How political power is maintained*
9. *The reason for oligarchies in political institutions*
10. *The sources of political power*
11. *The differing viewpoints on whether a power elite exists or not*

Political Horsepower

LOOKING BENEATH THE SURFACE

During the educational process, each of us learns about the formal structure of the American political system. We learn that the government of the United States is composed of a federal system of states based on democratic principles and a constitution. This constitution defines the functions of the three branches of government—executive, legislative, and judicial—stressing a system of checks and balances which guards against the domination by one branch over the other.

While all this is true, the political institution is much more than just a formal structure. To fully understand the political process we must relate the political structure to the entire social structure. Hence, the political process should not be viewed like a diagram titled "how a bill becomes law," but rather as a dynamic process of interaction, conflict, and compromise. Often, the most interesting political activity occurs before action is taken on a bill. In many cases, the vote itself is anticlimatic compared to the attempts by non-political, unofficial organizations to place pressure upon the public and legislators to support their viewpoint. The vote tally is more than just a score; it represents endless hours of bargaining, trading votes, collecting IOUs, and making deals which often result in unusual coalitions.

Political sociology is a branch of sociology which deals with the social and political conflicts that lead to changes in the distribution of power. Thus, political sociologists focus on the following questions:

How does a person become politically socialized? What factors are related to political participation and specifically to decisions in voting behavior? What is the role of self-interest, personal ambition, and egoistic interests in political life? What factors determine the outcome when political interests clash? Each of these questions can best be understood and discussed within the context of political struggle. Inevitably, the political interests of some men come into conflict with the political interests of other men, resulting in political struggle. Sometimes the struggle is a short one with the most powerful group dominating the battle throughout; other times the battle is long and there are no clearcut winners.

It is inevitable that groups will engage in political battle because of the manner in which their attitudes differ, the degree to which they feel that they can gather public support for their side, and the investment each group has in the issue at hand. Thus, to look for the answers to questions asked by political sociologists, we must look at differing perspectives that lead to conflict and the changes in political power due to the outcome of these struggles.

Journalistic efforts to analyze political struggles, like those which appear on the editorial pages of the daily newspaper, should not be confused with the efforts of political sociologists. The writings of the political columnist are based upon hearsay, rumor, and speculation and their major purpose is to influence their readers' opinions by interpreting current political activities in light of conservative or liberal perspectives. The political sociologist, on the other hand, is more dependent upon empirical data (when available) and his major purpose is to interpret current political activities in light of changes in the norms of the political institution.

LEARNING POLITICAL BELIEFS

As previously noted, political struggle has its source in the discrepancies between views on basic political issues and solutions. The source of these beliefs can be traced back to early childhood, where the basic orientations through which political happenings are interpreted are developed. It is not until later, however, that a person is able to appreciate the complexities of political life and to understand his role as a participant in the political life of the country.

Our basic political orientation consists of an emotional sense of belonging to a specific political community. Patriotism and national loyalty are learned at an early age, as are similar types of orientations about other political institutions (e.g., Democratic Party and Republican Party), symbols (e.g., American flag, bald eagle), and various social groups (e.g., the poor, the ethnic minorities, farmers). These basic orientations will later influence what the individual comes to believe about politics. The family is the source of most of the basic interpretive orientations through which politics comes to make sense. During the child's formative years, much of his political learning is indirect and unintentional. The child picks up views regarding the political world from things said in his family. These early political views which stem from the family continue to have an effect on an individual throughout life. Ultimately the influence of the family is mixed with that of the school and other groups in developing the political outlook of the individual.

From childhood on, the individual picks up facts and information and attempts to evaluate the meaning of what he learns. In early adolescence, peer groups become more important than the family in socialization, taking on an important role which they retain through adult life. During this stage political teaching is more deliberate. In school, the individual is confronted with direct and systematic attempts to ensure that political values and information appropriate for adult citizenship are acquired.

Finally, in later years, most political socialization takes place through secondary groups and direct experiences with the political world. The family and the school become less influential as the political self begins to respond directly to political campaigns, political debate, and political personalities. Thus, the maturing individual establishes a relationship with immediate political activities rather than with the political institution. These responses are affected by those basic orientations which, years before, launched that individual into political life.

POLITICAL DISILLUSIONMENT

In an ideal world where all things occur as predicted, one might imagine a child growing up in a home where his parents comment on the evening news that the Republican politician is a "good man." In the course of time he learns that being a Republican means favoring certain types of policies and group interests to the exclusion of others. As an adult, he formulates opinions supporting Republican leaders and votes for Republican candidates. If all this occurred as stated, then the person's political behavior could be formed during childhood and youth.[1]

In the real world, however, persons often fail to act as predicted. A common occurrence today is to find a lack of correspondence between the political orientations of many youth and the political orientations of their parents. How can this occur?

Dawson and Prewitt note that the earliest political socialization agencies have *authority over* the growing child. At this stage, the child is a receiver of messages, cues, instructions and so forth. During this stage parents transmit their political orientations to the impressionable child. The child does not evaluate the information received but merely assumes that the information received is correct. At a later point, the political socializing agencies stand in *positions of equality* with the learner. These equal level agents—mainly peer group and reference group associates—are responsible for adding content to the basic framework shaped during earlier years. From these relationships, future citizens acquire most of the special knowledge and attitudes that makes effective political life possible. At this stage the learner is more likely to question the sources of the information. He is no longer entirely accepting of all information received. Some of the information received is rejected while other information is questioned.

Still later, political socialization becomes a matter of *experiences* with the political system. Every form of direct contact (i.e., voting, paying taxes, obeying laws, receiving benefits) is an example of this stage. Some refer to this stage as a "period of testing reality." Despite the fact that one's parents and grandparents have always been conservative, liberal, or of any mixture of the two, if that orientation fails to be of assistance in comprehending and understanding the political world directly experienced, then basic alterations may occur in one's core orientations.

Some persons find that the political world fails to operate as they had expected it to operate. A common solution in such a circumstance is to replace one's feeling of trust and optimism with cynicism. In the same way, a young adult brought up to believe that political activity is futile may discover that political participation can be effective in bringing about changes. For most persons, the reality testing stage of political maturation results in only marginal adjustments. Except in situations where the political learning of childhood proves to be drastically inadequate, the adult years do little more than add to the political self attitudes relevant for direct participation in political life.[2]

In summary, political socialization begins at early childhood and continues throughout one's lifetime. Whether one will maintain the original perspective taught to him by his parents is, however, dependent upon how well that orientation helps the individual understand political activities. If the orientation assists in interpreting events, then it will remain intact. If the orientation is not useful in understanding political activities, then alterations will occur in the original perspective.

CONFLICTING PERSPECTIVES

To illustrate two conflicting basic orientations learned in the political socialization process, the *order perspective* will be contrasted with the *process perspective.* These two perspectives will be used because they represent the most common approaches toward political action.

A person who holds an order perspective assumes that every society tends toward a state of stability or balance. This person would value stability and authority (i.e., law and order) above conflict and strain. All events which result in disequilibrium or tension are regarded by this person as harmful to society and in need of immediate attention. Hence, when faced by a situation which unbalances the preferred state, this person tends to depend upon change in the leadership as a solution. Groups of "order approach persons" are satisfied to work within the system. Their most common tactic is to retain stability through stricter enforcement of the laws which support the status quo.

Persons who hold a process perspective assume that "every state of human affairs is likely to contain within it the seeds of its transformation into a new and different state."[3] Society is viewed as a continuous struggle between groups with opposed aims and goals. The powerful like things as they are, while the powerless want to have them changed. Advocates of the process approach believe that this struggle for power is the essence of political activities and, in general, characterizes the total social condition. Struggles imply, first, that there are winners and losers, and, second, that continuous change is inevitable. Overall, advocates of this approach have a positive attitude toward change since disequilibrium (viewed as harmful by proponents of the order perspective) is viewed as possibly progressive and leading to desired changes in existing conditions.

An example of these two approaches can be seen in the discussions about the effect of the civil rights movement in the 1960s. To those who have an order perspective, the black revolution was a disruptive period which destroyed effective social control and led to disorganized race relations throughout the United States. The legal victories won in the courts to end discrimination resulted in serious imbalances in the existing social system and created problems which persisted into the 1970s (e.g., the busing of children miles away from their neighborhood schools). This same set of historical events, however, was viewed by advocates of the process approach as necessary to dismantle a system of illegitimate social control (e.g., Jim Crow laws) which was used to exploit a minority group.

Order theory can only account for change in one direction (toward some point of ultimate stability) and so cannot explain how an increasingly deteriorating state of affairs may lead to a revolutionary explosion. On the other hand, despite the fact that process theory contends that every society harbors the seeds of its own destruction, the process perspective also assumes some form of internal social order. Thus, both order and process theory illuminate important segments of social reality, and a mixture of the two is necessary for a complete explanation.

Political Ideologies

One does not often hear a specific politician referred to as a man who possesses an order perspective. Rather politicians are categorized as belonging in one of three categories: conservative, liberal, or radical. While in reality there are countless gradations which exist between the extremes, these categories are most often utilized to describe the overall political views of a person. Few politicians are consistently liberal or conservative, yet it is inevitable that the media (and the voters) will label one candidate as more (or less) liberal than another candidate. Conservatism, liberalism, and radicalism represent ideologies with differing perspectives.

Conservatism and the order prospective have much in common. Government is viewed as an instrument to maintain law and order and to integrate the various parts of society into a balanced state. Conservatives believe social change should be kept to a minimum and only changes based on traditional values are allowable.

Liberalism sees government as a tool for change toward desired goals. The ultimate goal, however, remains the reality of an open society where all men are equal. It emphasizes the belief that all men should be able to take part in political decision making. Change always is to take place within the order of existing institutions and without a total restructuring of society's way of life.

The radical viewpoint rejects the idea that the electorate can ever agree on the proper goals for a society. Government rule is considered to benefit only a few men, rather than the needs of the public. Because radicals perceive a continuous struggle between the have and have nots, they feel that governmental power should be decreased and the power of the people increased. Those of radical viewpoint frequently call for total dismantling of social structure and complete reorganization of institutional patterns.

These ideologies should be considered as competing views of the struggle to gain political power. To some extent, ideologies also serve as rationalizations, especially for those already in positions of power. Those who benefit from the existing political order will try to convince the public that it is in their best interest to keep things as they are. Groups opposed to the existing political order must be convinced that reforms they desire can be gained in a gradual but peaceful manner. Inevitably, however, a few will remain unconvinced and will resort to violence to subvert the existing order.

RULES FOR CONFLICT

Americans tend to overlook the fact that political activities—like all other social activities—take place within a normative system. Conservatives and liberals who differ in perspective are allowed to clash openly, but the types of permissible conflict are limited by the rules of the political game. For example, two candidates for the same office are permitted to debate one another, to publicly campaign, to present speeches to all who will listen, to advocate their own position and criticize their opponent's positions, to advertise their candidacy, and so forth. These same two candidates, however, are not allowed to duel to decide the outcome, to lie about their abilities, to disrupt each other's rallies, to keep their opponent's supporters from casting ballots, or to bribe election officials. Thus, despite the distance between them on political issues, opposing candidates agree on the forms of conflict which are permitted in a political campaign.

Revolutionaries share with the political party presently out of office the desire to change the existing political leadership. The difference between them is that the disposed political party will observe the political norms and seek only to replace the leaders in office with their own leaders through the electoral process, while revolutionaries reject the established political norms. By not recognizing the rules, they feel free to resort to bombings, violence, and riots to express their dissatisfaction with the existing leadership. Often, revolutionaries seek to overthrow the entire government structure and replace it with a "better" form of government or none at all.

Revolutionary activities are not necessarily harmful. The civil rights movement in America utilized some rather revolutionary methods of change such as sit-ins, passive resistance, and poor people marches. These methods were supplemented by more traditional and acceptable measures such as law-suits, and together they brought about changes in American society which could not have been accomplished in the same amount of time by traditional methods alone.

Thus, revolutionaries are not persons with extreme political views so much as they are individuals who utilize other than traditional procedures for improving or changing the existing government. For this reason, writers have noted that stable governmental rule is dependent upon a consensus among opposing political candidates or parties with regard to basic governmental beliefs and norms. When the rules of the political game are no longer accepted by a significant number of people, that country may be said to have entered a pre-revolutionary stage. Therefore a revolution in any country must be preceded by a large-scale rejection of the normative political system. If this occurs, then "anything goes."

POLITICAL POWER

No society in recorded history has been able to avoid the effects and consequences of political power. Power, as defined by Max Weber, refers to the ability of a person, group, or institution to achieve its goals even when opposed.[4] Political power is a related concept with two major differences. First, political power is a scarce commodity. The president of the United States, the mayor of New York, the governor of Florida, as well as local commissioners and city councilmen, hold positions which can only be held by one man at a time. These positions are in turn important because the men who hold them have a say in the affairs of the state. (The term "state" is used by political sociologists in the same manner as government.) Second, political power is based upon the monopoly which each state holds on coercive force. Only the state can arrest a man, incarcerate a man, execute a man, raise an army, or go to war. These powers are entrusted to those men who manage somehow to attain one of those scarce positions of leadership. In sum, political power refers to the ability to attain positions (or to influence those who attain positions) which have control over the use of societal coercion.

Methods of Maintaining Power

The state may utilize three methods in various combinations to maintain power.

Violence is the most effective short-range method of retaining power. Over a long period of time, however, violence tends to decrease in effectiveness since the continuous use of physical force is self-defeating. The state is compelled to utilize increasingly severe methods which breed resistance.

Material benefits is a method by which a state may "buy" loyalty. If the state has a monopoly on the distribution of valuable goods, then it may maintain its power position by repaying loyalty. An obvious disadvantage of this method is that a complete monopoly on goods is impossible since those persons who receive the valuable goods from the state for their loyalty may, in turn, distribute them to others who may be loyal to their benefactors rather than to the state. Another disadvantage is that rebellion can also be bought for a price (presumably higher) by others.

Persuasion is the least expensive method because it does not require a large enforcement agency (i.e., police, army) or a complex system of collection and distribution. With this method the state attempts to hold power by enlisting the willing acceptance of at least a majority of the people over whom this power is exercised. Thus, persuasion is utilized to convince the majority that the authority and power held by the state is legitimate, justified, and beneficial. Weber has noted that in modern industrial societies any form of government must legitimate itself to the people in order to survive. In complex societies persuasion is the method most commonly used to achieve legitimation (and to maintain power). Accordingly, the citizens give the government legitimacy. They accept the government's right to exercise coercion and also believe that the state will use its power rightfully.

ATTITUDES TOWARD POLITICS

It should not surprise us that there exist various attitudes toward political power. At least two viewpoints may be suggested.

Politics Are Evil

Some take the attitude that political power is evil in origin and purpose. Augustine, in the fourth century, took the position that it was "unnatural" for man to rule over man, and that withdrawal from all things political in nature is mandatory. Thus, all forms of government and their objectives are viewed the same, regardless of how they are organized, who exerts political power, and for what purposes it is used. This viewpoint can be illustrated in modern America by those persons who believe that politics is a separate business of society apart from other societal functions. Therefore, any political power which maintains a minimum level of stability and which permits the individual to continue his daily social existence is legitimate.

Politics as a Tool

Thomas Aquinas countered Augustine's position by arguing that power relationships are not unnatural. This point of view looks upon political power as necessary, but is distrustful of political power and is concerned with controlling it. Control is accomplished by diluting power into legal relationships which elimate personal rule. Since political power is viewed as embracing all activities of man, government is viewed as a rational instrument to be used for desired and desirable ends. While this attitude resists the total politicizing of life and insists on the separate character of political power, it is concerned with the potential for a rational use of political power.

WHO HAS POLITICAL POWER?

One of the reasons for negative attitudes toward political power is the realization that political power is normally concentrated in the hands of a few persons. Neumann gives an explanation of the circumstances which lead to the concentration of power.[5] He notes that as a society becomes more complex, power groups will increasingly utilize secret techniques of rule. Since secrecy can best be preserved by a few persons, small ruling groups plot strategy. As a result, opposing parties must also resort to secrecy to effectively counter the moves by the opposition. The increasing complexity of society also leads to increasing stratification, which in turn causes a greater concentration of political power in certain groups. These small ruling groups, called oligarchies, are often composed of economically powerful men. Yet not all wealthy men are part of the power group. How do certain men obtain political power?

Obtaining Influence

Economic wealth does not guarantee political power unless one is able to translate economic power into influence. Influence can be obtained through countless methods and is potentially available to all.

You don't have to be rich to be President, but it helps

Some obtain influence by virtue of their ownership of property or the means of production. By owning a piece of land or a manufacturing plant, an owner can influence how the land will be used and who will be employed in the plant. Generally, the more a person owns, the greater will be his influence on the labor and commodity market. Influence over the economic realm often indirectly influences the political realm when the state finds economic growth desirable.

For non-owners, influence is generally obtained through organizations. Thus like-minded persons may speak out as a group rather than as individuals to have a greater impact. Generally, the larger the group the greater its influence. Examples of this type of influence are organized labor, cooperatives, and special interest groups. Owners also utilize organizations to obtain influence. The local Chambers of Commerce, employer's associations, and lobby groups organized by special interests act as pressure groups to influence local, state and national legislatures. The exact manner by which any group of men obtains influence varies considerably depending on local economic structure and social stratification of the community.

Political parties are the most obvious examples of organizations which attempt to obtain influence and translate it into political power. Political parties are headed by notable men with personal influence and attempt to recruit the assistance of thousands of volunteers, especially during elections years. Campaign workers collectively strive for mass support. The political party whose candidates are victorious regards itself as influential in determining the policies of the elected candidate. In this case, influence is directly related to political power.

Party politics serves to check egoistic interests. The democratic process requires that majority support be sought and thus political parties must present their interests (in the form of party platforms) as national interests. The fact that our political process requires candidates to take a stand on issues and the fact that party leaders must convince their regulars that these stands are to the best interest of the country prevents the domination of the party by the interests of a few men.

POWER POLITICS

Two questions can be asked with regard to the structure of power. First, since politics is not a neutral process and the politics of groups is a procedure that seems to operate to the advantage of some groups and to the disadvantage of other groups, it brings up this question: Which groups are favored? Second, power is patterned according to the interest structure of existing groups. That is, power tends to be shared among groups whose interests coincide. In the same manner, groups whose interests differ divide power between themselves. This generates this question: "Whose interests coincide?" As we shall see, these two questions are answered in distinct ways by opposing views on the structure of power.

American history has been categorized according to periods which are related to changes in the structure of power.[6] From the founding of the republic to the Jacksonian era, there was a clearly distinct and recognizable ruling group made up of wealthy land owners who produced the dominant crops (e.g., tobacco, cotton, corn) or shipped the goods to Europe and England. These members of the ruling class dominated not only the economic institutions but also the military, political, and social life of the early colonial period. One has only to look at the aristocratic background of our early Presidents to realize the important role played by a few notable families.

From the decline of Federalist leadership to the Civil War, power became more widely dispersed. During this period it was no longer possible to identify a sharply defined ruling group. While each community had its group of dominants, none were as powerful as certain groups had been during the colonial period.

From the Civil War to the Depression, American history showed a period of uncontrolled growth and supremacy of corporate economic power. Fueled by the industrial revolution, power and wealth once again became more concentrated. Interestingly enough, corporate power was largely a matter of economic domination with little influence upon other institutions.

There are two conflicting views of what has occurred in America since the Depression. C. Wright Mills sees the rise of the military-industrial complex as the major change in the structure of power. This mutually beneficial arrangement, Mills notes, now clearly dominates the American political system.[7] David Reisman, on the other hand, notes that one of the outcomes of the New Deal was a system of power which can best be described as a balance of pressure groups. Thus for Reisman the major change in the structure of power has been the rise of veto groups and rule by coalitions.[8]

These two points of view have resulted in a debate over who rules America. Mills contends that a small unified group of persons composed of top government officials, military officials, and corporation directors make up a "power elite." This group, according to Mills, is maintained through a series of interlocking directorates. This refers to the large number of boards of directors, boards of trustees, and other groups of decision makers which invariably include two or more of the power elite. Meetings of these groups provide opportunities for cooperation between businessmen and military officials, for example, in agreeing on policies which will solidify the coincidence of interests between themselves. Beneath the power elite, Mills describes two other levels of power. The middle level is composed of diverse interest groups who jockey among themselves in an effort to enlist the power elite on their side. At the lowest level are the powerless masses of unorganized people who are controlled and dominated by the power elite.

This viewpoint of elite ruling groups remains controversial for it questions the democratic procedures of this country. Democracy implies, according to Mills, that those vitally affected by any decision have an effective voice in that decision. In turn, this means that all power to make such decisions must be publicly legitimized and that the makers of such decisions must be held publicly accountable. Mills admits that the United States is generally a democratic nation, mainly in its legal structure and in its expectations, but small groups of men often make major decisions affecting our lives and an apathetic public allows these groups to continue making decisions for them. Furthermore, since these men hold non-official positions, they cannot be voted out of office nor are they necessarily responsible to the public or its needs.

Those who disagree with Mills argue that a power elite does not exist. They see major decisions as resulting from pressures placed on public officials by interest groups. The fact that each interest group is primarily concerned with its own particular necessities means that cooperation between interest groups will seldom occur. In fact, interest groups act as veto groups in that they work to prevent any other interest group from dominating. Thus, the self-interest of each group which conflicts with the self-interest of other groups prevents a power elite from forming. Since there is no power elite, there are only two levels of power in this scheme. The first level is the interest groups. The second level is composed of the masses of people whose support is sought by the various interest groups. (They are not seen as dominated, as in Mills' viewpoint.)

Recent community studies on decision making tend to support this viewpoint. A pyramidical leadership, one in which a few men make all the decisions, has not been frequently discovered. Instead most of these studies have found three basic decision making patterns. (1) Caucus—this is the situation where a relatively large group of individuals exist who make decisions through consensus. That is, they make decisions based on popular and widespread acceptance of their actions. (2) Polylith—in this situation, separate power structures are found for major spheres of community activity. Thus, government decisions are made by professional politicians, questions related to education are made by educators and related voluntary associations (e.g., PTA). In short, this pattern of decision making places the power for decision making in community service organizations which are in the hands of the business and professional subcommunity without large scale overlap. (3) Amorphous—in this situation there is no discernible or enduring pattern of decision making.

By now one can see that the two questions asked at the beginning of this section can indeed be answered differently. Mills would argue that the interests of the military establishment, top corporation heads, and top governmental officials coincide, and this power elite benefits to the disadvantage of the masses. Reisman would argue that power is divided between groups with differing interests and that the masses of people benefit as these groups seek support from the public for their viewpoints.

Elites, Mass Media, and Political Parties

The debate over the existence or nonexistence of ruling elites has resulted in some rather interesting debates on various other related topics. An example is the concept of the role of mass media. Mills believes that newspapers, radio, magazines, and especially television lull the masses by suppressing political topics and emphasizing entertainment. He believes that restricting political news and events to news programs keeps the public ignorant and unaware of what is really going on in the political world. As such, Mills looks at the mass media as a powerful tool. In the hands of the power elite it is used to keep the masses unaware, but in the hands of the non-elite it could be utilized to educate and mobilize the masses.

In contrast, Reisman believes that the mass media gives more attention to political affairs, political personalities, and political interpretations than the audience cares to see. As such, the media conveys what Reisman regards as a false impression that there is more interest in public affairs than really exists. Reisman does not regard the media as an important political instrument. He could note, for example, that despite the extensive coverage of national conventions and campaigns only about 55 percent of the eligible voters made it to the polls in the 1972 presidential election.

Still another contrast between these points of view can be made with regard to political parties. Mills views political parties as oligarchic organizations who allow the average citizen to exercise his rights to citizenship only when he votes between the alternatives presented to him by the competing organizations. Thus, voting is not a sufficient means of dealing with power in an age characterized by economic concentration and manipulation by huge military-industrial structures.

Reisman, on the other hand, reminds us that politics in a democratic society is primarily a struggle. The fact that each political party must appeal to an electorate larger than the immediate interest group (which may have a large say in party leadership) compels various interests to compromise or at least make adjustments. In the end, political parties are dependent upon support from an electorate who must be convinced that their proposed policies and candidates are also to their benefit and consistent with the democratic ideals in America.

SUMMARY

To understand political events, the political structure must be related to the entire social structure. Political sociology is concerned with social and political conflicts that lead to changes in the distribution of power. Political sociologists are also interested in the process of political socialization by which one is taught to interpret political activities. The family, schools, and peer groups help to form early attitudes but direct experience with the political realm determines if one will retain these attitudes or modify them.

Order perspectives were contrasted with process perspectives in their approach to political action. Conservativism, liberalism, and radicalism were described. It was noted that revolutionaries do not recognize the traditional norms and procedures for improving the existing political order.

Political power refers to the ability of groups to attain positions which include control over the use of force to influence change or squash resistance. Political power may be maintained by violence, material benefits, or persuasion. Attitudes toward political power may be negative in that politics may be viewed as evil and to be avoided, or politics may be viewed as a tool to be used for desired change.

Oligarchy refers to a situation in which rule and decision making is placed in the hands of a select few. Oligarchies exist because political struggle requires secrecy on matters of tactics, and secrecy can best be preserved by a few. Oligarchies are composed of men who are able to translate economic power into social power. This transformation is accomplished by the use of lobby groups, pressure groups, and political parties.

Politics is not a neutral process. Some groups are favored over other groups. Power is normally shared by groups with similar interests and divided between groups with differing interests. There are conflicting views as to which groups have been favored over other groups. C. W. Mills believes that a power elite exists composed of military leaders, top corporation heads, and top governmental officials. David Reisman contends that veto groups successfully prevent any interest group from dominating. These two contrasting views were illustrated to show how these viewpoints lead to differing conclusions about life in a democratic nation.

Notes

1. Richard E. Dawson and Kenneth Prewitt, *Political Socialization* (Boston; Little, Brown, 1969).

2. Ibid., p. 206.

3. Barrington Moore, Jr., "Sociological Theory and Contemporary Politics," *American Journal of Sociology* 61 (September 1955): 107–15.

4. Max Weber, *Essays in Sociology,* ed. H. H. Gerth and C. W. Mills (New York: Oxford University Press, 1946).

5. F. Neumann, "Approaches to the Study of Political Power," *Political Science Quarterly* 65 (June 1950): 161–80.

6. William Kornhauser, "Power Elite or Veto Groups," *in Culture and Social Character,* ed. S. Lipset and L. Lowenthal (New York: Free Press, 1961).

7. C. Wright Mills, *The Power Elite* (New York: Oxford University Press, 1956).

8. David Reisman, *The Lonely Crowd* (New York: Doubleday Anchor, 1953).

Thinking
Sociologically

1.   Ask your parents who the most powerful man in America is. Do you think many of them will say, "the president"? Ask them why they think so and record their answers. Compare your results with those from other students.

2.   Look at some campaign speeches and look for quotes or statements meant to appeal to the national interest.

3.   Look in your newspaper for decisions made by "somebody out there" that affect the lives of many people including yourself. How can you explain the fact that you were not asked for your opinion?

4.   Some people say that anyone can grow up to be president. Is it likely that you will be president of the United States? Why or why not?

5.   Write a brief political speech for a candidate who wants a bill passed to permit ownership of slaves. Keep in mind that the majority of people would have to vote in favor of the bill for it to become law.

Chapter 12

Cognitive
Objectives

This chapter is designed to acquaint you with a sociological perspective on religion. Without drawing conclusions on the truth or untruth of any religion or denomination, the sociologist examines religion as one element of human behavior. He looks for patterns of behavior, similarities, and differences in religious expression. Look for the following as you read this chapter:

1. *The diversity of religious expression*
2. *The meaning of the term "surrogate religion"*
3. *The meaning of the terms "sacred" and "profane"*
4. *The meaning of the term "religion" as defined by Durkheim and how he related religion to "totemism"*
5. *The social functions of religion*
6. *The characteristics of "institutionalized religion" and the "routinization of charisma"*
7. *The difference between a church and a sect*
8. *The meaning of the terms cult, myth, and theology*
9. *The effect of secularization on religion*
10. *The effect of urbanization upon the expression of religion in our society*

Hell Fire
and
Holy Water

The sociologist, whether or not he is himself a religious person, is interested in religious expression as one aspect of human behavior. Some of the questions which he asks about religion in our society would include the following: What purposes (or functions) does religion perform in a society? How is religion expressed in human behavior and what effect does religion have on that behavior? How does social structure affect religion? What effects does religion have on social structure?

DEFINING RELIGION

Before we begin to look at the expression of religion in society, perhaps a word of clarification is necessary. Religion is a difficult subject to define. This is true not only because easily identifiable religious activity is so diverse, but because irreligious, even anti-religious activity can take on such a "religious" outlook in attitude and behavior that it may be viewed as surrogate (or substitute) religion. Fanatical believers can be attracted to a political movement, an ideological cause, or even an athletic event. These persons' evangelistic fervor and adherence to a body of dogmatic principles can look a lot like "religious" conviction. Even communism, with its commitment to atheism, has been referred to as a "religion." With all the diversity of specifically religious expression and the multitude of non-religious "religions," to what does a sociologist refer when he speaks of religion?

Emile Durkheim, a French sociologist writing in the early part of this century, differentiated between the *sacred* and the *profane.* Sacred, for him, meant those aspects of "what men think" or believe which are "set apart or forbidden." Sacredness has to do with transcendent or ultimate things. The profane, on the other hand, is concerned with everything else. It is the realm of commonplace things, the routine, the everyday. The sacred transcends the profane.

For Durkheim, religion is any belief system, with its appropriate behavior, which helps man define and relate to the sacred. The world's "great" religions such as Buddhism, Judaism, Islam, Christianity, Hinduism, as well as the religious or other-worldly beliefs of primitive societies, are examples of man's efforts to define the sacred. Churches, mosques, and temples become instruments or material vehicles which help man relate to the sacred. Theologies as well as rites and rituals are designed to enable the adherents of a religion to behave and believe in accordance with their definition of the sacred.

Durkheim argued that religion had its source in primitive "totemism." This term is used to describe the practice of choosing a sacred animal or object as the embodiment of the sacred. Primitive tribes

Many activities can have "religious" aspects.

select as their totem some animate or inaminate object and look upon it as the representation of their definition of the sacred. The religion of the group is tied up in the totem. The prescribed methods of relating to the sacred become identified with the totem and the displeasure of the spirit world can be incurred by offending the totem with some kind of disobedience. Rituals of appeasement were useful for reducing the ire of the totem and returning the group to the totem's good pleasure. Modern societies of western civilization continue to have their totem, said Durkheim. The totem is, however, the non-objectified (unseen) monotheistic God.

In so arguing Durkheim has made an interesting point. The totem among primitives is the voice and will of the society. The group defines the content and nature of the sacred as well as the correct manner of behaving in relationship with the sacred. The totem only represents the definition. God's voice, it follows, is then the voice of society. Group norms, as well as the definition of the content of sacredness, is made known through the voice and will of God.[1]

It is interesting to note, with respect to Durkheim's argument, that the word religion comes from a Latin word which means "to bind." Religion is a force that preserves norms of belief and behavior which help to bind the individual and the society into solidarity. The sacred makes demands upon the believer and is binding in its ethical imperatives and moral obligations.

To summarize, religion may be defined as a system of belief, with its appropriate behavior, which helps man define and relate to the sacred. The expression of religion within a society is made through rites and rituals as well as through the manipulation of external objects (such as buildings, crosses, sacred books, and statues) in accordance with the belief system.

THE SOCIAL FUNCTIONS OF RELIGION

The question at this point is what religion does for the individual and for society. We may assume that those patterns of behavior which do not have a function in society either cease to exist or enjoy no more than marginal existence. Since religion is an integral part of every known society, we may also assume that it helps provide for the fulfillment of necessary functions in the social fabric. Religion functions in a socially needed way or it would not have the universal appeal which it demonstrably enjoys. What then are those functions?

Explanation of Suffering
Beliefs which are more or less systematized and have to do with the content of appropriate behavior in given situations offer strength and

consolation to the individual. One aspect of religion is that it is concerned, at least in part, with the explanation of human suffering. Buddhism, for example, is based upon the overcoming of suffering associated with death, starvation, old age, and illness. The Christian religion places the death of Christ at the center of its belief system, and Jesus' concern with the old, infirm, and outcast takes up a major portion of the gospels.

Religion gives significance to unexplainable events of hardship and misery which are a part of the human experience. One suffers because God punishes sin or "tries" a person's faith. The sudden destructive storm, the death of a child, a war, an incurable illness, even the loss of a job can be placed within some framework of religious meaning. The result for the individual is support, consolation, and strength in the face of his own (or other's) adversity.

Marx felt that the consoling role of religion can function as an opiate in society. That is, the injustices of the social structure which are responsible for some types of human misery are left intact and

Religion can console and give strength.

unchallenged because they are "God's will." Such feelings impede social reform by placing the attention of those who suffer most from earthly injustice on heavenly rewards. The result for society is a more stable and less changing social environment.

Strengthening Norms

Social control stemming from the binding nature of religion has already been mentioned. Societal stability is further enhanced by religion's capacity to "sacralize" the norms and values prevalent in the social order. The religious organization is a principle agent in the socialization process. In our society, the values of hard work, honesty, diligence, achievement, success, and individual progress are emphasized in religious services and teachings. These social values are made sacred by placing them in a religious context.

The believer is taught the content of "wrongdoing" or sin. He learns the appropriate feelings of guilt associated with a specific act of disobedience. His religion also communicates to him methods of eliminating these feelings of guilt. In such a manner, the church contributes to social control and indirectly to the stability of the society.

Couching these secular norms in religious terms creates the impression of absolute or eternal truth. Such is the source of one dilemma of the church in modern society. Changing circumstances of social existence may cause some canons of "absolute" truth to lose their appropriateness. Since truth is supposed to be eternal, it is difficult for the church to adapt to a changing society. Religion must often defend outdated dogma in the midst of a rapidly developing society. For example, the Christian church for centuries condemned the theory that the earth revolved around the sun. Darwin's theory of evolution was likewise stubbornly rejected. More recently, even in the face of widespread overpopulation, "artificial" birth control is prohibited by some religious establishments. Making certain norms "sacred" contributes to social stability, but it can place religion in conflict with a rapidly changing society.

Individual Identity

To the degree that religious organizations are successful in socializing individuals into the normative structure, they contribute to the development of the individual's self-concept. By his acceptance of the societal norms for behavior, the individual learns what is expected of him and is given a standard by which to measure how well he is doing with reference to these expectations. Religion therefore helps him develop a self-image. Continual participation in religious ceremonies

I'm a good boy if I don't do it and a bad boy if I do

reinforces the individual's self-understanding. These ceremonies also give him opportunity to relieve the guilt associated with failure to live up to expectations. By being "forgiven," he can maintain a positive self-image.

The identity of the individual is expanded in connection with the concept of the ultimate. That is, believers are tied to the ultimate in the sense that the eternal becomes a part of himself and he a part of the eternal. The Christian religion's emphasis on God's providence and God's "plan" for the world are instances of this kind of thinking. Within the framework of God's plan, the Christian lives out his life. As Kingsley Davis puts it, "religion gives the individual a sense of identity with the distant past and the limitless future. It expands his ego by making his spirit significant for the universe and the universe significant for him."[2]

Identifying Others

Religion provides a further social function by assisting individuals to identify and position others. Will Herberg speaks of the "three religions of democracy," referring to Protestantism, Catholicism, and Judaism.[3] The answer to the question "What is your religion?" usually falls within one of the three categories and becomes a cue to the questioner which helps him, on the basis of his perception of these three religious systems, to understand and position the answerer. The respondent's specific denomination or his degree of adherence to his specific religious system may be explained as the conversation continues. Who the other person is and how he relates to his world, as well as much of the normative structure which guides his behavior, may be determined by his religous perspective. In a fast moving urban society where contact is frequently brief and cursory and where relationships are quickly made and just as rapidly broken, such cues for identity are necessary. Religion provides one such avenue for rapidly positioning those we meet in such contexts.

Societal Criticism

Religion may be the source of criticisms of the existing social order. O'Dea says, "Religion may also provide standards of value in terms of which institutionalized norms may be critically examined and found seriously wanting."[4] For example, some Old Testament prophets, as well as Jesus and many early followers of the Christian religion, engaged in social protest of established governmental and societal forms. More recently, priests, rabbis, and ministers have played different types of leadership and supportive roles in the civil rights movement in this country.

Most frequently, this function of religion is performed by isolated individuals and their band of followers. Organized religion in the form of denominational churches infrequently engage in social protest. Furthermore, it is not at all infrequent that social dissenters face the brunt of social sanctions from the religious denomination of which they are a part. It is true, of course, that leadership for the early civil rights movements came from black religious leaders and that meetings for black protests were frequently held in black churches. This was true not so much because of the nature of the denominational religion of the blacks as simply because the ministers were among the best educated of the blacks, and few buildings other than churches were available for black meetings.

Religion, in summary, performs a consoling and strengthing function for the individual and it enables him to make a religious interpretation of the problems he and others confront in life. By sacralizing the norms of the society, religion performs a socializing function and is effective in social control. The socializing function of religion helps to create a normative structure for the individual within which he developes a self-image and, therefore, functions in the area of individual identity. Religious affiliation of other individuals is useful in placing them within categories. Finally, religion may help to create individuals who are critical of the established social, political, and economic conditions prevalent within a society.

THE INSTITUTIONALIZATION OF RELIGION

Religious expression for the majority of Americans is experienced through the major denominations of Christianity. These denominations of Christianity represent organized religion in the form of well-defined groups with entrenched denominational boundaries, ordered worship services, dogmatic creeds, ethical imperatives, and an established professional religious leadership. In our society, then, there are organizations whose reason for being is essentially religious.

Such a pattern of religious expression, known as institutionalized religion, may be distinguished from the pattern characteristic of primitive societies and some subcultures of American society. In these groups, religious functions are not relegated to a specific organization. Religious acts are more diffuse and cut across all aspects of the culture. The family, the work group, recreational organizations, and other forms of human association have important responsibilities of a religious nature. There may be individuals such as witch doctors who are religious (or magical) specialists. However, the explicitly religious organization is rare.

The Routinization of Charisma

Institutionalization of religion involves, according to O'Dea, "a stable set of statuses and roles, defined in terms of function, upon which are rights and obligations. There arises a structure of offices which involves a stratified set of rewards in terms of prestige, life opportunities, and material compensation."[5] In other words, institutionalized religion demands, at a minimum, a professional clergy. The development of professional religious leadership and the creation of institutionalized religion was referred to by Max Weber as "the routinization of charisma."

Religions, Weber observed, are founded by a charismatic leader and a band of followers. The authority of the leader stems from his charismatic appeal, which is spontaneously acknowledged by his disciples. With the death or disappearance of the leader, the group experiences a crisis of continuity. Who or what shall constitute the authority originally associated with the leader's charisma? The desire to continue the group and its original religious experience makes necessary the establishment of new approaches to the charisma and the authority it carries. The extablishment of a permanent, stable community of followers necessitates the development of traditions linked to the original leader and the establishment of new leaders to whom the mantle of the original leader's authority has passed. These new leaders will speak in the old leader's name and interpret his words, most of which are soon canonized in a holy book. This position is based upon the fact that they were chosen by the original leader or by those previously holding the position. Tactics such as apostolic succession assure the continuation of a leadership which is authoritative. Most denominations have some ritual of ordination in which specific acts are performed to symbolize the transmission of authority.

The history of the Christian church has followed the pathway of the routinization of Jesus' charisma. Denominations in protestantism have similar histories; for example, the development of Lutheranism from Martin Luther, Presbyterianism from John Calvin, and Methodism from John Wesley.

Sects and Churches

Ernest Troeltsch, the German sociologist, has distinguished between what he called a *sect* and a *church*.[6] Put at its simplest, the *church* is a large, formal association with an elaborate hierarchy of professional leaders. It seeks to perpetuate its dogma, to expand its core of spiritual influence, and to maintain itself within the social system. Its order of worship, symbols and rituals, and ethical demands are firmly fixed and well known to its constituents.

Troeltsch described the church as having a broad membership base, i.e., drawing its adherents from all parts of a society. Further, a church develops political alignments with the government and the ruling classes. These facts, taken together, dictate that a certain type of pliability be characteristic of a church. Troeltsch recognized the function of the church in stablizing the existing order by developing these alignments. However, in weaving the state and ruling classes into her fabric, the church becomes dependent upon the upper classes and must be sensitive to change and developments in these classes. This dependency means that the church must always be ready to *compromise*.

The church is also characterized by rigidity of ecclesiastical structure. Established relationships in the heirarchy are inflexible and unchanging. Rigidity is the case, likewise, in the area of dogma. Eternal truth, it seems, must change slowly and the church is saddled with the anomaly of protecting against any heretic the absoluteness of absolute truth.

Sects, on the other hand, are groups which arise to challenge and repudiate the compromises and/or the inflexible heirarchy and dogma of the church. They are protesters (the source of the word "protestant").

Sects are loosely organized, usually around a leader, a few lieutenants, and a band of followers. They are nummerically small. Power and status rankings are not clear and worship is spontaneous, unorganized, often loud, and sometimes hysterical.

Repeatedly the history of the Christian church has underscored the tendency of sects to become churches. Second- and third-generation members of sectarian movements are removed from the original problems giving rise to their sect. Sooner or later the positions of authority are rigidified, dogma becomes inflexible, and the sect, as the church from which it seceded, becomes unable to meet the human needs it confronts. At such a point, conditions are ripe for the emergence of a new sect.

Cult, Myth, and Theology

The expression of religion in either a sect or a church involves symbols of worship in the form of rituals and liturgies, a set of beliefs which are perpetuated, and, in the more institutionalized organizations, a rational and systematic statement of theology. These three forms of religious expression may be termed cult, myth, and theology.

Cult refers to the gestures, words, and other symbols which are used in worship. These symbols are the acting out of feelings and are understood by worshippers to have specific meanings. For example,

Statues may be a part of the "cult" of a religion.

the practice of bowing one's head or kneeling during prayer is ostensibly the expression of a feeling of reverence and contriteness in the presence of the Almighty.

Cultic acts are the core of worship. The liturgy of worship surrounds the enactment of symbolic acts and involves the manipulation of physical vehicles (like crosses or books or water) that are an intergal part of the expression of feelings. Songs, sermons, sacrifice, prayer, and Bible reading are all cultic acts. Baptism and the Eucharistic meal (Communion or the Lord's Supper) are cultic acts in all Christian denominations as are the other sacraments of the Roman Catholic church. The cult becomes important in celebrating important events such as puberty, marriage, illness, or death.

Standardization of the cult is a normal part of the institutionalization of religion. These acts normally begin as spontaneous expressions of feeling and gradually are rigidified into systematic forms. Each new generation of believers must be taught the proper forms of cultic expression as well as their meaning. There remains the danger that standard symbols become routinized and lose their meaning. Symbolic acts become perfunctory and are carried out as an end in themselves rather than as an expression of what they symbolize. The symbol loses its power to create the feelings and attitudes for which it was originally designated.

It would perhaps be more proper to say that, rather than symbols losing their meaning, new meanings become associated with cultic acts. Communion was probably a time of fellowship for early Christians which commemorated the resurrection of Jesus. It was associated with spontaneous worship. Communion for modern Christians does not take this form and probably does not have the symbolic meaning it had for the early Christians. Today it is a rite, associated with proper worship of God. One partakes to please God (for what reason he is not sure), but partaking leaves the believer with the sure knowledge that he has in fact done what God requires. Thus communion today may symbolize no more than the believer's good intent.

Myth, on the other hand, has to do with beliefs. At the simplest level, myth is the effort to express in words the believer's understanding of the nature of God, the world, the meaning of life, and the meaning of death. Myth is not based upon logic or rational thought. It is expressive of emotional thought. The statement "God loves man" is an example of myth. This is the statement of a belief at a feeling level. The speaker is emotionally assured that the statement is true. It is a belief for which there can be no empirical verification. The parable of creation with which the Bible opens is another example. The writer of these stories was expressing a feeling that a rather loving and all powerful being brought all that he saw about him into existence.

The effort to rationalize myth leads to a *theology.* Religious specialists in the form of professional clergy attempt to systematize myth into a logical and coherent whole. The result of their efforts is a more or less consistent and reasoned statement of the religious tradition and beliefs of the faith. A rational ethic or statement of morals accompanies the development of a systematic theology.

The intellectualized theology created by the clergy is, to a limited degree, transmitted to the laity. However, there remains in the mind of the believer, because of his lack of formal religious training, a mixture of myth and theology.

The effort to develop a rational theology may be one way the church has sought to remain relevant in a changing society. The German theologian Rudolph Bultmann has made an appeal for what he calls demythologizing christianity.[7] He explains this term as the effort to strip away the inconsistencies of the primitive statements of myth and to restate the core of truth found within the myth in a more modern way. Ancient truth (the church, you see, continues to proclaim the idea of an unchanging truth) can be revealed to modern man in a more palatable fashion through demythologizing.

SOCIAL TRENDS AFFECTING RELIGION

Secularization

O'Dea points out that the role of the church with reference to secularization is varied. He states, "the highly religious life of the medieval university and the medieval city, so much a product of the ideas of Christianity, was the locus of considerable secularization and prepared for the more marked secularization of the Renaissance. The church sponsored activities in intellectual life, in art, in political life, and even in business, which hastened and contributed to the process." The church then was both sponsor and opponent of the increase in rationality in the thinking of men.

That religion was a partial sponsor of secularization is borne out by historical research. Yet, to a large degree the process of secularization is a force that moved through western civilization which the church was forced to confront and to which it ultimately had to conform. Secularization involves the diminishing of the sacred. Explanations of phenomena are increasingly based upon rational, logical thinking and the cause and effects of tenets of science. "This worldly" rather than "other worldly" value orientations have become increasingly more important, especially in Protestant denominations. Involvement of clergymen in nonreligious community affairs is an outstanding example of this development. Their interest in civil rights, drug addiction, marital problems, crime, and other social problems is evidence of their increasing "this worldly" perspective. The religious overtones and popularity of such things as the "power of positive thinking" and "peace of mind" movements show the layman's willingness to have "other worldly" religious truth secularized.

Rather than forecasting the ultimate demise of religion, secularization may be one explanation for the increasing popularity of religion in American society. The reinterpretation of Christian truth in secular terms represents an effort of the church to change with a changing society. Such change makes religion more relevant to modern man, and insures the continuation of the appearance of religious and devotional literature on best-seller lists.

Some arms of the church have, however, refused to go along with this trend toward a secular religion. Advocates of this more fundamentalist approach have offered a conservative, nostalgic return to the past. Individuals who are overwhelmed by the rapid pace of a changing urban society may find a welcome relief in the appeal to rural values and an idealized, unchanging religion. Terms, phrases, liturgies, and hymns which they experienced as children (or during more stable periods of their life) may, because of simple familiarity, be of comfort. The refusal to secularize in religion may be denial of the secularization of the total society in which they live.

Urbanization

The impact of urbanization on social arrangements in general will be discussed in chapter 13. The religious institution has felt this impact. A study of the conversion of Puerto Ricans in New York City to Pentacostlism is an illustration of the effect of urbanization on religion.[9] The authors of this study report that new migrants experienced maltreatment in the large city. They were alone, uprooted from old groups, and surrounded by strange customs and peoples. Storefront churches of the Pentacostal variety of Protestantism offered warm friendship and close ties to the estranged newcomers. Values of Pentacostalism were espoused enthusiastically by church members. "Regeneration" in the form of breaking with the old life and beginning anew was offered to those wishing to accept it. Converts among the Puerto Ricans were numerous.

According to the authors, there was a sinfulness–conversion–regeneration cycle which conformed with the actual life experiences of the converts. The sense of loss, confusion, and uncertainty which accompanied their migration to New York represents the period of disorganization referred to in their repeated testimonials of sinfulness. Conversion means the sense of reorganization which they experienced in finding and joining the warm Pentacostal community of believers. Regeneration is descriptive of their new life immersed in the values of the highly supportive fellowship of their new group. Evidently, the anxieties and disorientation characteristic of new migrants to large cities creates a vacuum into which fundamentalist faiths may pour their message of sin, conversion, and regeneration. The quest for meaningful community in strange surroundings is fulfilled by these religious groups.

Demographic changes within cities have also demanded commensurate changes in churches. The mass "white flight" of middle class citizens to the suburbs has caused the movement of white middle class (usually Protestant) churches to the same areas. The proliferation of churches of various denominational brands and their phenomenal growth in membership and budgets is explained, at least in part, by the equally phenomenal growth of white suburbia.

SUMMARY

The purpose of this chapter has been to present the meaning, functions, and changes within religion as viewed from the sociological point of view. Religion, it was said, may be defined as any belief system, along with its rituals and ethical standards, which defines and enables man to relate to the "sacred." The sacred is the area of the ultimate which transcends the profane or the routine. What is defined as sacred is socially determined and, therefore, may vary from one society (or subculture) to another. It follows that the rituals, ethics, and vehicles for expressing religion will differ according to the nature of that defined as sacred.

Religion serves a number of useful functions for the individual and the society. In the face of the harsh facts of human suffering, religion may give consolation and strength through "explaining" crises from some framework of meaning. By sacralizing some norms and values in a society, religion socializes its adherents to the normative structure and, by imposing such factors as guilt, is effective in social control. In such a manner, religion helps to stabilize a society. Additionally, the socializing of individuals is effective in helping the person to develop a self-identity. Religion may also serve as a cue to identify and position others one may meet in society. Finally, religion may function in a capacity of social criticism.

In American society, religion is largely institutionalized. This fact means that there are organized groups whose functional speciality is religious in essence. Authority in these organizations has undergone what is called the routinization of charisma. Traditions have developed by which the charismatic authority of some persons in the past has been conferred upon individuals who occupy a specified social position in the organization. Churches, the sociological term used to designate these large formal structures, are to be distinguished from sects. The latter are more spontaneous, loosely organized, and created as splinter groups to protest alleged failures and discrepancies in the churches. Sects, it seems, have a history of developing into churches.

Religious expression includes cult, myth, and theology. Cult refers to the ritual practices and manipulation of physical objects which symbolize feelings and become vehicles for expressing these emotions. Myth is used to describe the beliefs of religious emotion, while theology is the result of an effort to put the myths into a logical or systematic order.

Secularization and urbanization appear to be two important social forces which have significant impact upon religion in American society. Secularization involves a diminishing of the sacred. More and more phenomena are explained by logical reasoning and the cause and effect tenets of science. Religion is forced to make compensating changes which effect its own secularization. Urbanization may have a disorganizing effect upon recent immigrants which results not infrequently in their seeking out religious communities. Demographic changes in the city, and especially the flight of white middle-class citizens, have led to the suburbanizing of religion. The vacuum left within the city has created the opportunity for sectarian growth of the fundamentalist type.

Notes

1. Emile Durkheim, *The Elementary Forms of Religious Life* (New York: Macmillan, 1926).

2. Kingsley Davis, *Human Society* (New York: Macmillan, 1948), p. 531.

3. Will Herberg, *Protestant, Catholic, Jew* (Garden City, N.Y.: Doubleday, 1955).

4. Thomas O'Dea, *The Sociology of Religion* (Englewood Cliffs, N.J.: Prentice-Hall, 1966), p. 14.

5. Ibid., p. 91.

6. Ernest Troeltsch, *The Social Teaching of the Christian Churches* (New York: Macmillan, 1931).

7. Rudolph Bultmann, *Primitive Christianity* (New York: Merican Books, 1956).

8. O'Dea, *The Sociology of Religion*, p. 88.

9. Renato Poblete, S. J. and Thomas O'Dea, "Anomie and the Quest for Community: The Formation of Sects Among the Puerto Ricans of New York," *American Catholic Sociological Review* 21 (1960): 25–32.

Thinking
Sociologically

1.   Some social observers suggest that religion, especially Protestantism, in rural America of a few decades ago was a chief form of entertainment. That is, going to church was a form of community gathering, offered opportunity for self-expression in leadership roles, and provided an important avenue of community solidarity. Can you think of organizations which, in urban American, have in some ways supplanted this entertainment role of the church? Can you think of ways which modern Christianity has changed to counter these developments in order to maintain its social role?

2.   Cult, as was suggested, refers to ritual acts and physical objects which are expressions or symbols of religious feelings. Attend a religious service and look for cultic acts and objects. Start with the building itself and follow the entire worship service. What words, phrases, and objects are used to convey religious symbolism? Notice also the various ways in which cultic acts reinforce popular values of our society.

3.   Religion serves society by functioning as an agent of social control. This is true for ardent religious persons. Is it also true for those who are not professing religious individuals? Can you think of ways in which the existence of religious organizations in a community have an impact on the life of the total community? Can you think of ways in which government uses religion as an agent of control? What about ways in which religion uses government through which to express its control?

4.   Some people, including religious persons, have a negative and critical view of religion. Assume that you had the power to improve the religious system. Write a brief description of what your improved version would be like.

PART SIX

Urban Sociology and Bureaucracy

Chapter 13

Cognitive
Objectives

This chapter will present the sociological view of the city. As you will note, sociologists attempt to view the city as one setting within which human behavior takes place. Among the important ideas which you should look for are the following:

1. *The factors necessary before a city may appear*
2. *Some of the ways that cities have been defined*
3. *The definition of the term "city"*
4. *What cities have in common*
5. *How cities differ from one another*
6. *The characteristics of urban living*
7. *The meaning of the term human ecology*
8. *The problems at the root of the urban crisis*
9. *What city planning is*

Cement City

THE ORIGINS OF THE CITY

One overwhelming characteristic of our modern era is urbanization. Some historians note that the city appeared at about the time that man made the transition from wandering, food-gathering bands to a settled existence. Thus some conclude that the city represents one of the great achievements of man and deserves to be ranked along with the discovery of fire, agriculture, and the wheel. Perhaps this is overstating the case, but there is no doubt that the appearance of the first cities represents that period of time when man advanced his civilization to a height never before attained.

Consider what is required for a city to appear. First of all, agricultural technology (the methods of growing food crops) must be advanced enough to result in a surplus. If each family can produce only enough to provide for their own existence, the lack of excess food requires that all others also engage in farming to feed themselves. When a food surplus does exist, a person may devote all or part of his time to non-agricultural trades or tasks such as weaving, tailoring, candlemaking, or pottery making. Obviously, if it takes ten farmers to feed one city-dwelling candlemaker, then only a limited number of persons may give up an agricultural life in favor of candlemaking or any other non-farm job. As farming methods improve, it becomes possible for greater numbers of people to live together spending most of their time producing goods which were traded to the farmer in return for food.

249

Not only is a surplus of food necessary—a surplus of people is also essential. In all societies, population growth can only occur when the number of babies born exceed the number of deaths in the group. Early tribes experienced times of plenty and periods of famine. Thus, although birth rates by our standards today were exceedingly high, so were the rates of infant deaths, deaths resulting from childbearing, and deaths resulting from disease, infection, and epidemics. This irregular pattern of births and deaths counteracting each other made numerical growth a slow and uneven process dependent upon the harshness of the environment. In order for cities to appear, a civilization must attain some control over the major causes of death, while maintaining approximately the same rate of births in order to have people who need not work in the fields but can devote their life to producing goods in exchange for food.

Thus, in summary, we can see that before the first city ever appeared, civilized man had achieved a high enough level of agriculture to support a non-agricultural segment. In addition, medical technology had advanced to the point that births exceeded deaths by a significant number. Not discussed, but also important, are advancements in communication and transportation both essential to allow access from the city to the surrounding areas.

WHAT IS NOT A CITY?

No one who has been in a large metropolitan city where millions of people live could question whether that place should be called a city. But what about those places that surround most metropolitan cities that are smaller and which appear to have only some of the characteristics of that city? Exactly at what point does a populated area become a city? Writers have tried various definitions to decide what is a city and what is not a city. The following discussion follows the arguments of Tomlinson and notes the problems involved with several of the most common criteria for a city.[1]

Population

A minimum number of people is used by the Census Bureau to officially designate a city. If a place has 2500 or more people then the Census Bureau considers that place to be a city. The fact that people may be distributed in a rather small area or in a rather large area has resulted in various other minimum numbers. For example, in Denmark a country with limited space and small population, only 200 people are required for a place to be officially considered to be a city.

On the other hand, in Greece, a country with limited space but a large population, 10,000 people are required for a place to officially be called a city. Thus the minimum population necessary for a city is not the same in every country, but depends upon the amount of land and the size of the population of each country.

Structures

Some have suggested that cities should be defined as a place where the buildings, roads and houses are so built up that they blot out the natural countryside. Anyone who has ever driven from the country to the city realizes that the city does, indeed, block out most of the natural environment. With today's modern land moving equipment it is possible to fill in valleys, flatten hills, cut a gap through a mountain, or even create a lake. The methods we use to construct buildings, such as reinforced concrete and elevators, allow us to build larger, taller, and more awesome structures which dominate our view and block out the countryside.

A city's structures dominate the horizon.

The problem with a definition such as this is that it tries to define a city in terms of things instead of people. Using this definition, it is possible that an oil refinery or grain elevators located in an empty field could be defined as cities, since their size and breadth also block out the natural countryside. Thus it is not sufficient merely to look at buildings—one must also take urban dwellers into account.

Occupations

It has been suggested that the best way to define cities is by looking at the kinds of jobs held by the inhabitants. It is well known that urban dwelling people do not farm, but work at industrial, commercial, and service occupations. Thus it is suggested that if we compare the number of people in industrial, commercial, and service occupations with the number in agricultural occupations, it will be possible to determine if the people of this place in question are urban or rural. There are several difficulties with this definition, the most obvious of which is the fact that there are no guidelines as to the percentage of workers who must be engaged in non-agricultural jobs before a place may be considered to be a city. Another problem is that it is possible for a small company town, where most of the jobs available are at the local factory, to be considered a city since the majority of workers are industrial workers. Under this criteria, mining towns and coal towns would have to be considered to be cities, which is unrealistic.

Center of Activities

Some have suggested that cities are the place where government and religious functions tend to focus, and thus cities may be defined by locating the religious and political centers for each region. This definition may have been useful in the past, when cathedrals and palaces were inevitably located in the largest and most important centers, but in the United States it is not uncommon to find the capital of a state in a medium-sized city, not in the largest and most important economic center in that state. For example, the capitals of the states of New York, Florida, California, and Texas are located in cities which are small in comparison to the metropolises of New York City, Miami, Los Angeles, and Houston. The exceptions rule out the usefulness of this method for defining cities.

Life Styles

Still another way to define what is or is not a city has been suggested by those who point to the fact that the city is more than anything else a way of life. They note that city life is characterized by indifference, impersonal relationships, and secondary controls. Thus, they suggest that a city can be distinguished from a non-city by studying the life styles of the inhabitants. If the inhabitants of a place act like city dwellers, then that place should be considered a city whatever its size, or occupations. It should be obvious to you that determining if people are not friendly enough or how often people have indifferent attitudes is not at all simple. Such problems make it difficult to use this definition.

Combinations

Having looked at a few of the past attempts, let's ask our original question, "What is a city?" Perhaps the best manner of answering the question is to combine what appears to be the most central concepts of the previously discussed ideas. Thus, a city is a large number of people living in a built-up area, working at non-agricultural jobs, producing goods and supplying services, and distributing those goods and services in exchange for raw materials and food; and who, as a result of working in a complex metropolitan center, develop a way of life characterized by anonymity, impersonal contacts with others, and secondary controls.[2]

This definition of the city recognizes that a large number of people are essential, without specifying a minimum number. It also takes into consideration the occupations usually held by urban dwellers and, finally, it takes into account the style of life characteristic of urban dwellers in general. All three must be present, to some degree, if a place is to be called a city. Now that we have some idea of what a city is, let us discuss the way cities are similar and the ways they differ.

CITIES: SIMILARITIES AND DIFFERENCES

There are several common features that characterize all cities, whether one is talking about ancient Athens, imperial Rome, or modern London. Among these common features are the following: no city is self-supporting. The fact that a city exists implies that farmers also exist somewhere with a surplus to feed the urbanites. Every city dominates a region, drawing raw materials and people from it in return for providing services not normally available to the people in the rural areas. Every city is located at the intersection of important roads and highways, which are essential for the efficient exchange of urban products for agricultural goods. Each city is also dependent upon other neighboring cities for products and trained people not available in the immediate area. An example of this dependence would be the city of Detroit and its massive auto industry. But the steel needed for the body of the car is made in Pittsburg or Bethlehem, Pennsylvania. The tires come from Akron, Ohio and the transmission, brakes, and suspension are all produced in still other cities.

In all cities, the division of labor is more complex than in rural areas. This means that there are a greater number of occupations and a greater specialization within occupations. Think about the number of jobs available to a person in one large office building in any metropolitan center. At the top of the occupational scale, there must be executives, vice presidents, managers, and administrative assistants. There must also be some secretaries, file clerks, salesmen, draftsmen and commercial artists. Finally, at the bottom of the scale, there is a need for mailroom clerks, elevator operators, and janitors. All the jobs cannot be listed here, but these illustrate the many levels of occupations found in most large business offices. When you take factories, restrauants, theatres, and shopping centers into account, the number of occupations rises considerably. There is also increased specializa-

tion, which refers to the situation in which a person is responsible for one narrow and specific task. Thus, in the office building we discussed above, it is not unusual to find a vice president in charge of sales, one in charge of production, still another in charge of personnel and possibly six or seven others with different responsibilities. The idea behind specialization is that by focusing upon one concern the person can do a better job. The facts also tend to imply that the generalist or the person who knows a little about everything is not as desirable as a person who knows a lot about only one thing.

Another common feature of most cities is that inhabitants of cities tend to be heterogeneous, that is, different from one another. They are more often from diverse origins and cultures, they are racially and physically distinct, and have a great deal of variation in their religious beliefs, political attitudes, and the ways in which they spend their free time.

All cities at all times have been characterized by internal disorder to some degree. Thus no cities have ever existed which did not make provisions for policing the population. Finally, all cities develop characteristic institutions such as markets, shops, and law courts to insure the continuation of business. Some of these institutions serve the purpose of preserving the culture (i.e., schools and museums), others serve a ceremonial purpose (i.e., parade grounds, arenas, auditoriums), and other institutions serve the needs of the people (i.e., hospitals, gymnasiums, laundaries, beauty salons, and hotels).

There are several ways to look at the manner in which cities differ. We could, for example, focus upon the beauty or cleanliness of cities, or any other criteria based on the impression or image they give us. Perhaps a better method, however, is to look at cities in terms of their function. Cities may be separated into (1) administrative centers (Washington, D.C.); (2) industrial centers (Pittsburg); (3) commercial cities (New York City); (4) museum cities (Williamsburg); (5) resort cities (Miami); (6) university cities (Madison or Princeton); and (7) port cities (Charleston or Houston). These categories could be broken down even further. For example, resort cities could be subdivided into those suited for summer recreation (summer homes in beach resort towns) while others are suited for winter recreation (skiing areas with lifts and lodges).

Thus cities may be characterized by function and physical traits. Another way to classify them is by the life style of their inhabitants.

CITY LIFE

Although the study of the modern city is still in its early stages, several distinctive directions have been taken by investigators. One variety of

social scientists continue to stress the ways in which urbanites learn to cope with their environment. Not surprisingly, they study neighborhoods and focus upon visiting patterns and friendships. A number of studies have tried to discover why some areas have a feeling of community or "weness," while other neighborhoods contain strangers living together. Friendship patterns in large cities are also receiving attention mainly because urban friendship appears to be based on mutual interests rather than nearness or proximity. Thus, it has been noted, urbanites are willing to drive all the way across town, sometimes further than they are willing to drive to go shopping, just to see friends with whom they share interests in sports, dancing, art, swimming, or any other such activity.

Apartment living has also received attention since it has become a rather common living experience for greater numbers of Americans. Some apartments, due to their stairway patterns and parking lots, tend to encourage tenants to talk to one another, while other apartment buildings tend to discourage friendships. Apartment dwelling also appears to be related to an acceptance of temporary, flexible living patterns.

Suburban subdivisions which surround all of our cities today represent efforts on the part of many to escape from the consequences of living in the city. Suburban living is regarded as preferable to living closer to the downtown area since the suburbanite can take advantage of diverse services and activities available only in the city while not having to be concerned with overcrowding, congestion, parking, and understaffed schools. The image that comes to mind is of a person who works in a hurried, active, pressured job getting in his car and heading to a quiet, winding street lined with comfortable homes. Each house has a well-trimmed lawn, a double garage, and a child's bicycle in the driveway. Despite the pleasant images, present day suburbanites find that they also have problems for which they cannot escape. Traffic congestion during rush hours means that besides eight hours on the job, the suburbanite must spend one to three hours on the road. Burglaries, automobile thefts, and vandalism commonly occur in all suburbs and have led to the use of private police to guard these areas. High property taxes, poor construction, and poor planning (resulting in flooded areas, mudslides, or shifting land) as well as neighbors one detests, are problems from which one cannot easily escape. If one moves to another subdivision some of his problems may be solved, but other problems take their place.

There is no doubt a great deal to be learned from studies of the everyday life of the urban dweller. But these studies are limited to the extent that human beings react in their own peculiar ways to the same problem. Another method of study utilized by social scientists is that which focuses upon the nonsocial aspects of the city.

CITY STRUCTURE

This method of study is concerned with describing the differences between communities according to their structural properties, such as location, population, and changes in the distribution of inhabitants. To understand the "ecological" approach, as it is called, it is necessary to understand spatial organization which is related to the dynamic processes of growth. Spatial organization, according to the urban ecologist, is the result of competition. The fact that there is a limited amount of land available in the city means that a struggle for land use is inevitable between persons or groups who desire it for different purposes. Some groups, however, have more power and thus are able to win most of these struggles and dominate. For example, if you wished to buy a desirable plot of land in a downtown area upon which to build an apartment building, you may have to compete with several business groups who wish to construct office buildings on that site. Since the cost of land in the downtown area is extremely high, let us say ten dollars per square foot, it is not difficult to believe that the business corporation would be more likely to afford the cost and thus continue the business dominance of the central business area. Thus, the location of industry, business offices, homes, and schools can be explained by looking at the struggle between competing groups for land. The dynamic processes of growth may be summarized by looking at the following five concepts.

Concentration—People tend to congregate. The fact that ninety percent of the American population live on ten percent of the available land gives us some idea of the concentration characteristic in our society. History has recorded the story of this concentration. In the early 1900s, during immigrant waves from Europe, entering groups tended to concentrate on the Eastern seaboard. Blacks from the

Southern states concentrated in the northern industrial centers. The concentration of the population into small areas is explained by the competition for jobs, inexpensive housing, and the dominance of certain groups in certain areas.

Centralization—People cluster around a particular point. Thus most American cities are built around a central business district, town square, or main street. Competition for valuable land leads to the particular form which the downtown areas tend to take. Because land is so expensive, the only worthwhile investment is a tall structure which increases the number of people and businesses which can utilize that land. Businesses which serve those who work in the central business district (such as hotels, auditoriums, travel agencies) are also found close to the downtown area. The problem of centralization is that it tends to result in the congestion of people and cars.

Decentralization—This refers to people who have a tendency to move away from the central business district. We refer to this process today as suburbanization. With the advent of the automobile, a person's

Only tall buildings are worthwhile investments in a city.

place of work and place of residence no longer had to be close to one another. Once again, competition for the best place to live outside, but not too far from, the city causes more expensive homes to be built in some areas and not in others.

Segregation—Groups who share a common attribute tend to concentrate in one area. We normally think of segregation as related to groups who share racial characteristics, but it may also be true of religious groupings, occupational groupings, and subcultures.

Invasion—This term refers to areas which are dominated by a particular group or function (apartments, rooming houses, hotels) but which are threatened by a competing group or function. Thus, a segregated area of whites may be invaded by blacks, or an apartment rooming house area may be invaded by small businesses. *Succession* is the conclusion of the invasion process, and occurs when the invading group or function becomes the dominant one.

These processes are used by the ecologists because they can be measured objectively, using population data like that provided by the Census Bureau. This view of impersonal and uncontrolled processes has been criticized by those who point out that space is culturally defined. The result is that at times some areas of the city do not fit the impersonal patterns expected on the basis of competition. Spatial determinism cannot explain park areas like Central Park or the Boston Commons existing on the most valuable land in the central city area of New York or Boston. Neither can it explain why some cities attempt to save historical sites rather than remove them and replace them with supermarkets or hamburger stands.

In conclusion, it appears that the ecological approach is useful in the study of cities, but without consideration of social factors the view obtained will remain incomplete. A combination of approaches might be used, for example, in the study of "rural enclaves" or areas in the city which are rural in outlook. These areas could be located by discovering where rural migrants tend to reside. Only a look at social factors can explain how these areas serve as a buffer, teaching rural migrants how to act in urban areas while continuing to give them a taste of "country-style" hospitality.

There is no reason to debate the question of whether living in the city is good or not. The fact of the matter is that the vast majority of Americans live in cities now and will probably continue to live in cities in the future. The advantages of living in the cities, including being close to business, recreational, and cultural centers, and being able to choose from many alternate styles of life, are still preferred to a rural existence.

URBAN CRISIS

The news media constantly speaks of the urban crisis. Just how did the cities arrive at this crisis stage? Several processes, some historical in nature and others presently occurring, may be pointed out as contributing to the present situation.

Rural-Urban Migration

Perhaps the source of our urban problems can be found in the fact that this nation industrialized in a rather short period of time. Increased industrialization created a demand for factory labor. At the same time, mechanization of agriculture released many rural-oriented, unskilled farm workers from the fields. The obvious place to go was to where the jobs were—the city.

Inner City Slums

Slum areas formed as the rural-to-urban migration continued. The reason for the formation of these enclaves is rather simple. They offered the newcomer to the city inexpensive and readily available (although crowded) housing and a comfortable feeling that he was among "his own kind." A slum dwelling, when it is the only housing one can afford, is sufficient. However, when the migrant had the desire (and money) to move out but could not because of segregated housing patterns, the density and the feeling of being trapped increased.

Neglect on the part of the landlord, the failure of local officials to enforce housing codes, and the crowded conditions result in decaying inner city slum areas composed of the deprived and the trapped.[3] Slum dwellers were also faced with higher unemployment, less access to transportation, and an educational system unprepared for the student from the slum subculture.

Crime

The problems of alcoholism and drug abuse in slum areas made them unsafe. The city streets became battlegrounds for teenage gangs. Without secure jobs or the hope for job opportunities, many slum dwellers turned to illegal activities in an attempt to attain the economic means to survive. Increased criminal activity resulted in a response from enforcement agencies. Increased patrolling, tougher enforcement, and severe criminal justice led to cries of harassment from the community.

The Urban Family

In the face of this environment, some families found their influence over their own children decreasing. Teenage gangs became influential peer groups because they offered protection and a sense of importance, as well as a value system somewhat at odds with the "normal" rules of behavior. Many families broke apart as men unable to support their families left in search of better opportunities, never to return. The matriarchal family began to dominate. The lower-class family became a multiple-problem family faced with pessimism, low educational attainment, and the inability to recognize available opportunities.

White Flight

In the face of the decaying central city and the increasing proportion of minority group members, most whites (those who could afford it) chose to move out of the central city into the safer areas. The suburbs offered a living arrangment where one did not have to worry about being mugged or having to send their children to inferior schools. The movement to the suburbs caused the expansion of slum areas into new sections of town and the formation of still more suburbs further away.

Congestion

Suburban living made possible by the automobile also created the problem of traffic jams. Freeways or expressways, parking garages,

Freeways are a fact of city life.

and economy cars are efforts to ease this problem. Middle class workers (with the exception of New York City) apparently prefer to drive their cars to work rather than to utilize mass transit systems. The problems of smog in our major cities has caused reconsideration of methods to change our style of life to one in which we are less dependent upon the car.

Urban Turbulence

The gap between the haves and have-nots became greater as whites abandoned the central city. The slum dweller became frustrated, trapped, and angry and expressed his discontent during a period of violent rioting and looting. No doubt these actions called to the attention of the nation the drastic changes needed, but the actual changes which have occured in cities torn by riots in the 1960s appear to be minimal.

Municipal Finances

As the city grows, its people require new schools, bigger hospitals, more utilities, and so forth. But how can the city raise the money through taxation to provide these services when it contains most of the unskilled labor and large numbers of the unemployed? The more affluent now reside in the suburbs, and the city, with great needs, has the weakest tax base from which to draw. The result is that severe problems cannot be solved when the funds needed for the study, initiation, and implementation of solutions are not available to city government. Thus, the problems remain.

PLANNING FOR THE FUTURE

Because of the size and complexity of the modern city, solving the problems of poverty, slums, unemployment, city schools and so forth appears to require many changes and innovations. As a result, the last decade has seen the advent of new mechanisms such as planned communities, city planning, and metropolitan government.

Planned communities are cities created and organized in the mind of the planners long before the first cornerstone is laid. Street patterns, shopping areas, neighborhood schools, and parking are all planned in advance using the criterion of convenience. The purpose of these new towns is to make cities livable again by insuring that they will meet the needs of the people who live in them.

City planning today is a major part of city government. The planners use a master plan of the city as their guide. The master plan determines the best future utilization of land based on its topographical features (hills, soil composition, watershed) and the expected growth patterns of surrounding areas.

To enable the city government to have some control over future growth patterns, zoning laws have been enacted which require that the owner of a plot of land receive permission from local authorities to build a business on a plot zoned as residential, or to build a factory on a plot zoned as commercial. Zoning should only be looked upon as a instrument to be used by planners to control growth patterns and prevent a railroad yard or a stockyard from being built next to a residential area. Another great concern of planners is allowing for sufficient "green space" or parks, natural areas, and playgrounds for the convenience of all urban dwellers.

SUMMARY

The city did not suddenly appear. Civilized man had to reach a rather advanced stage in his development before city life was possible. The city was defined as a place where a large number of people live in a built-up area, work at non-agricultural jobs, produce goods and supply services, distribute those goods and services in exchange for raw materials and food, and develop a way of life characterized by aloofness, impersonal relationships and secondary controls. All cities have some characteristics in common, such as dependence upon other cities and rural areas, complex division of labor, heterogeneity, diversity, and some degree of internal disorder. Cities also differ from one another according to size, street patterns, beauty, and function.

Neighborhood studies focus upon the manner in which urban dwellers cope with their environment. Ecological studies look at non-social aspects of city life based on concepts such as concentration, centralization, decentralization, segregation, and invasion. The urban crisis should be viewed not as a new phenomenon, but as an increasingly more severe problem having its roots in the historical processes of rural and urban migration, slum formation, white flight to the suburbs, and a lack of municipal funds.

Notes

1. Ralph Tomlinson, *Urban Social Structure* (New York: Random House, 1969).

2. Ibid.

3. Herbert J. Gans, *The Urban Villagers* (New York: Free Press of Glencoe, 1962).

Thinking
Sociologically

1.   Go to the center of a large metropolitan area and make observations from the center to the outskirts of the city. Use the mileage indicator on the car and stop at half-mile intervals for the first two miles, and then at one mile intervals until you reach the rural areas. Avoid freeways, expressways, and interstate highways. Make observations on at least the following;
   1.   How tall is the tallest building around?
   2.   How much space is there between buildings?
   3.   What kind of architecture seems to predominate?
   4.   How are most people dressed?
   5.   What colors seem to dominate (green grassy areas, grey concrete highways, etc.)?

2.   Take a street map of a large city and, using the yellow pages of its telephone directory, locate on the map the following:
   1.   hospitals
   2.   banks
   3.   flower shops
   4.   stock brokerage firms
   5.   pawn shops
   6.   branches of the public library
   Do you see any patterns in the locations of the above listed places? Select several other places of business or shops and note to what extent they tend to concentrate in one area of the town.

3.   Even in our urban society, rural values like open spaces and a return to nature are emphasized. Advertising promotion for various products uses these factors to help sell their merchandise. Select a specific magazine and gather examples of advertisements which utilize rural scenes and appeal to nature to entice prospective buyers. Why do advertisers think these ads will appeal to the general public, most of whom live in an urban setting?

Chapter 14

Cognitive
Objectives

"Big government" and "big business" are often-criticized elements of our society, along with bureaucratic "red tape." This chapter is designed to help you understand the origin of these phenomena, how they work in our society, and their positive, as well as negative, effects. Look for the following as you read the chapter:

1. *To what do the terms "the expansion of society" and the "national community" refer? What is increase in scale? To what do horizontal and vertical patterns of relationship refer? What is the importance of their relative strength? What are four results of the expansion of society?*
2. *What is bureaucracy?*
3. *What are the characteristics of bureaucracy?*
4. *What are the elements in bureaucracy which increase its efficiency? Do these factors contribute to its inefficiency?*
5. *How has bureaucratic authority changed?*
6. *What are informal mechanisms of control?*
7. *What is alienation? How do the nature of work, bureaucracy, and consumption patterns contribute to alienation? What is a ritualist? What is executive dropout? What are the characteristics of alienation?*
8. *How does bureaucracy contribute to security?*

Bureaucratic Ceramics and Cracked Pots

Discussing the historical events of the seventeenth and eighteenth centuries in western civilization, Becker and Barnes describe the discoveries of the biologists, the explorers, the ethnographers (early anthropologists), and the astronomers. The revelation and knowledge made available during these centuries had the effect of releasing man from old boundaries and, at the same time, displacing him from his proud throne as even his earth was reduced to a speck of dust in an immeasurable universe. They conclude, "the world became larger, and the earth became smaller."[1]

Something of the same may be said for developments in America during the nineteenth and twentieth centuries. Individuals were released from the boundaries of small agrarian communities. They roamed the entire nation. The drudgery of hard manual work for both man and woman was replaced by automated labor saving machines and devices. Americans now consume products from around the world. Sights, smells, foods, and artifacts from distant cultures are available in neighborhood markets. Television brings national and international personalities and events into the living room. Technological discoveries and their implementation into the social fabric have resulted in a drastic reduction in the size of the earth and an amazing increase in man's control of his environment.

No one may say for sure if life is more complex for the individual today than it was two hundred years ago in this country. Precise records of measurement of life's complexity are unavailable and definitions of what is and is not complex are not that clear. Individuals struggled for existence then as now. Making a living, raising children, expressing faith, and facing the exigencies of life were difficult and complex for individuals in the idealized days of the past as they are in our times.

Perhaps what may be said is that social forms are more diverse today and the range of choices available for the individual is greater now than in America's agrarian past. Society is, therefore, more complex and life for the individual is different from, if not more complex than, that of his forefather.

"Bigness" is the single word most appropriate to describe modern man's perception of his society. Big business, big government, and big society are most frequently mentioned. These are complemented by commercialized religion, recreation, and education. Perhaps what is being said is that the individual feels less in control of events that shape one's life and more at the mercy of impersonal forces that pervade the society. While a person may watch events occurring on the opposite side of the globe on television, he feels that he has no viable control over how these events affect his life. It is true that an individual no longer has to wield a shovel to dig a ditch. Rather, the worker manipulates an expensive machine that cuts through the earth's surface. Yet the people who determine whether or not he works, how much he is paid, and the conditions under which he works sit in far away offices and are only indirectly aware of his existence. To paraphrase Becker and Barnes, "Society gets bigger and the individual becomes smaller."

The purpose of this chapter is to discuss the implication of the social events which have expanded society's complexity and decreased man's perception of himself in the urban context. The chapter will begin with a brief description of social expansion and then turn to a discussion of bureaucracy and alienation.

SOCIAL EXPANSION

The chapter on social change underscored the intertwined nature of forces which create societal change. Factors in the economic or industrial area are influenced by, and seem to influence, population growth and distribution. Changes in values and ideology stimulate and are responsive to changes in urbanization trends. Each factor of change is both a cause and a result of other factors of change. One must be careful, therefore, not to commit the fallacy of reductionism and suggest that the point at which American society stands today is the result of any single force.

As the organization of life becomes more complex, the individual becomes more powerless.

However, some starting point is necessary to describe the historical factors which have made us what we are today. For this starting point, let us begin with the economic sphere. Since the mid-nineteenth century, at least three important changes have occurred. (1) In industry there has been an increasing use of nonhuman sources of energy. Human muscle has been increasingly replaced by machines, assembly-line production, and computers. (2) The organizations which have coordinated the men and machines in the productive and distributive processes have increased in size and influence. (3) Productivity for each human participant in the industrial process has drastically increased and resulted in certain occupational changes. Fewer blue collar workers are needed relative to the numbers of white collar workers. This fact has resulted in the proliferation of white collar and service occupations. Greater specialization of tasks to be performed in the economic order has demanded more specialized training and increased quality and quantity of education for members of the work force. More pay for fewer hours per week has created a better market for products, as well as the individual affluence to consume industry's products. According to John Kenneth Galbraith, industry's manipulation of the market has caused "rational buying" to end. Corporations are as much in the business of creating demand as they are involved in producing consumable goods.[2]

Scott Greer described these three changes and their social repercussions.[3] Greer coined the term "increase in scale" to describe the cumulative effects of these changes in the economic order. Man's technological advances have "reduced the space-time ratio of energy transformation." What this means is that the whole nation can get the immense supply of gas and oil necessary to run its factories and automobiles from one or two locations. Citrus fruits and other perishable commodities can be plucked from their trees and bushes on one day and be transported before they spoil to all parts of the country. The mass media "cans" entertainment in a few specific centers in the nation and sends it out to almost every home in the country.

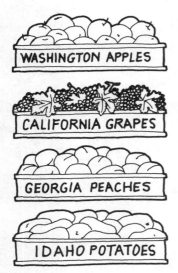

Increase in scale means, then, that widely separated geographical areas are being brought together into increasingly smaller networks of coordination and integration. The term refers to the dependence of communities upon the rest of the nation as well as the dependence of all communities upon certain centralized sources of food, fiber, entertainment, or other necessary services. The map of the nation is being changed from a set of relatively isolated communities exercising a degree of antonomy into a collectivity which is a single or national community.

Roland Warren describes the same phenomenon with his concept of the relative strength of what he calls horizontal and vertical relationships. In his scheme, horizontal relationships refer to intercommunity relations of sentiments, attitudes, values, and interactions. Vertical ties are those which exist between organizations within the community and extra-community agencies. For example, relations between a local school and the local bank and churches is a horizontal relationship. Vertical relationships, on the other hand, are the ties of the local school to the county school board, and to educational boards at the state and national level. Warren's point is that while vertical relationships are increasing in strength, those of a horizontal nature are weakening. What he means, by way of illustration, is that many decisions within the local school are influenced by rules, standards, and laws which stem from outside the community rather than what the local patrons (or even the local banker) might wish. Wages at the local factory are influenced by national unions and federal laws. Branch plants of national firms close, change products, or mechanize at the wishes of boards or directors which meet in distant places rather than at the actual work site. The interdependence of communities, associated with national community, is underscored by the relative increase in strength of these vertical relationships.

The expansion of society, perceived as the development of a national community, results in at least four factors which affect the way life is lived in our society.

There is increased impersonality and loss of freedom. As the activity of individuals widely separated by geographical space is coordinated by a giant corporation, people become collective means to individual ends. Increasingly one lives, shops, worships, and works beside strangers about whom one knows or cares little.

The increased range and content of communications broadens the base of socialization. More diffuse and less concentrated socialization creates the probability that individuals will be subjected to conflicting norms. Ambiguity in behavioral expectation can be an important source of conflict in the individual's self-concept.

The fragmentation of the normative structure changes the patterns of social control. On the one hand, anonymity decreases the potential strength of public opinion as an effective element of social control. An individual does not respond to sanctions from a stranger as readily as one does from a person who is well known. Compliance to expectations, on the other hand, takes more organizational outlook. The organization man, in William H. Whyte's term, conforms to organization patterns which may be dictated from afar.

Finally, the national community results in mass society. The mass, or a great number of people, are recruited and regimented for political or economic purposes. They are organized by exposure to common and far-reaching techniques of communication for the purpose of artifically stimulating patterns of consumption. The result is a standardization of tastes. On the surface, mass society appears to offer a diversity of choices. After all, there are three major television networks, four major automobile manufactors, and two major political parties. On a closer look, however, the range of choices is not infrequently a matter of prescribed alternatives which share more similarities than differences.

Society's expansion, or the increase in scale, is a term used to describe the increasing complexity of society which is based upon the growing interdependence of each part upon all others. The effect of the expansivensss of society is increased impersonality, conflicting socialization, organizational social control, and mass society. The growth of the organizational networks which coordinate the vast numbers of people, equipment, and records necessary for the increasing interdependence has been nothing short of phenomenal. But it has been matched by the growth of an administrative tool which is both a result of organizational expansion and a contributor to that very expansion. Bureaucracy is the term by which this administration tool is known. Let us turn now to that subject.

THE BUREAUCRATIZATION OF SOCIETY

Let us suppose that you had the task of collecting tickets for a home-town basketball game in a gym that held only a few hundred people. Your task would be rather simple. You might simply let everyone go in and after the game started, pass among the spectators to pick up their tickets. Or you might sit at the only entrance to the gym and collect their tickets as they came in.

Now let us suppose that you were responsible for collecting tickets to a college football game in a stadium that would seat fifty thousand people. It would be possible, of course, to close all gates except one and force all spectators to enter at that point. You could then sit there and collect their tickets as they passed by. Such a procedure would, however, reduce efficiency since spectators would have to stand in long lines and getting them all into the stadium would take hours. To avoid the confusion and inconvenience caused by this inefficient method of ticket collection, you would probably organize the whole operation. To do this, you might hire a score of people to assist you and they would be given specific instructions including when to arrive at the stadium, which gate to man, and the procedure for turning in the money and tickets which they might collect. In other words, you would need organization to insure the orderly and efficient accomplishment of your task.

This hypothetical example is an illustration of bureaucracy, as well as the social condition which makes bureaucracy necessary. In fact, bureaucracy may be defined as "the type of organization designed to accomplish large-scale administrative tasks by systematically coordinating the work of many individuals."[4]

Cursed for its red tape and inefficiency and, conversely, for its ruthless efficiency and impersonality, bureaucracy is a fact of life. Few things in the life of the average American are not dependent, directly or indirectly, upon some bureaucracy. Government, military, business, mass communication, industry, education, labor unions, churches, recreation, and social services are all bureaucratized. The individual employed in these areas, as well as the individual affected by the service (or lack of service) offered by these agencies, is touched by bureaucracy. Bureaucracy is a way of life in our society.

Organizing large numbers of tasks and individuals often requires a bureaucracy.

THE CHARACTERISTICS OF BUREAUCRACY

Bureaucracy is a phenomenon almost as old as civilization itself. The complex task of irrigating the fertile but arid regions of ancient Egypt gave rise to the first known large-scale bureaucracy in history. Ancient empires were faced with the task of organizing an effective army and collecting taxes for its support. Bureaucratic methods were introduced to solve the problems involved in these two ventures. Bureaucracy itself is old. What is new is the total bureaucratization of a society. This development has occurred during the last two centuries in western civilization and our society is a perfect example of the rise of bureaucratization.

Innovative changes in technology made possible the rapid rise in standard of living experienced by the citizens of this nation. Mechanization had to be matched by administrative innovations to insure the mass production and distribution of goods and service. The coordination of thousands of workers (sometimes separated by great geographical distance) and complex machinery necessitated the development of an intricate administrative organization. To meet these needs, the rational and orderly tool known as bureaucracy was developed.

Max Weber, who wrote in the early 1900s when bureaucracy was in its infancy, proposed the following characteristics of bureaucracy.

1. There is a minute *division of labor* based upon specialization in a given task and a clearcut hierarchy of authority. The activities which one is to perform are standardized, and impersonal rules, usually written, govern the performance of tasks.

2. Positions, especially on the top end of the hierarchy, are filled by full-time appointed officials. These persons are selected for their tasks on the basis of special qualifications that have to do with training and preparation rather than mere ability.

3. The performance of duty is independent of personal sentiments and opinions. Favoritism is to be avoided and political and religious ideologies are not to interfere with the obedient performance of the tasks one is assigned.

4. A system of merit awards assures the faithful accomplishment of tasks. Such things as promotion, salary increments, pensions, insurance, stable careers, and other fringe benefits insure loyalty to the organization.

5. Orders are issued in written form in order to fix responsibility and to help insure uniformity. There is an emphasis on quota and formal reports, which likewise insure uniformity, and, in addition, heighten the type of impersonality upon which bureaucracy is based.

Blau and Meyer reduce Weber's lengthy list to four factors which characterize bureaucracy. They say, "these four factors—specialization, a heirarchy of authority, a system of rules, and impersonality—are the basic characteristics of bureaucratic organization."[5]

It should be noted at this point that the basis of bureaucracy, and its most essential characteristic, is rationality. What this means is that bureaucratic organization, with all its characteristics, is a rational procedure designed to accomplish a goal or set of objectives in the most efficient manner. The impersonality, the specialization, the heirarchy of authority, and the formalized set of rules heighten efficiency in accomplishing the task. Bureaucracy is a tool which arose in response to man's need for an efficient way of organizing to accomplish specific goals. It is a rational technology designed to move people and products, and to cordinate men and machines in such a way as to avoid confusion, mistakes, useless waiting, and activity which does not help achieve designated goals and objectives. We now turn to the question of the efficiency of bureaucracy.

BUREAUCRACY AND EFFICIENCY

Weber states, "Experience tends universally to show that the purely bureaucratic type of administrative organization . . . is, from a purely technical point of view, capable of attaining the highest degree of efficiency."[6] Bureaucratic organizations compare, Weber says, with other types of administrative organizations as machine technology compares with pre-modernized means of production. The discipline which bureaucracy brings with its formal rules and its hierarchy of authority, as well as the speciality which each member supplies, allows the organization to be efficient.

Rigid rules and set procedures for promotion, however, may hinder employee creativity and stifle the tendency to innovation. Blau and Meyer comment:

> Although the formally established structure and procedures are designed to further efficiency, some of these emergent processes defeat the formal design and create bureaucratic rigidity, which interferes with adaptation to changing conditions and impeded efficiency. Other internal processes have the opposite effect and create informal adjustments to new situations and problems that arise, thus furthering effective operations. A fundamental dilemma of bureaucratic administration is that the very arrangements officially instituted to improve efficiency often have by-products that impede it. Centralized authority, even if it results in superior decisions, undermines the ability of middle managers to assume responsibilities. Detailed rules, even if they improve performance, prevent adaptation to changing situations. Strict discipline, even if it facilitates managerial direction, creates resentments that reduce effort. Generally, there are no formal arrangements that can assure efficiency because it depends on flexible adjustments to varying and changing conditions in the organization. What formal arrangements can and should do, however, is create conditions in the organization that foster processes of adjustment. The main task of management is not to lay down rules on how to do the work but to maintain conditions in which adjustments spontaneously occur when new problems arise and to protect these conditions from bureaucratic processes of ossification.[7]

Most criticisms of bureaucratic inefficiency stem, at least for the general populace, from individuals who are clients of the organization. Ironically, the accusations of inefficiency of bureaucratic machinery are leveled at those aspects of bureaucracy which make the organization *more* efficient. Filling out lengthy forms which for the most part are irrelevant to the client involves time and effort and, not infrequently, appears to delay the delivery of service. Lengthy forms, however, often speed service and help prevent costly and time-wasting mistakes. Individuals sometimes resent the impersonality of bureaucracy's extensive use of computer cards. Computer usage, however, speeds up the process of service delivery and, despite the occasional computer mistake, enhances the keeping of correct records.

The individual experiences a sense of helplessness and frustration in the face of the impersonality of bureaucracy. Rules are made to apply to everyone and the special circumstances which the individual feels are applicable to his own situation are totally disregarded by the bureaucracy. Decisions which vitally affect the individual are made by the powerful machinery of bureaucracy on the basis of the impersonal rules and without regard to the special interests of the individual. The frustrations which stem from this feeling of impotence result often in verbal attack on "bureaucratic red tape" and "petty bureaucrats." Such tactics, it seems, are produced by the individual's real or perceived disadvantage in the face of bureaucracy's ruthless and impersonal efficiency, rather than actual inefficiency.

Bureaucracy, in summary, is an administrative tool which has both advantages and disadvantages for those who work within it as well as for those served by it. Its strength lies in its impersonal efficiency and its rigid system of rules and hierarchy of authority. Its weakness lies in these same characteristics. It is inflexible, rigid, and goal oriented. Not infrequently, its rigidity prevents innovation and its goal orientation blocks the accomplishment of other significant goals. Its impersonality isolates the individual and helps produce a sense of frustration and impotence. But, conversely, bureaucracy makes possible the most efficient use of technology to supply needed goods and services. The education of the young, the provision of religious training, the political participation and information needs of mass society, and the maintainance of a sometimes cumbersome and plodding government are all made possible in our society by this organizational tool.

BUREAUCRACY AND AUTHORITY

Nineteenth century bureaucracy was based, as noted earlier, upon a chain of command in which the person or persons up each notch of the hierarchy held acknowledged authority over those below them. Unquestioning obedience was the expected response to this authority. Note for example, Fredrick W. Taylor's illustration of the supervisor's control over a hypothetical worker named Schmidt:

"Schmidt, are you a high-priced man?"
"Vell, I don't know vat you mean."
"Oh yes, you do. What I want to know is whether you are a high-priced man or not."

"Vell, I don't know what you mean."

"Oh, come now, you answer my questions. What I want to find out is whether you are a high-priced man or one of these cheap fellows here. What I want to find out is whether you want to earn $1.85 a day or whether you are satisfied with $1.15, just the same as all those cheap fellows are getting."

"Did I vant $1.85 a day. Vas dot a high-priced man? Vell, yes, I vas a high-priced man."

"Oh, you're aggravating me. Of course you want $1.85 as—everyone wants it! You know perfectly well that that has very little to do with your being a high-priced man. For goodness sake, answer my questions, and don't waste any more of my time. Now come over here. You see that pile of pig iron?"

"Yes."

"You see that car?"

"Yes."

"Well, if you are a high-priced man, you will load that pig iron on that car tomorrow for $1.85. Now do wake up and answer my question. Tell me whether you are a high-priced man or not."

"Vell—did I get $1.85 for loading dot pig iron on dot car tomorrow?"

"Yes, of course you do, and you get $1.85 for loading a pile like that every day right through the year. That is what a high-priced man does, and you know it just as well as I do."

"Vell, dot's all right. I could load dot pig iron on the car tomorrow for $1.85, and I get every day, don't I?"

"Certainly you do—certainly you do."

"Vell, den, I vas a high-priced man."

"Now, hold on, hold on. You know just as well as I do that a high-priced man has to do exactly as he's told from morning to night. You have seen this man here before, haven't you?"

"No, I never saw him."

"Well, if you are a high-priced man, you will do exactly as this man tells you tomorrow, from morning till night. When he tells you to pick up a pig and walk, you pick it up and you walk, and when he tells you to sit down and rest, you sit down. You do that right straight through the day. And what's more, no back talk. Now a high-priced man does just what he's told to do, and no back talk. Do you understand that. When this man tells you to walk, you walk; when he tells you to sit down, you sit down, and you don't talk back to him. Now you come on to work here tomorrow morning and I'll know before night whether you are really a high-priced man or not."*

Two major changes, one in the bureaucracy itself and the other in the technology which supports the hierarcy, have changed the nature

*From pp. 44–46 in "The Principles of Scientific Management" from *Scientific Management* by Fredrick Winslow Taylor. Copyright, 1911 by Fredrick W. Taylor; renewed, 1939 by Louise M. S. Taylor. By permission of Harper & Row, Publishers, Inc.

of bureaucratic authority. First, within the bureaucracy, the tendency toward greater specialization has been heightened. Supervisors in an administrative capacity now preside over specialists whose performance is so specialized that the supervisor is at a loss to direct it. The supervisor, himself a specialist in administration, must depend upon the specialist to direct himself in his area of competence. Sometimes such a supervisor is responsible for administering the work of a number of specialists trained in several different areas of speciality. His authority is extremely diffused due to his lack of competence in the intricate work of the specialists.

Second, improved technology has produced machines upon which coordination of work depends. Machines not only perform tasks, but supply information necessary for direction of work. Supervisors, along with other workers, wait on the machine to give orders. Such a situation reduces the need for and the legitimation of the supervisor giving directives, and therefore reduces the authority of those in command. Science fiction movies frequently play on this theme. While in outer space, for example, the computer which runs the space ship may "take over" command and jeopardize the lives of the crew.

Due to these two major changes, impersonal mechanisms of control (including formalized codes and procedures) have increasingly replaced direct command in methods of directing duties and operations. These are more subject to challenge and subsequently to change which further alters the make-up of authority in the bureaucracy. What all this means is that authority remains within the organization but has been depersonalized. Discipline associated with blind obedience to direct authority is replaced by more impersonal types of control.

BUREAUCRACY AND ALIENATION

Eric and Mary Josephson begin their book, *Man Alone,* with the words,

> Our present age of pessimism, despair and uncertainty succeeds a quite different earlier period of optimism, hope and certainty—a period when man believed in himself and the work of his hands, had faith in the powers of reason and science, trusted his gods, and conceived his own capacity for growth as endless and his widening horizons limitless. Bold in his desires for freedom, equality, social justice and brotherhood, he imagined that ignorance alone stood in the way of these desires. But tumult and violence have unseated these traditional beliefs and values. Knowledge has spread, but it has not abolished war, or fear; not has it made all men brothers. Instead, men find themselves more isolated, anxious and uneasy than ever.*

They note that former times saw its share of depression, anxiety, and frustration. The medieval age, ordered by a rigid church and an equally rigid system of social stratification, did not fail to produce instances of unhappiness and pessimism. Yet they argue, in the words of Eric Kahler, that while inhumanity has been largely a matter of man's entire history, modern times are characterized by *ahumanity*. For evidence of the heightened degree and unique type of pessimism which pervades modern society they offer:

> So it is not to gross statistics that we look, but to the untold "lives of quiet desperation" that mark our age—the multitudes of factory and white-collar workers who find their jobs monotonous and degrading; the voters and nonvoters who feel hopeless or "don't care"; the juveniles who commit "senseless" acts of violence; the growing army of idle and lonely old people; the Negroes who "want to be treated like men," the stupefied audiences of mass media; the people who reject the prevailing values of our culture but cannot—or may not—find any alternatives, the escapists, the retreatists, the nihilists, and the desperate citizens who would "solve" all major political problems by moving our society underground and blowing up the planet. There are few statistics to tell us about them, especially as many continue to function with the appearance of normality. Yet even with indirect evidence it seems safe to assume that there is something in common between them, something that touches the very roots of our social order.*

The sources of alienation (the term used to describe these feelings of "quiet desperation") and its origin in modern society stem from at least three sources: the nature of work, bureaucracy, and consumption patterns. Let us discuss first the nature of work as a source of alienation.

The term alienation was originally applied to the loss of control which workers experienced with the developments of industrialization under capitalism. Karl Marx in 1844 saw the alienation of workers as a product of the social forces in which they lived. The economic order had changed from the guild system in which the workers owned their own tools, bought their own raw materials, made their products either in their own homes or in shops near their home, and sold the work of their hands to their neighbors. By Marx's time, the factory system of production dominated the economic order. The workers left their home to go to a shop, usually located in the city, to labor with other workers to produce a product owned by someone else. Neither the tools, raw materials, nor the product were the property of the worker.

---

*From the Introduction to *Man Alone* edited by Eric and Mary Josephson. Copyright © 1962 by Dell Publishing Co., Inc. Used by permission of the publisher.

A feeling of being alone is part of alienation.

In such a situation, Marx said, the worker was alienated. The workers had lost control of the forces shaping their lives. Specifically, Marx said, the worker was alienated from the product, from work, and from himself; the first because the item produced was not his own but someone else's, the second because the work was laborious and noncreative and, therefore, external to the worker, and the last because the worker had become an object manipulated by others and, hence, belonging to another—the workers had lost themselves.

Recent research indicates that the unpleasant nature of work has increased rather than abated since Marx's time. Work is not a central life interest despite the fact that such a large slice of the day is dedicated to it. Much attention is given to occupational choices, and labor is characterized by machines that do the work, time-saving devices, vacations, spiraling wages and salaries, and fringe benefits. It remains, however, an unpleasant chore to be accomplished in order to get the money to buy the things and do the things one really wants. Few escape the unhappy trap of a monotonous job. Rather, more and more American families take on additional jobs in order to keep up with the rising cost of living. Josephson and Josephson describe the dehumanizing effect of work in our society:

> Increasing division of labor, greater mechanization, the growth of giant industrial and financial enterprises—these are the agents of our economic power and also of individual powerlessness. For evidence we need only look at men on the job. They must work, but how and for what? Few of them have known the pursuit of individual crafts. But millions of men and women labor in large-scale enterprises where work is monotonous and repetitive and where the decreasing need for skilled workers and an increasing division of labor place both the processes and the products of work for beyond their control.[8]

Beyond the effect of the economic order and its work structure on the worker, a second source of alienation in modern society may be listed—bureaucracy. Weber noted that bureaucratic organization had the same effect of separation as did the capitalistic enterprise. Individuals face the bureaucratic machinery from a relatively powerless position. Bureaucracy, it seems, is a way of life which is demanding upon the total person. And to be successful, one must repress some tendencies in order to emphasize those qualities which more nearly fit the bureaucratic mold. C. Wright Mills speaks of the salesman ethic which requires a pretended interest in others in order to manipulate them. This results in a compulsive sociability where one depends upon a "friendly" personality to ingratiate oneself to others. What is being spoken of here is a loss of sincerity in which friendliness becomes, rather than an end in itself, a tool to accomplish an end. On the other hand, one's personality becomes a merchandisable product which is "sold" at the price of the goal which one hopes to accomplish. In other words, while seeking to make instruments of the other person, one makes an instrument of himself and loses control of, or is alienated from, himself.

Ritualist is the term used to describe the individual who has totally surrendered to demands of the bureaucracy. Such a person is committed almost unwaveringly to the details of routine which are often encountered in bureaucracy. Usually, the ritualist avoids making a decision until certain that the proper rules are not being broken. In cases involving uncertainty, they may "pass the buck" to someone else's sphere of jurisdiction. For the ritualist, absolute observance of bureaucratic rules is raised to the primary objective of bureaucratic activity.

Bureaucratic alienation is also fostered by the sheer size of the organization which the individual faces, as well as the impersonal practices which the individual confronts. Consider the difference involved in correcting a ten-dollar mistake in billing at a corner grocery store and correcting the same mistake in one of the large, nationwide mail-order department stores.

Boredom and helpless frustration may result in what is called an "executive dropout." Some observers believe that dissatisfaction and alienation in the bureaucratic organization will make such dropouts a familiar phenomenon. As an example, a recent magazine advertisement for John Hancock Insurance contains the picture of a robust middle-aged man, his beautiful blond-haired wife, and their teen-aged daughter. The three are relaxing against a wooden rail fence in the backyard of a rambling, two-story farm home. In the background are trees and open spaces. The headline for the advertisement reads, "How John Hancock helped Ed Noyes become a successful dropout." The narrative describing the insurance company's part in Ed Noyes' escape from the executive rat race begins:

> Ed Noyes chucked it all.
>
> He gave up his up-and-coming career as an executive in industrial plastics.
>
> He gave up his jangling, city-stirred nerves.
>
> And best of all, he traded his complicated life for a simpler one. In the serene rolling hills of Ipswich, Massachusetts.
>
> Ed bought a County Federal farmhouse built around 1800, and started remodeling it for his family. After the house was fixed up, Ed and his family started a modest ski shop in the basement.

Increasing numbers of young people are also disenchanted with the isolation and "materialism" associated with the economic order in our society. They prefer what is called a "hang loose" ethic in which many of the basic values of capitalism are questioned or denied. Nostalgic dreams and, sometimes, realistic plans to escape back to nature in small bands or communities based upon less material values are espoused and practiced. These young persons feel oppressed by the sheer bigness of the social structure surrounding them. They describe the interpersonal relationships characteristic of those structures as hypocritical and inhuman. Their desire to return to nature is based upon a yearning for simple things and the optimistic belief that in small communities made up of others who share their feelings a life style can be created based upon caring that transcends motivation.

A final source of alienation in our society is patterns of consumption. Americans have a tendency to extend their identity into or acquire their identity from the things which they possess. This is true, in part, because our system of stratification is based upon the acquisition and manipulation of status symbols. Material objects become claims for prestige and status. Seeking status from others, people then have a tendency to measure themselves in terms of the objects which they consume, e.g., the size and quality of their home, their neighborhood, the length and content of their vacation, the clubs and associations to which they belong, and the age and size of the automobile which they drive.

The extent to which the average person identifies with material objects can be seen in the innocent and not infrequently asked question, "Where are you parked?" Obviously, the person is not parked anywhere—his automobile is. The question and its usual answer, however, identifies the owner with the car.

When one is identified with material objects, one's identity lies outside oneself. It is vested in objects external to oneself and that most precious of all human possessions—personhood—is depersonalized and estranged.

THE CHARACTERISTICS OF ALIENATION

Alienation appears to be characterized by specific feelings which the individual experiences. Following Melvin Seeman, these feelings may be listed as follows:[9]

1. The individual feels powerless, and believes his behavior is unimportant in determining the outcome of any activity. His fate lies in the hands of others or with some impersonal force (or forces) over which he exercises little or no control.
2. The individual experiences no meaning or purpose to his life. What a man wants he cannot get, or when he does achieve goals, they are not satisfying. He cannot begin to answer the question "Who am I?"
3. The individual has a sense of loneliness. While he may be surrounded by crowds, he feels cut off from the sense of direction or joy which they appear to be experiencing.
4. A man is unsure of what is expected of him. Norms are unclear, ambiguous, or conflicting. Melvin Seeman notes that there is a high expectancy that socially unapproved behavior is required to achieve socially sanctioned goals.
5. Finally, the individual feels separated from himself. He must do things, he feels, which he does not want to do in order to do things which he wants to do. In such a manner, a person loses control of himself.

It should be noted that alienation is a matter of degree that varies in intensity from time to time and from person to person. Few individuals experience all five of these characteristics at their fullest at any given time. One experiences a greater or lesser degree of alienation at any given time based upon the situation at hand. Yet the dull thud of anxiety which is associated with these characteristics is potentially present, consciously or subconsciously, in many average American lives.

BUREAUCRACY AND SECURITY

The paradoxical role of bureaucracy in our society is seen in the fact that while the bureaucratic organization is a potential source of alienation, it is also a potential source of security. The bureaucratic world is, ideally at least, fairly stable and predictable. Procedure is fixed, promotion is routinized, tenure and seniority are built in, and generally wages and salaries are protected from drastic fluctuations. Uncertainity and insecurity are ruled out by definition in formalized work descriptions and written procedure.

While consumption of goods and services may, as suggested above, be a potential source of alienation, bureaucratic administration (along with advanced technology) insures a constant flow of goods and services to be consumed. Individuals may measure their sense of importance by a handful of trinkets. Be this as it may, bureaucracy helps to assure that, with the exception of some minorities, there are plenty of trinkets to go around.

Beyond that, a sense of powerlessness and a lack of control over events may be psychologically functional. Blame for failure or mistakes is shifted from the individual to the procedure or the organization. Adequate compensation for the lack of freedom to decide and act upon one's decision may be found for many individuals in the simple fact that decisions are made by others and responsibility is, therefore, upon their shoulders. Mistakes may be attributed to a defect in the rules. If so, the rules, not the individual, are at fault. The individual, therefore, may be a slave since he is not free to act. But, due to the warm security of the bureaucratic blanket, he may be a happy slave.

SUMMARY

Societal expansion is a term used in this chapter to describe the increasing complexity of society and the growing dependence of each part on all the others. The interdependence of parts is witnessed by the rapid transition of this country from a network of somewhat isolated and autonomous communities to a single, national community. Societal expansion, it was suggested, may be described in Scott Greer's term "increase in scale" and has resulted in (1) increased impersonality and loss of freedom, (2) expanded range and content of communication and therefore, conflicting socialization and obfuscation of norms, (3) changing patterns of social control, and (4) mass society.

Earlier chapters have noted the contribution of technological development in facilitating social expansion. The role played by bureaucracy in this process of growth is discussed in this chapter. Bureaucracy is defined as an administrative organization designed to systematize and coordinate the efforts of large numbers of people and machines. It is characterized by a heirarchy of authority, specialization, impersonality, and formal rules. Above all it is based upon rationality. This means no more than that the question, "What's the fastest and cheapest way to do this?" stands at the heart of bureaucracy.

In efficiency, bureaucracy has both advantages and disadvantages. Its ruthless impersonality is a major strength and a major weakness. Rigidity and goal orientation make the bureaucratic organization appear heartless, but assist it in delivery of goods. Bureaucracy overshadows the isolated individual and leaves one impotent and frustrated, but, conversely, it harnesses technology to deliver the mass of goods and services when inundate life.

Bureaucracy, along with technology and consumption patterns, is an alienating force in this society. Pre-bureaucratic tendencies must be submerged and the individual sees himself as a merchandizable product. The loss of control or powerlessness associated with the bureaucratic way of life is matched by four other characteristics of alienation: (1) lack of meaning or purpose in life, (2) a sense of aloneness, (3) uncertainity of expectations due to unclear or conflicting norms, and (4) the feeling of being estranged from oneself.

Paradoxically, bureaucracy contributes not only to alienation of individuals, but to their security. Uncertainty is ruled out by fixed promotion, salaries, and fringe benefits. An endless flow of products makes "playthings" readily available to most Americans and thereby facilitates, at least on the surface, a satisfying way of life. Socialized to seek status through material objects, the average citizen has many objects to consume. Finally, bureaucracy allows responsibility for decision making to be shifted from the individual to the organization. The freedom to decide and act are surrendered, but perhaps not unwillingly, and are replaced by the secure knowledge that, while others tell one what to do, they also are responsible.

Notes

1. Howard Becker and Harry Elmer Barnes, *Social Thought from Lore to Science* Vol. I (New York: Dover Publications, 1961), p. 341.

2. J. K. Galbraith, *The New Industrial State* (Boston: Houghton Mifflin, 1967).

3. Scott Greer, *The Emerging City* (New York: The Free Press, 1962).

4. Peter M. Blau and Marshall W. Meyer, *Bureaucracy in Modern Society* (New York: Random House, 1971), p. 4.

5. Ibid., p. 9.

6. Max Weber, *The Theory of Social and Economic Organization,* trans. A. M. Henderson and Talcott Parsons (New York: Oxford University Press, 1947), p. 337.

7. Blau and Meyer, *Bureaucracy in Modern Society,* pp. 58–59.

8. Eric and Mary Josephson, eds., *Man Alone* (New York: Harper and Row, 1962).

9. Melvin Seeman, "On the Meaning of Alienation," *American Sociological Review* 24 (1959): 783–91.

Thinking
Sociologically

1.   Asking the individual to become "aware" of the bureaucracy that surrounds him and sustains his physical and social life may be as impossible as asking the fish to become aware of the water in which he swims. Yet it may be interesting to try.

Count the number of credit cards you carry with you. Consider the type of entertainment which you enjoy most frequently. Think of your job, your school, your church, your clubs. Picture the places where you shop for groceries and clothes. Each of these things touches you in some way everyday and, most likely, they are all bureaucratic organizations.

Do we participate in bureaucracies, despite our negative attitudes, because we chose to or because no real alternatives are provided in our society? In other words, could you purchase commodities and services which you need for daily existence without the bureaucratic apparatus? Further, what changes would be necessary in your life and what conveniences would you be without if you chose not to be involved with bureaucracy?

2.   Loneliness is a significant problem in contemporary society. Because of this most newspapers carry at least one ad in the classified section which begins with something like "Need someone to listen?" See if any local paper carries such an ad and, if so, contact the agency which performs this service. Determine the type people who take advantage of this service. Are they primarily old, young, male, female, married, or single? What problems are most frequently mentioned? Are there any similarities in the loneliness they describe and the characteristics of alienation mentioned in this chapter?

If no such listening service is available in your town you might want to contact a minister, priest, psychologist, or other counselors. Ask about the loneliness which people complain about. Attempt to determine the social causes of the feelings about which troubled persons complain.

3.   Can you think of avenues open to individuals to escape the impersonality of mass society? How can one find groups which enable

him to overcome the alienating effect of modern society? Does the family, informal friendships at work or play, or other primary groups help? Is it possible that to avoid the dehumanizing effects of bureaucracy, we set up other organizations (like the YMCA, Masons, or fraternities) which themselves develop into impersonal bureaucratic organizations? How do you establish personal contacts and how do you help others to do the same?

Index